1000
Most Important
Words

1000
Most Important
Words

Norman W. Schur

Ballantine Books • New York

Library of Congress Catalog Card Number: 82-8801

ISBN 0-345-29863-2

First Edition: August 1982
Second Printing: June 1983

To my poor wife, Marjorie, who has had to suffer the almost unbearable loss of my company during the writing of this book.

No dictionary of a living tongue can ever be perfect.... In this work, when it shall be found that much is omitted, let it not be forgotten that much likewise is performed.

—Samuel Johnson

Is there a wretch whose crimes a sentence crave
Of toil and torture, till he reach the grave?
Let not the mill *his wasted body wear,*
Let not the mine *immerse him in despair.*
'Make dictionaries' be the doom assigned;
All other punishments are there combined.

—Lord Neaves
(Translation of a poem in Latin by the French scholar Joseph Scaliger, 1540–1609)

Acknowledgment

I must express my heartfelt thanks to my old friend Ralph Berton, who went over the proofs with *his* usual (i.e., *un*usual) thoroughness, perspicacity—and wit.

Preface

The purpose of this book is to enrich your life by enriching your vocabulary. Anthropologists have long maintained that man's uniqueness in the animal world is based on his gift of speech. Most of us haven't taken proper advantage of it.

We all have, in the words of Professor of Linguistics John Lyon of the University of Edinburgh, two kinds of vocabularies: the "active" and the "passive." The active one consists of the words we use; the passive one includes the words we more or less recognize when we meet them but fail to use for one reason or another, be it uncertainty, timidity, or laziness. It is to be hoped that this book will activate the passive.

Words have been included that I have found particularly expressive or especially rewarding, words that are adornments to speech or writing, words that mark you as one who makes good use of his special anthropological gift.

The usual practice in dictionaries is to present a number, sometimes a large and confusing number, of meanings for each entry. In this volume, I have attempted to choose the one or few most significant and useful meanings in contemporary usage.

From time to time you will run across the word *figurative* in the text. Many words are used figuratively as well as literally. The literal meaning of a word is its strict material meaning. The figurative use presents a symbolic picture. *Boomerang* is a good example. We know what it means literally: a bent wooden club that, when thrown, returns to the thrower. In its figurative sense, it means something that comes back to hurt you, not physically, but symbolically: something you may have said a long time ago, for example, that can now be used against you, perhaps long after you've reversed your opinion.

Or take the word *pedestrian*. We all know what a pedestrian is. The word comes from the Latin word *pedester*, meaning "on foot." But *pedestrian* has a figurative sense as well: "dull, commonplace, uninspired and uninspiring," or "run-of-the-mill," as in, *He gave a pedestrian account of what must have been a hair-raising experience*. Here we see the figurative use of the word, related to the literal only in the image of a person ploddingly putting one foot in front of another rather than someone running, jumping, springing, full of vitality.

In setting forth pronunciation, only one phonetic symbol has been used—the *schwa*, represented by an upside down *e*, thus: ə. It indicates the indefinite sound—almost none at all—of a vowel in an unaccented syllable, as in these examples: the *a* in *ago*, *woman*; the first *a* in *escalator*; the second *a* in *palace*, and the *a* in *solace*; the *e* in *open* or *agent*; the *i* in *admirable*, *edible*, *pencil*; the second *i* in *imperil*; the *o* in *gallop* and *scallop*; the *u* in *focus* and both of them in *hocus-pocus*.

I have tried to show the derivation of each word without being too technical. The derivation, or source or origin, I think, adds to your deeper understanding of the word. You will see that the overwhelmingly frequent source is Latin; next Greek, then French and the other Romance languages (Italian and Spanish); then Old and Middle English. As to Latin, I should define some terms: *Latin* means *classical* Latin, the language of the Roman Empire prior to A.D. 300; *Late Latin* is that in use A.D. 300–700; *Middle Latin* (also called *Medieval Latin*) is that in use A.D. 700–1500; *New Latin* (or *Neo-Latin*) is that which came into use around 1500, appearing chiefly in scientific writing; and *Vulgar Latin* was the vernacular (i.e., popular, as opposed to literary) Latin of the people. The word *Vulgar*, in this usage, means "popular," from the Latin noun *vulgus*, meaning "the common people," and does not mean "vulgar" in the usual sense of the word.

Old English is that of A.D. 450–1150; *Middle English* covers the years A.D. 1150–1475; *Old French* covers the ninth to the thirteenth century; *Middle French* the fourteenth to the sixteenth century.

Where derivation is from the Latin, I have given the grammatical form that I think most clearly demonstrates the derivation. This requires some further definition. The term *inflection* means the "changing of the form" of a word required by its grammatical function, i.e., by its place and use in the sentence. Thus, our word *love* undergoes changes to *loves* or *love's* when it is a noun and to *loves*, *loving*, or *loved* as a verb; *weave*, as a verb, changes to *weaves*, *weaving*, *wove*, *woven*; *woman* becomes *woman's*, *women*, *women's*; *child* takes a number of forms: *children*, *children's*, etc. Latin, like classical Greek and most modern languages, is a much more highly inflected language than English; the forms of words in those languages are much more numerous than those of an English word. Our words may be derived from any one of a number of forms of a Latin or other foreign word.

Where derivation is from a Latin noun, i have occasionally selected the possessive case (called the "genitive" in most Latin grammars), which shows the stem or root of the word. For example, in the case of the English word *generic*, instead of merely showing the Latin word *genus*, I have selected *generis* (the possessive case of *genus*) as the form closest to the English derivative. Where a Latin or other verb is involved, I have similarly chosen the form best suited to the purpose. Thus, for *effulgent*, I have selected *effulgens*, a form of the verb *effulgere* (to glitter); in the case of *elucidate*, I have used *elucidatus*, a form of the verb *elucidare* (to enlighten). Showing the form of the Latin or other foreign word closest to the English derivative is the most effective way of demonstrating the derivation.

This book may be used in a variety of ways. When you come across a word only vaguely familiar, or wholly unfamiliar, look for it here (if you can't find it, go to your standard dictionary); or go through this book methodically and enrich your arsenal of words by learning one or two new ones a day, and then make them your own by *using* them; or browse through it just for the fun of it—and some of it will stick.

There are no characters, no plot, no climax, no denouement; its only unifying feature is the alphabet; it is just words, and only a thousand—a very small fraction of the contents of your college or desk dictionary—but enough to enhance and upgrade your vocabulary for a lifetime.

I expect criticisms about my choice of entries or definitions, some kindly, others (based on past experience in this field) less so. Whatever they may be, they will be welcome and seriously considered in the preparation of future editions.

Norman W. Schur
Weston, Connecticut, 1982

Author's Note

Occasionally, one of the "1000 Most Important Words" appears in the explanatory comment under an entry. If you run across an unfamiliar word in the text, look it up first in this dictionary. If it isn't one of the "1000," look it up in the *Random Hous* *Dictionary*.

abashed (ǝ basht') *adj.* *Abashed* indicates a state of embarrassment. A person *abashed* feels disconcerted and, to a certain degree, put to shame. One would feel *abashed* if his poor grades were posted on the classroom wall. A fund-raising committee would feel *abashed* if its campaign fell on its face. From Middle English *abashen*, which is thought to have come from Middle French *abaisser* (to be dumbfounded).

abate (ǝ bate') *vb.* To *abate* is to lessen or diminish. A group starts out to scale a mountain, and is unsuccessful time after time; their enthusiasm about meeting the challenge eventually *abates*. A storm that blows over *abates*. One becomes attached to a person of the opposite sex; after meeting with the family one's initial zeal sometimes *abates*. This verb can take an object: The government *abated* the burdensome tax. When there isn't enough money in an estate (after paying taxes, debts, and expenses) to pay all the legacies in full, the executor distributes what's available *pro rata* among the legatees; in this case, the legacies are said to be *abated*. From the Old French *abattre* (to knock down), which was based on Latin *battuere* (to beat or knock).

abdicate (ab' dǝ kate) *vb.* To *abdicate* is to step down, as from a throne, or give something up. The word can stand by itself: Edward VIII *abdicated* in 1936; or it can be used with a noun: Edward VIII *abdicated* the throne of England. *Abdicate* doesn't apply merely to thrones: you can *abdicate* power, authority, or a claim to something. If a chairman regularly fails to attend committee meetings, he can be said to have *abdicated* his responsibility. All it means in this sense is "renounce," i.e., "give up." The act itself is called *abdication* (ab dǝ kay' shǝn). From *abdicatus*, a form of Latin *abdicare* (to renounce, abdicate).

aberrant (a berr' ǝnt) *adj.* This is a rather sad word, often found in the phrases *aberrant conduct*, *aberrant behavior*. As you will see from the derivation given below, its literal meaning implies a straying from the normal, usual, or customary way. Its meaning is close to *unusual* or *uncharacteristic*. If a person normally sociable and gregarious suddenly turns away from friends and society in general, his conduct might be described as *aberrant* and difficult to explain. *Aberrant* acts are known as *aberrations* (a bǝ ray' shǝnz). Don't confuse *aberrant* with *abhorrent* (ab hor' ǝnt), which means "loathsome," although *aberrant* acts committed by normally law-abiding citizens, such as assault, rape, or assassination, can be abhorrent at the same time. From *aberrans*, a form of Latin *aberrare* (to wander, lose one's way).

abominate (ə bom' ə nate) *vb.* When you *abominate* something or somebody, you loathe, hate, abhor, detest him, her or it. People normally *abominate* the very thought of treason, for instance, or kidnapping. Such acts are *abominable* (ə bom' ən ə bəl—*adj.*); they are *abominations* (ə bom ə nay' shəns—*n.*). The treatment of our hostages by the Iranians was an *abomination* in the eyes of the civilized world. On a less dramatic level, Aunt Jane simply *abominates* bad manners. From *abominatus*, a form of Latin *abominari* (to hate).

abrasive (bray' siv) *n.*, *adj.* An *abrasive* is any substance that can be used for polishing or grinding, like sandpaper or pumice. Used literally as an adjective, it describes any such material; but figuratively, it applies to people and their personalities, in the sense of "irritatingly or annoyingly harsh and grating." *Abrasive* peole rub you the wrong way. They are aggressive boors, who ignore or ridicule other people's feelings. "In the person of George Downing (the man who gave his name to Downing Street, London, where the Prime Minister lives at No. 10) the English for the first time confronted a specimen of that *abrasive* new breed, genus Yankee." (Ormonde de Kay, in an article in the March–April 1981 issue of *Harvard Magazine*.) An ex-Yankee who is often described in the press as *abrasive* is baseball manager Billy Martin, well-known for his short temper and his arguments with umpires. From *abrasus*, a form of Latin *abradere* (to scrape off), which gave us also the verb *to abrade*, meaning "wear away by rubbing or scraping."

abrogate (ab' rə gate) *vb.* When a law is *abrogated*, it is repealed. You can *abrogate* a contract as well, if the agreement has been violated. Prevailing customs may be *abrogated*, i.e., discontinued. *Abrogation* (ab rə gay' shən) is the noun; it implies all these things: repeal, annulment, cancellation. In some states there used to be a poll tax, which had to be paid before one could vote. In others there were "Blue Laws," like the Massachusetts statute that made it illegal to kiss your wife on Sunday. Laws like those have been *abrogated*, i.e., officially cancelled. From *abrogatus*, a form of Latin *abrogare* (to repeal).

abstemious (ab stee' mee əs) *adj.* An *abstemious* person is not necessarily a teetotaler; he eats and drinks sparingly. This word, describing such moderation, comes from the Latin adjective *abstemius*, which means, literally, "away from drink," but in English applies to food as well. People who live to a ripe old age often attribute their longevity to an *abstemious* life. The word evokes the image of a thin, conservative, rather picky person, the very opposite of a glutton.

abstinent (ab' stən ənt) *adj.* The quality of self-control in the matter of alcohol is commonly implied by this word. Its general meaning is "self-denying, self-restraining," but more specifically and commonly, control in the matter of the intake of alcohol is to be inferred. The noun is *abstinence* (ab' stən əns) and is often found in the term *total abstinence*, describing a teetotaler. The related words *abstain* and *abstention* are more general and refer to holding oneself back in any situation, whether from eating too much or voting at the United Nations. From *abstinens*, a form of Latin *abstinere* (to hold back, to keep away from).

abstruse (ab stroos') *adj. Abstruse* explanations of theories may be clear to the person expounding them, but unintelligible to those on the receiving end. The theories and formulas of atomic physicists are, to the general public, so *abstruse* as to be incomprehensible. If you found James Joyce's *Ulysses* in parts *abstruse*, wait until you wade into *Finnegan's Wake*. From *abstrusus*, a form of Latin *abstrudere* (to hide); *abstrusus* means "hidden," therefore "secret," therefore *abstruse*.

accolade (ak ə lade' or ak' ə lade) *n. Accolade* means "great praise, enthusiastic approval." It is the technical term for the sovereign's ceremonial tap on the shoulder with a sword, conferring knighthood on a subject. Since knighthood is a reward for merit, it is easy to see how *accolade* came into general use as a term of emphatic approval. It is often used in the plural. One reads that a play was greeted with *accolades* by the critics, or that a politician's course of action received *accolades* from the liberal press. Actors thrive on *accolades* (who doesn't?). From *accollata*, a form of Italian *accollare* (to hug around the neck). (*Collo* is "neck" in Italian, from which we get *collar*.)

acerbic (ə sir' bik) *adj. Acerbic* describes the scowl on the face of a sourpuss or curmudgeon. People who don't like people walk around with an *acerbic* expression—sour, bitter, harsh. Political speeches in the heat of those endless campaigns are all too often *acerbic*. People often write *acerbic* letters to their local newspapers. A boss with an *acerbic* expression can make the whole office staff uneasy. Even humor can be *acerbic*. When Isadora Duncan proposed to G.B. Shaw that they have a child, because with her beauty and his brains it would be nearly perfect, he replied, "Yes, my dear, but what if the child has my beauty and your brains?"— an example of *acerbic* humor, if there ever was one. From Latin *acerbus* (bitter).

acme (ak' mee) *n. Akme* is classical Greek for "highest point." The *acme* of anything is its summit, its utmost limit. Thus, people who have "arrived" are spoken of as having reached the *acme* of success. Before his defeat at Moscow, Napoleon had attained the *acme* of his power. The word has been cheapened somewhat by its use here and about in the names of small local businesses, like "The New *Acme* Diner." Used that way, it is all too often a gross exaggeration.

acolyte (ak' ə lite) *n*. Originally, an *acolyte* was a priest's attendant at church, an altar boy. It has come to mean any "follower" or "attendant" of an important personage. The chairman of the board struts in followed by his *acolytes*, and the meeting can now begin. The term is sometimes used sarcastically and pejoratively, imparting the flavor of *toady*. Boxing champions and rock stars often travel with a dozen or more *acolytes*, which may explain why so many of them wind up broke in their declining years. From Greek *akolouthos* (follower, attendant).

acquiesce (ak wee ess') *vb*. Usually followed by the preposition *in*, it means to "agree with," "consent to," "comply with." Diehard fundamentalists still refuse to *acquiesce* in the matter of Darwin's theory of evolution. The noun *acquiescence* (ak wee ess' əns) implies silent agreement or passive submission or compliance. The term is used in a technical sense in the field of tax litigation: When the Tax Court of the United States hands down an opinion, the Internal Revenue Service sometimes publishes its *"Acquiescence"* (meaning that it will comply) or *"Nonacquiescence"* (it will not, and it will appeal or take the next case on the subject to court). From Latin *adquiescere* (to rest; by extension, to be pleased with).

acrimonious (ak rə moe' nee əs) *adj. Acrimonious* remarks are bitter and cutting. Sometimes an innocent question, well meant but misunderstood, gets an *acrimonious* answer. "Friendly" divorce proceedings all too often turn *acrimonious*. *Acrimo-*

nious remarks are often the result of a hot temper and the kind you're frequently sorry you made. From Middle Latin *acrimoniosus*, based on Latin *acer* (sharp, cutting) and *acerbus* (bitter). cf. *acerbic*.

acronym (ak′ rə nim) *n*. An *acronym* is a word formed from the initial letters of a group of words, like *WAC* (Women's Army Corps); *radar* (radio detecting and ranging); or *laser* (light amplification by stimulated emission of radiation). *Acronyms* start out by being strings of initials and end by becoming familiar words (if they're found to be remotely pronounceable). *OPEC* (Organization of Petroleum Exporting Countries) is all too familiar. *NATO* (North American Treaty Organization) is more reassuring. From a combination of two Greek words, *akros* (topmost, i.e., the initial letter of a word) and *onoma* (name, word).

adage (ad′ ij) *n*. An *adage* is a proverb, or a traditional saying. It is a wise child who knows his own father. Spare the rod and spoil the child. A stitch in time saves nine. These are all *adages*, also known as *old saws*, *maxims*, or *aphorisms*. Some people can muster an *adage* to suit any occasion. *Adages* may make you yawn, but they are sometimes the most effective way to characterize or sum up a situation. From a combination of Latin prefix *ad-* and a form of *aio* (I say).

admonitory (ad mon′ ə tor ee) *adj*. Anything that is *admonitory* provides a warning. An *admonitory* movement or gesture or tone of voice warns us that something unpleasant or dangerous is going to happen. A lioness about to spring often emits an *admonitory* growl. When a principal asks a schoolboy into his office he often greets him with an *admonitory* look. The related word *admonish* (ad mon′ ish) means "to caution." *Admonition* (ad mə nish′ ən) is the noun and means "warning." From Latin *admonitus*, a form of *admonere* (to remind, advise), which in turn is based on *monere* (to warn).

adroit (ə droyt′) *adj*. An *adroit* person is skillful, resourceful, quick to seize upon the right move in a situation, especially a tricky one. A good debater has to be *adroit*. The word can also be applied to the resourceful act itself. The rescue at Entebbe was one of the most *adroit* exploits in recent history. The word comes from *à droit*, French for "right" in the sense of "proper." *Adroit* is the opposite of *gauche*. In French, *à droite* means "on the right"; *à gauche* means "on the left." This use of *adroit* and *gauche* has to do with the old superstition about left-handed people being somehow less capable. See *dexterous; maladroit*.

adulation (aj ə lay′ shən) *n.* Anyone who feels *adulation* is likely to display fawning adoration or devotion. It's a state of idolization, or servile and excessive admiration. The *adulation* of rock stars by vast audiences is a display that puzzles earlier generations. Feline pride and self-sufficiency are nobler traits than canine *adulation*. From Latin *adulatio* (fawning). The verb is *adulate* (aj′ ə late), from Latin *adulatus*, a form of *adulare* (to fawn). Some people *adulate* baseball players, while others *adulate* movie stars.

adversity (ad vur′ sə tee) *n. Adversity* is a condition marked by bad luck, troubles, woes, hard times. *Adversity* was widespread during the Great Depression of the Thirties. After years of *adversity* on the farm, a couple may pull up stakes and move into a little house in town. The word is an extension of the adjective *adverse* (ad vurs′), which describes anyone or anything acting against your interests, or anything unfavorable, as in the phrase, *adverse circumstances*. A related word is *adversary* (ad′ vər serr ee), which means "opponent" (*n.*) or "opposing" (*adj.*). *Adversity* is the opposite of *prosperity*, and comes from Latin *adversitas*.

aegis (ee′ jis) *n.* The Aegis in Greek mythology was a shield of Zeus and a symbol of protection. Thus the word came into common use meaning "sponsorship" or "patronage." An acting career may prosper under the *aegis* of a truly great impresario. When we travel abroad, we feel safe under the *aegis* of our government, despite the poor treatment accorded U.S. citizens in some countries. When a recital is presented under the *aegis* of the local music club, the word expresses the sense of "sponsorship" rather than that of "protection."

affable (af′ ə bəl) *adj.* We are all fond of friends who are *affable*; they're pleasant, friendly, and easy to talk to. The English are a courteous, *affable* people. Candidates often charm audiences with an open and *affable* manner. From Latin *adfabilis* (easy to speak to).

aficionado (ə fees yə nah′ doe) *n.* This word was taken over unchanged from the Spanish. (Purists, conscious of its Spanish origin, like to pronounce the second syllable *feeth*.) An *aficionado* is a devotee, an ardent follower, a fan. A person who never misses a single game of the home team is an *aficionado*. People who read a detective story a week are *aficionados*. Hemingway popularized the word in his novel, *The Sun Also Rises*. There, of course, he was talking about bullfighting, and "Papa" was one of the sport's most ardent *aficionados*.

affinity (ə fin' ə tee) *n*. When we have an *affinity* for someone or something, we experience a natural liking and feel an attraction. Sometimes one is barely introduced to a person but immediately feels an *affinity* for him. Virginia Woolf spoke of the "odd *affinities* [she] had with people she had never spoken to." Born actors have an *affinity* for the stage. From Latin *adfinitas* (literally, relationship by marriage; by extension, union).

aggrandize (ə gran' dïzo) *vb*. When you *aggrandize* something, you magnify it, inflate it, or increase it. Hilaire Belloc (1870–1953) wrote of one whose only desire "was to *aggrandize* his estate." The noun is *aggrandizement* (ə gran' diz mənt). Justice Benjamin N. Cardozo (1870–1938), of the United States Supreme Court, answered the "critics of [his] *aggrandizement* of federal power." *Aggrandize* sometimes takes on the meaning of making, or trying to make, people or things greater than they are. *Self-aggrandizement* is used this way, of people of little talent who exaggerate their own importance. People who win many promotions in a company are often given to *self-aggrandizement*, which sometimes never abates, even after retirement. Muhammad Ali ("I am the greatest!") is a conspicuous practitioner of the art. From Middle French *aggrandissement*, based on Latin *grandis* (great, large).

alacrity (ə lak' ri tee) *n*. This word is usually seen in the phrase *with alacrity*. Anything done *with alacrity* is done with cheerful or eager readiness, the opposite of reluctance. When the boss invites you to lunch, you are likely to accept *with alacrity*. When good things come our way, like free theatre tickets, tax rebates, or Christmas bonuses, we respond *with alacrity*. From Latin *alacritas* (liveliness).

allay (ə lay') *vb*. To *allay* something is to calm or quiet it, or relieve it, depending on the context. One *allays* suspicion (that is, quiets it or puts it to rest) by proving it to be unjustified. Pain may be *allayed* (relieved) by medicine or massage. The right psychologist may be able to *allay* (calm) anxieties. A child's fears may be *allayed* (pacified) by tender, loving care. *Allay* is a soothing word, full of kindness and hope. From Middle English *alayen*.

allegory (al' ə gor ee) *n*. An *allegory* is a symbolic narrative; it is a tale that is not to be taken literally, but is told to present a moral lesson or a universal truth. John Keats (1795–1821) wrote in an 1819 letter, "A man's life of any worth is a continual *allegory* ...." He meant that moral generalizations could be drawn from the story of a worthwhile life. *Pilgrim's Progress* (John Bunyan, 1628–1688) is an *allegory*. *Everyman* (full title, *The Summoning of Everyman*), a fifteenth-century morality play, is an *allegory*. A short *allegory* using animals as characters is called a *fable*. The examples by Aesop and La Fontaine are famous. From Greek *allegoria*, which was based on the Greek verb *allegorein* (to speak figuratively; that is, to speak in such a way as to imply something else).

alleviate (ə lee' vee ate) *vb*. Anything that *alleviates* relieves or lessens. Aspirin *alleviates* fever. When something *alleviates* pain or sorrow, it makes it easier to bear. In *Don Quixote*, Cervantes writes about the "strange charm in the thoughts of a good legacy" that "wondrously *alleviates* the sorrow that men would otherwise feel for the death of friends." An apology, or an explanation, can often *alleviate* the strain in a relationship. From Late Latin *alleviatus*, a form of *alleviare* (to lighten, diminish).

alliteration (ə lit ə ray' shən) *n*. The repetition of a sound or letter in two or more words in a sequence is an *alliteration*. Examples: Sing a song of sixpence; wild and woolly; bewitched and bewildered; a dime a dozen. The so-called tongue twisters are based primarily on *alliteration*: rubber baby buggy bumpers; she sells seashells by the seashore; Peter Piper picked a peck of pickled peppers. From Middle Latin *alliteratio*.

amanuensis (ə man yoo en' sis: *pl*. -seez) *n*. Secretary; one who takes dictation or copies (in these days, types) a manuscript. Note the syllables *manu-* in both words, *manuscript* and *amanuensis*. They come from *manus*, Latin for *hand*, which gives us *manual*, *manufacture*, and other words involving the use of the hands. This is not a common word, but it makes an elegant addition to one's vocabulary. There are writers whose faithful *amanuenses* have typed their manuscripts every day for decades. The author of this humble dictionary is deeply indebted to his *amanuenses*, who have had to struggle with Latin, Greek, the pesky omnipresent schwa (see Preface), and Lord knows what else. Taken over intact from the Latin.

ambience (am' bee əns) *n. Ambience* is the mood, character, or atmosphere of an environment; the quality of the surroundings or milieu. Tourists love the charming Old World *ambience* of little villages all over Europe. Quaint ethnic restaurants offer authentic *ambiences*; would that the food always lived up to the atmosphere! Many people don't feel comfortable in certain kinds of *ambience*, like the great open spaces of large banks. There are those who are too sophisticated to be happy in a provincial *ambience*—and vice-versa. Also spelled *ambiance*, which is the French noun from which *ambience* is taken.

ambiguous (am big' yoo əs) *adj.* Anything *ambiguous* is capable of more than one meaning and, therefore, unclear. *Overlook*, for example, can mean either "oversee," i.e., "inspect and supervise," or "fail to see." An unfortunately *ambiguous* sign at an Edwardian beach reads: "Gentlemen are requested not to overlook the ladies' Bathing Place." *Ambiguous* language is the enemy of clarity, leaving the reader or hearer puzzled. Its use in contracts and laws, especially tax laws, has resulted in much litigation; in treaties, it has led to international complications. The noun, *ambiguity* (am bih gyoo' ə tee), is not to be confused with *ambivalence*. From Latin *ambiguus* (literally, moving from side to side). *Ambi-* is a Latin prefix meaning "both," as in *ambidextrous*, *ambivalence*, etc.

ambivalent (am biv' ə lənt) *adj.* When a person is *ambivalent* about something, he is indecisive, unable to make up his mind, wavering between two courses of action or opposing opinions, favoring, at one and the same time, both yes and no. Some youngsters are *ambivalent* about college; they want the education but hate to leave home. The noun is *ambivalence* (am biv' ə ləns). The late Jimmy Durante used to sing a wonderfully funny song that went: "Dija evah have the feelin' that ya wanted ta go, and yet ya had the feelin' ya wanted to stay, go, stay, go, stay," etc. (Every time he said "go" he picked up his battered hat off the piano and started up off the stool; every time he said "stay" he darted back, sat down and dumped his hat back on the piano.) The love-hate syndrome is an example of *ambivalence*. The Roman poet Catullus (87 B.C.–54 B.C.) wrote: "I hate and I love. Why...I know not, but I feel it and am in torment." Do not confuse *ambivalent* with *ambiguous*. From a combination of *ambi-* (Latin prefix meaning "both" and *valens*, a form of Latin *valere* (to be strong); in other words, *both* inclinations are equally *strong*.

ambulatory (am' byə lə tor ee) *adj.* One who is *ambulatory* is able to walk, as opposed to being bedridden. It is a term heard often in hospitals. Nowadays, patients are *ambulatory* much sooner after an operation than used to be the case. *Amble* and *ambulance* come from the same Latin word, *ambulare* (to walk). (Ambulances don't walk, but they do get about.) *Ambulatory* has a special meaning in law; an *ambulatory document* is one that can be changed at will, like a will.

ameliorate (ə meel' yə rate) *vb.* When you *ameliorate* something, you improve it or make it better. We get the word from *melior*, which is Latin for "better." This word is often found in the expression *ameliorate the situation*. A timely apology can *ameliorate* a relationship that has gone sour because one party has taken offense. Good economic news or an optimistic message from the President usually *ameliorates* the condition of the stock market. The noun is *amelioration* (ə meel yə ray' shən). It is to be hoped that renewal of the SALT talks will result in the *amelioration* of Soviet-American relations.

amenable (ə mee' nə bəl, ə men' ə bəl) *adj.* An *amenable* person is agreeable, willing to be persuaded, to listen to reason, and to follow advice. If you argue your point of view and obtain the other party's agreement promptly, you can say that he was quickly *amenable*. In this sense, *amenable* is the opposite of *stubborn*. *Amenable* has another and different meaning not often met with, "liable," "answerable." When you borrow money you are *amenable* for the debt incurred, i.e., answerable for it. When you commit an offense, you are *amenable* to the authorities involved. From a combination of the Latin prefix *ad-* and the verb *minare* (to lead to) plus the Latin ending *-abilis*, from which we get *-able*.

amenity (ə men' i tee) *n. Amenity*, generally speaking, connotes pleasantness and agreeableness. One can speak of the *amenity* of a certain part of the countryside. In the plural, it can mean "gracious manners." We all enjoy the *amenities* of civilized society. In the plural it can also have the sense of "conveniences": Nowadays, in America, most dwellings are provided with all the *amenities* (hot and cold running water, oil heat, proximity to shops, a lovely view, etc.). From Latin *amoenitas* (pleasantness).

amorous (am' ə rəs) *adj*. A word with many facets: affectionate; having a tendency to love; obsessed by sexuality; smitten; showing love. This word has all those nuances. Samuel Johnson (1709–1784) told David Garrick, the famous actor (1717–1779), that he wouldn't go backstage "for the silk stockings and white bosoms of your actresses excite my *amorous* propensities." Some men are *amorous* of every pretty woman they meet. When Valentino appeared on screen, he instantly triggered the *amorous* impulses of the women in the audience, or at least those under eighty-five. From Latin *amorosus*.

amorphous (ə morf' əs) *adj*. This word describes anything without definite shape or form; formless. Somebody sees an *amorphous* shadow in the doorway; can it be the family ghost? Clouds that constantly change shape can be said to be *amorphous*. The shifting crowd that squeezes its way out of the stadium after a big game is *amorphous*. The philosopher John Dewey (1859–1952) spoke of "that indefinite and *amorphous* thing called the consuming public." A work of art can be called *amorphous*, whether an abstract painting or a play in the idiom of the theater of the absurd. From Greek *amorphos* (shapeless).

anachronism (ə nak' rə niz əm) *n*. This term applies to any person, institution, custom, concept, etc., that belongs to another age. An old London pub surrounded by giant skyscrapers is a pleasant *anachronism*. An absolute monarchy is an *anachronism* in this day and age. The Yankee in King Arthur's court was a contrived dramatic *anachronism*. The Edwardian clothes affected by some contemporary young men are an *anachronism*. James Morris, in *Farewell the Trumpets* (Faber & Faber, London, 1978), said of India in the 1920s: "It was becoming an awkward *anachronism*." The adjective is *anachronistic* (ə nak rə nis' tik). The wigs and gowns of English judges and barristers are an *anachronistic* bit of fancy dress that signify the continuity and dignity of English justice. From Latin *anachronismus*, taken from Greek *anachronismos* (wrong time reference).

anagram (an' ə gram) *n*. An *anagram* is a word formed from a rearrangement of the letters of another word. *Evil* is an anagram of *vile*; *able* and *bale* are anagrams of each other; so are *carthorse* and *orchestra*. From New Latin *anagramma*.

analogy (ə nal' ə jee) *n*. This word is used to describe a resemblance based on the similarity between certain features of two things, like the human heart and a mechanical pump. Social science teachers often draw an *analogy* between the nation and the family. Samuel Butler (1835–1902) said, "... *analogy* is often misleading." The things compared are called *analogues* (an' ə logs) and *analogize* (ə nal' ə jize) is the verb, meaning to point out the similarities. Lawyers draw *analogies*, between the facts of decided cases and the facts of the specific case before them, in order to predict the outcome. Business people are often chided for their love of sports *analogies*: "Most of the salesmen are singles hitters, but Atkins is capable of the long ball. He lands the big accounts." And the world finally wearied of the Nixon administration's "game plan." *Analogous* (ə nal' ə gəs) is the adjective: The wings of an airplane are *analogous* to those of a bird. From Latin *analogia*, based on Greek *analogos*.

anathema (ə nath' ə mə) *n*. *Anathema* is commonly used to describe a detestable thing or person. Literally, an *anathema* is a curse laid on by the Church and usually follows excommunication. Figuratively, it is used to describe anyone or anything detestable or loathsome. Cigarette smoke at the dinner table is *anathema* to most diners. Those television commercials are getting worse and worse; they're becoming *anathema* to sensitive viewers. The world seems increasingly full of *anathemas*: radiation, acid rain, beachfront condominiums—where have all the flowers gone? From Latin *anathema*, taken from the same Greek word (thing accursed).

ancillary (an' sə ler ee) *adj*. This word means the same thing as "auxiliary" and describes anything that serves as an accessory. The word is based on the Latin word for "maidservant," *ancilla*. Inventories are sometimes stored in a main warehouse and *ancillary* locations. When one takes up the study of physics, math and chemistry are *ancillary* requirements. Textbooks are often supplemented by workbooks and other *ancillary* materials.

animus (an' ə məs) *n*. When a person experiences *animus*, he is filled with hostility and antagonism. We get the word *animosity* from *animus*. On a controversial subject, a speaker may create a good deal of *animus* among the audience. The use of *animus* implies, generally, that the ill will, though unexpressed, is deepseated. One might, by observing a jury, detect its *animus* against the plaintiff or a witness. William Ralph Inge (1806–1954), Dean of St. Paul's in London, known as "the Gloomy Dean," wrote about the large school of thought that cherished "...a certain *animus* against what it calls intellectualism...." From Latin *animus* (soul, feeling, wrath).

annals (an' əlz) *n. pl.* Annals are historical records. Gray's *Elegy Written in a Country Churchyard* (Thomas Gray 1716–1771) spoke of "...the short and simple *annals* of the poor." "Happy the people whose *annals* are blank in history books," wrote Thomas Carlyle (1795–1881), referring to the absence of wars, revolutions, upheavals, etc. (This brings to mind the old Chinese curse: "May you live in interesting times!") Politicians are fond of referring to "the *annals* of history" (They are apparently fond of redundancies.) And we've all heard of movies touted as "the greatest in the *annals* of show business." From Latin *annales* (yearly records); based on *annus* (year), from which we get *annual, anniversary,* etc.

anomaly (ə nom' ə lee) *n.* An *anomaly* is a deviation from the general rule or type; anything out of keeping with accepted ideas of how things should be. Shabby clothes worn by an impoverished earl on his magnificent estate would appear to be an *anomaly.* The sensitive face of a lovely maiden would be an *anomaly* in an otherwise brutish family. George Santayana (1863–1952), the philosopher, discussing the characteristics of the English, wrote, "England is the paradise of individuality, eccentricity...*anomalies*..." Among states, New Hampshire is an *anomaly*—and a pleasant one: it has no sales or income tax. The adjective is *anomalous* (ə nom' ə ləs): A lovely flower growing in a rubbish heap can be startlingly *anomalous.* From Latin *anomalia,* taken from the Greek.

antecedents (an tih see' dənts) *n.pl.* This word can mean both "ancestors" and "events of one's earlier life." The first meaning is illustrated in this sentence: His emotional problems are easily explained when one knows about his *antecedents.* The other meaning appears in the following example: The defense attorney hoped to suppress his client's *antecedents* during the trial. It is used in the singular as an adjective meaning "preceding" or "previous," as in the phrase *antecedent events* or *circumstances.* From Latin *antecedens,* a form of *antecedere* (to precede).

anthropology (an thrə pol' ə jee) *n. Anthropology* is the study of mankind, its origins, development, customs, and racial characteristics. A specialist in *anthropology* is an *anthropologist*. Margaret Mead (1901–1978) was one of America's greatest *anthropologists*. Sir James George Frazer (1854–1941), writing of primitive peoples in *The Golden Bough*, said, "The awe and dread with which the untutored savage contemplates his mother-in-law are amongst the most familiar facts of *anthropology*." From Greek *anthropos* (man) and *-logia*, a Greek suffix denoting study or science: hence, study or science of man.

anthropomorphic (an thrǝ pǝ mor' fik) *adj.* Any act or statement that ascribes human characteristics to gods, animals, and objects is *anthropomorphic*. To do so is to *anthropomorphize* (an thrǝ pǝ mor' fize) them. The ancient Greek and Roman descriptions of their gods as loving, drinking, fighting, etc., were *anthropomorphic*. People tend to *anthropomorphize* their pets and plants, addressing them as though they were human and ascribing human emotions to them. "My rhododendrons look tired." "Oh, poor goldfish. I hope you guys don't miss us while we're in Bermuda." Ships are referred to as "she" and are given human attributes, like pride, fatigue and, as in *Little Toot*, bravery.* From Greek *anthropos* (man) plus *morphe* (form); hence man-form, or human.

*And one comes across passages in prose or poetry like "The trees were sighing, the heavens were weeping."

antic (an' tik) *n., adj.* This word describes odd or eccentric behavior, amusing gestures, pranks, and capers. It is most often found in the plural: You never know what to expect from some people; they suddenly break into the strangest *antics*. There are those whose *antics* puzzle their friends. Puck, in *Midsummer Night's Dream*, is always represented as engaging in *antics*. From Latin *anticus* (in front; by extension, primitive). The adjective is now archaic.

antipathy (an tip' ǝ thee—*th* as in *thing*) *n.* An *antipathy* fills us with aversion and a strong dislike. He has an *antipathy* to travel. It can happen that people meet and feel a mutual *antipathy* almost at once. An *antipathy* is a strong, settled, unchanging feeling of abhorrence towards a particular person, activity, style, type of food, way of life, race, anything. The adjective *antipathetic* (an tǝ pǝ thet' ik) can be used to describe the person doing the loathing: Some people are *antipathetic* to change; or it can describe the object of the aversion: Certain kinds of behavior have always been *antipathetic* to particular individuals. From Greek *antipatheia*. Note also *sympathy*, from Greek *sympatheia*, and *empathy*, from *empatheia;* all the Greek originals being based on Greek *pathos* (sensation) plus appropriate prefixes *anti-* (against), *sym-* (with), *em-* (in, into).

antiquity (an tik' wih tee) *n*. This word has a number of uses. It can mean "ancient times,": The study of *antiquity* teaches us a great deal about our own times. It can denote the quality of ancientness: We know the pyramids are monuments of great *antiquity*. In the plural it describes relics of ancient times: Archeologists engage in the search for ancient coins, cooking utensils, fragments of buildings and monuments, and other *antiquities*. From Latin *antiquitas*.

antithesis (an tith' ə sis—*th* as in *thiny*) *n*. The *antithesis* of anything is its direct opposite. Fascism and communism are the *antithesis* of democracy. Good is the *antithesis* of evil. *Antithetic* (an tə thet' ik) and *antithetical* (an tə thet' ə kəl) are adjectives describing the things that are opposite to each other. If a wife loves to entertain, to go dancing, to travel, and her husband loves his fireside and slippers most of all, they can be described as the *antithesis* of each other. Taken over intact from the Greek.

aphorism (af' ə riz əm) *n*. An *aphorism* is a concise statement of a general truth. Unfortunately, it often happens that such statements have only a grain of truth. *Aphorisms* are also known by such names as *maxims, proverbs*, and *old saws*. "Nice guys finish last," is one of the more painful *aphorisms*. *Ars longa, vita brevis* (Art is long, and life is short) is a well-known warning, expressed in a Latin *aphorism*, that the production of great art takes a lifetime. "*There is no royal road to learning*," is an *aphorism* meaning that you've got to work hard, even if you're a king, to acquire knowledge. *Aphoristic* (af ə ris' tik) is the adjective, and some people curb their *aphoristic* tendencies with great difficulty. From Greek *aphorismos*, via Middle Latin *aphorismus* (definition).

aplomb (ə plom', or ə plum') *n*. *Aplomb* is self-assurance, poise, imperturbability. A person with *aplomb* is not fazed or disconcerted under the most trying circumstances. Sir Francis Drake (1540–1596) displayed his *aplomb* by playing at ninepins while the Spanish Armada was approaching. Walt Whitman (1819–1892) wrote, in *Democratic Vistas*: "It is native personality . . . that endows a man to stand before presidents or generals . . . with *aplomb* . . ." *Plomb* (from Latin *plumbum*) is French for "lead": *à plomb* means "vertical." People with *aplomb* stand up straight; they never cringe. (The weighted line used to establish the vertical is called a *plumb line* because the weight is usually a piece of lead.)

apocalypse (ə pok' ə lips) *n.* A dire word, describing disaster, cataclysm, the end of the world, Armageddon. *Apocalypse* (from an ancient Greek word meaning "to disclose") is the name of the *Revelation of St. John the Divine*, the last book of the New Testament, in which he describes the end of the world. Literally, an *apocalypse* is a revelation, but because of the biblical *Apocalypse*, the word is commonly used to describe any cataclysmic event. World War III could be the final *apocalypse*. Francis Ford Coppola aptly titled his film of the Vietnam War *Apocalypse Now*. On the other hand, with the war having ended several years before, perhaps the title should have been *Apocalypse Then*. *Apocalyptic* (ə pok ə lip' tik) is the adjective: St. John had an *apocalyptic* vision of Armageddon.

apocryphal (ə pok' rə fəl) *adj.* This word is used to describe things, usually stories or reports, of questionable authenticity. The legend of King Arthur and the Knights of the Round Table is, in that sense, *apocryphal*. The word can be used in a somewhat stronger way, to indicate spuriousness or falsity. Some people are given to the telling of *apocryphal* anecdotes whose falsities are transparent. The word comes from the *Apocrypha*, fourteen books of the Old Testament rejected by Jews and Protestants as of doubtful origin. Later, any writings of dubious authenticity were called *apocryphal*. One often hears the phrase *apocryphal story*, referring to those tales that are presented as true but seem too patently grisly or sentimental to be real. Clifford Irving's biography of Howard Hughes was more than apocryphal; it was a downright fabrication.

apogee (ap' ə jee) *n.* In astronomy, the *apogee* is the point in the orbit of any planet, satellite, the moon, etc. when it is farthest from the earth. The *perigee* (per' ə jee) is the nearest point. *Apogee* is used frequently to mean the "high point" of anything, and in that sense it can mean "climax" or "summit." Trade with China is just getting started; it will be a long time before it reaches its *apogee*. From Greek *apogaion* (off-earth) and *perigeion* (close to the earth), respectively.

apostate (ə pos' tate) *n.* An *apostate* is a person who renounces his faith, party, etc., a renegade or defector. Whitaker Chambers (1901–1961), who denounced Alger Hiss, was an *apostate* from Communism, John Connally, from the Democratic Party. The Roman emperor Flavius Claudius Julianus, who reigned from 361–363 A.D., is better known as *Julian the Apostate*, because in the course of his studies he abandoned Christianity. The act of renunciation is called *apostasy* (ə pos' tə see). Ronald Reagan has never regretted his *apostasy* from the Democratic Party. From Greek *apostates* (drawing away).

apotheosis (ə poth ee o' sis or a pə thee' ə sis—*th* as in *thing*) *n.* This word, in its literal use, describes deification, i.e., the raising of a person to divine rank. Roman emperors often underwent *apotheosis* upon death. Thus, for example, Claudius I, who reigned from A.D. 41–51, became Claudius the God upon his death, as indicated by the titles of the two novels about him by Robert Graves: *I Claudius* and *Claudius the God*. Nowadays, the term has come to mean, simply, "glorification." In this sense, on his death, John Lennon, like Rudolf Valentino and Elvis Presley before him, underwent *apotheosis*. But the word is more often used figuratively to mean glorification in the sense of "supreme example": John Wayne was the *apotheosis* of daring and courage to his adoring fans. The Queen Mother is the *apotheosis* of British womanhood. Taken over intact from the Greek, via Late Latin.

appellation (ap ə lay' shən) *n.* An *appellation* is a name or designation applied to somebody or something. The name *Cassius Clay* has been extinguished by the *appellation* "Muhammad Ali." We are all familiar with mud tracks that hardly deserve the *appellation* "road." "The Confessor" has become the common *appellation* of the English King Edward, who ruled from 1042–1066 and founded Westminster Abbey. From Latin *appellatio* (naming.).

apposite (ap' ə zit) *adj.* This is a term applied to something that is to the point, or well put. An *apposite* answer or remark is exactly right, on the nose. When a young thing asked Louis Armstrong what jazz was, he replied, "If you have to ask what jazz is, you'll never know." *That* was an *apposite* answer! So was Winston Churchill's riposte to George Bernard Shaw, who sent him two tickets to the opening night of a new Shaw play with a note reading, "Bring a friend, if you have one." Winston's answer came quickly: "I'm busy that night. Send me two tickets for the second night—if there is one." Churchill was good at *apposite* replies. Margot Asquith told him that if she were married to him, she would put poison in his coffee. Back he came, "If I were married to you, I'd drink it." From *appositus*, a form of Latin *apponere* (to put near).

apprehend (ap rə hend') *vb.* The common use of this word is as a somewhat more formal substitute for *catch* or *arrest*, in the sense of "take into custody." It has two subsidiary meanings: "to grasp the meaning of (something)," for which its sister word *comprehend* is usually used, and "to worry about, expect with fear and anxiety, dread." Police officers on television favor "big words" and like to speak of "*apprehending* the perpetrator" (catching the criminal). The related word *apprehensive* (ap rə hen' siv) means "uneasy," reflecting the second, subsidiary meaning mentioned above. Similarly, *apprehension* (ap rə hen' shən) is an *uneasiness* or fear about bad luck in the offing. *Misapprehension* has nothing to do with *arresting* or *uneasiness*: it simply means "mistake," reflecting the first subsidiary meaning shown above, and the same is true of the verb to *misapprehend*, not very commonly used in ordinary speech. To summarize: *apprehend* means "to catch"; *apprehensive* means "uneasy"; *apprehension* is "uneasiness"; and *misapprehension* means simply "mistake." From Latin *apprehendere* (to grasp).

appropriate (ə pro' pree ət) *adj.*, (ə pro' pree ate) *vb.* As an adjective (note pronunciation of last syllable), *appropriate* describes anything suitable for a particular purpose or occasion. A long evening gown is unquestionably *appropriate* for a soprano's debut as soloist. *Appropriate* can be used where the suitability is to the person rather than the occasion or purpose: In view of his inexperience, a newcomer to the staff should be sure to take an *appropriate* back seat at firm meetings. Modesty is an admirable quality and almost always an *appropriate* mode of behavior. The verb goes off in an entirely different direction: to *appropriate* something can mean merely to "set it aside" for a specific purpose, the way the Senate *appropriates* a million dollars for an investigation (we are familiar with the term *appropriation bill*) or a company *appropriates* a certain sum for research, but it can have a more sinister meaning, when, for example, dictators *appropriate* the property of the state or of private citizens; here, *appropriate* is a polite word for "steal." To *misappropriate* is to take or apply (property or funds) dishonestly, especially for one's own use, and here too we have a fancy synonym for "steal." (*Euphemism* might be a "nicer" word than *synonym*, but why be nice about it?) From Late Latin *appropriatus*, a form of *appropriare* (to make one's own), based on Latin prefix *ap-*, a variant of *ad-* (to) before *p*, plus *proprius* (one's own). Cf. *expropriate*.

apt (apt) *adj.* Apt has several meanings. In the sense of "inclined" (given to a particular behavior pattern), it might be used to describe a person who, when angry, is *apt* to snap at you. It can also mean "likely." If you scan the sky on a November night, you're *apt* to see a shooting star. The word can also describe the quality of being able to acquire knowledge quickly. Teachers are pleased by the quick reactions of *apt* pupils. Finally, *apt* can be used in the sense of "suitable," fit for a particular need, purpose, or occasion. Adlai Stevenson pleased his audiences with his *apt* remarks on the state of the world. In talking about the excesses of contemporary life, mention of the fate of ancient Rome might be an *apt* comparison. From Latin *aptus (fastened, fitting)*.

arbiter (ar' bi tər) *n.* Arbiter describes a final authority, one with the absolute power to decide. Emily Post, the *arbiter* of etiquette for generations, was succeeded by Amy Vanderbilt. "The press is increasingly becoming the *arbiter* of American life," says Louis Banks in *"The Rise of Newsocracy"* (January 1981 issue of the *Atlantic Monthly*). *Arbiter* is a Latin word, taken over into English unchanged. Gaius Petronius, the Roman satirist who died in A.D. 66, was known as *Petronius Arbiter* (short for *arbiter elegantiae* or *elegantiarum*—Petronius the Arbiter of Taste.)

arcane (ar kane') *adj.* This word characterizes something secret or obscure, with a hint of mystery. Mona Lisa's smile, usually described as mysterious or enigmatic, seems to be shielding *arcane* thoughts. What secret is she keeping? Things that are *arcane* are open only to those possessed of special, inside knowledge. In this sense, such things are esoteric. *Arcana* (ar kane' ah) is a very literary word for *mysteries*. *Arcane* comes from the Latin word *arcanus* (literally, shut, closed, and hence secret).

arch (arch) *adj.* This word can be used in a number of ways. By itself, it describes people who are mischievous or roguish, playfully saucy. John Barrymore was much given to witty remarks and *arch* smiles. Jane Austen wrote, "...that *arch* eye of yours! It sees through everything." *Arch* is also used in the sense of "outstanding," connected to the word it modifies: Everybody in the world knows that Hitler was an *arch*villain. It can be used as an intensive prefix, in the sense of "chief" or "principal," in words like *arch*bishop, *arch*deacon, and *arch*diocese. In *arch*angel it is pronounced *ark*; otherwise that word would be quite a mouthful. The sense of "mischievous or playful" is said to have come from the use of *arch-* as a prefix in such words as *archrogue, archwag*, with the connotations of *rogue, wag*, etc., flowing back, as it were, into the prefix. From Greek *arche-*, a prefix indicating excellence.

arduous (ar' joo əs) *adj. Arduous* can be used in a number of ways. Climbing Mt. Everest is an *arduous* undertaking. In this sense, the word takes on the coloration of "laborious," requiring great strength and perseverance. The Roman poet Horace (65–8 B.C.) wrote, "No height is too *arduous* for mortal men." The word has also the meaning of "strenuous": If you are destined to fail, all your *arduous* efforts will come to nothing. *Arduous* can also characterize something hard to bear: Springtime is welcome after an *arduous* winter. Those idyllic South Sea islands suffer from *arduous* typhoon seasons. Inflation is particularly *arduous* to those living on fixed incomes. From Latin *arduus* (high, steep, or difficult).

argot (ar' go or ar' gət) *n. Argot* is jargon, the idiom of a particular class or group. It is hard for older people to understand the *argot* of teen-agers. The term applies particularly to the underworld: the *argot* of thieves; the *argot* of pickpockets; but it can apply to any group, class, or profession, used in the same way as *jargon*: the *argot* of economists (Will somebody please write a glossary on that?), psychiatrists (and one on that?), etc. The word has been taken over unchanged from the French word for *slang*, pronounced *ar go'*.

arid (ar' id—*ar* as in *arrow*) *adj.* The literal meaning is "extremely dry": April, notable for its showers, can occasionally be an *arid* month. Farmers have a hard time producing crops from *arid* land. Used figuratively, *arid* means "dull and uninteresting": It is sometimes hard to stay awake during a brilliant scholar's *arid* lectures. Judges can be turned off by a lawyer's *arid* treatment of a case. From Latin *aridus*.

Armageddon (ar mə geh' dən) *n. Armageddon* is the biblical scene of the final battle between the forces of good and the forces of evil at the end of the world (Revelation 16: 16). The word is now used figuratively to characterize any decisive, final conflict. Many authorities believe that World War III would result in *Armageddon*.

arrant (ar' ənt—*ar* as in *arrow*) *adj.* This word is used to intensify a quality of a person or thing, in the sense of "out-and-out" or "downright": Al Capone was an *arrant* knave. Ed Wynn played the part of an *arrant* fool (his sobriquet was "the Perfect Fool"). Father Divine's speeches were jumbles of *arrant* nonsense. "George Downing: As Arrant a Rascal as Lives amongst Men" is the title of an article by Ormonde de Kay, in the March–April 1981 issue of *Harvard Magazine*. The word is a variant of *errant*, which comes from *errans*, a form of Latin *errare* (to rove, stray).

arrogate (ar' ə gate—*ar* as in *arrow*) *vb.* To *arrogate* something is to claim it as one's own without right. In these troubled times, the generals or the colonels are sometimes quick to *arrogate* supreme power on the death of the head of state. There are those *arrogant* people who *arrogate* the right to decide all questions. As you might expect, *arrogate* is related to *arrogant* (ar' ə gənt), which means "overbearing and presumptuous." From Latin prefix *ad-* plus *rogare* (to ask, request).

arsenal (ar' sə nəl) *n.* This word, which in its literal sense denotes a place for the storage of arms and ammunition, is used figuratively to describe a supply or collection or repertory of anything. There are people whose *arsenal* of anecdotes make them welcome dinner guests. There are entertainers like Rich Little and Lily Tomlin whose *arsenal* of impersonations enchant their audiences. Franklin D. Roosevelt, in his fireside chat of December 19, 1940, said, "We must be the great *arsenal* of democracy," using *arsenal* both ways: supplier of arms against the fascists, and storehouse of democratic rights. From Italian *arsenale* (dockyard).

artful (art' fəl) *adj.* An *artful* person is crafty, deceitful, and cunning, the exact opposite of *artless*. There are those ladies who owe their youthful appearance to the *artful* application of makeup. In *Oliver Twist*, we are introduced to the young "artful Dodger," Fagin's eager pupil, chief of the young troop of pickpockets. William Congreve (1670–1729), in *Amoret*, described a troubling lady as "careless...with *artful* care, affecting to seem unaffected." Do not misuse *artful* in the sense of "artistic." From Latin *artis*, a form of *ars* (cunning) plus suffix *-ful*.

artless (art' lis) *adj.* An *artless* person is free from deceit and guile; without craftiness or cunning, the very opposite of *artful*. Very young children are *artless*; they haven't yet learned to conceal their feelings, to put on a false face. *Artless* people aren't wise to the ways of the world. Christopher Columbus, in a letter to the King and Queen of Spain, described the savages of Hispaniola as "*artless* and free with all they possess." From *artis*, a form of Latin *ars* (cunning) plus suffix *-less*.

ascetic (ə set' ik) *n., adj.* An *ascetic* is a self-denying person. As an adjective it means "self-denying," rigorously refraining from the ordinary pleasures of life. People who partake of none of the simple pleasures can be said to lead an *ascetic* existence. Ralph Nader's lifestyle is frequently described as spare and *ascetic*. Monks who take the vows of poverty are *ascetics*. From Greek *asketikos* (rigorous, hardworking).

asperity (ə sperr' ə tee) *n. Asperity* is harshness and acrimony (see *acrimonious*). The harshness is of a kind expressed by tone or manner. In a heated argument, people often overreact and address each other with great *asperity*. United Nations debates are often characterized by such *asperity* as to leave one feeling pessimistic about the prospects of lasting world peace...or a lasting world for that matter. From Latin *asperitas*.

aspersion (ə spur' zhən) *n.* This word is usually found in the plural, meaning "damaging assertions" and "slandering vilifications." Its most common use is in the expression to *cast aspersions*. There is a growing movement among Hollywood celebrities to hold gossip magazines accountable for their reckless *aspersions*. From Latin *aspersio* (sprinkling).

assiduous (ə sih' joo əs) *adj.* This word, denoting perseverance and diligence, can apply to both people and such things as effort, attention, or devotion. Success in school requires *assiduous* application to one's studies. Faint heart never won fair lady— and *assiduous* devotion helps. There are many research projects that would not have succeeded without the help of *assiduous* assistants, who provided *assiduous* assistance. From Latin *assiduus* (sitting down to: by extension, settling down to).

assuage (ə swayj') *vb.* To *assuage* is to soothe and relieve. Thoughtful cards of sympathy can help to *assuage* grief. A conscientious nurse will do her best to *assuage* the patient's pain. Nothing *assuages* thirst like the cool water of a brook. In his famous letter to Mrs. Bixby (Nov. 21, 1864), who had lost her sons in the Civil War, President Lincoln wrote, "... I pray that our Heavenly Father may *assuage* the anguish of your bereavement...." From the Latin prefix *ad-*, becoming *as-* before *s*, plus *sauvis* (pleasant, agreeable).

atavistic (at ə vis' tik) *adj.* Anything *atavistic* exhibits the characteristics of one's forebears or of a primitive culture. It comes from the noun *atavism* (at' ə vi zəm), which denotes reversion to one's ancestors or to earlier cultures. Napoleon's attempt to conquer the world was prompted by an *atavistic* desire to emulate Alexander the Great and Attila the Hun. Violence on the streets today may be the result of *atavistic* impulses to relive jungle life. The American economist and sociologist Thorstein Veblen (1857–1929) said: "The adoption of the cap and gown is one of the striking *atavistic* features of modern college life." The adjective *atavistic* might well be applied also to the wigs worn by English judges and barristers. One frequently encounters the phrase *atavistic recall*, signifying a memory passed down from ancient ancestors to the present—a reference to Jung's "collective unconscious." From Latin *atavus* (great-great-great-grandfather).

atrophy (a' trə fee) *n.*, *vb.* *Atrophy* is wasting away or degeneration. Muscles suffer *atrophy* through lack of use or exercise. The rights and freedom of the German people underwent *atrophy* when they failed to resist the Nazis. *Atrophy* is used as a verb as well, in the sense of "waste away, wither away, or decline." Unused talent can *atrophy*. The liberty of a people may *atrophy* through lack of vigilance. From Greek *atrophos* (not fed).

attenuate (ə ten' yoo ate) *vb.* To *attenuate* something is to weaken it, to thin it out and reduce it in intensity or value. Inflation has drastically *attenuated* our purchasing power. Long familiarity with a lover can *attenuate* one's initial ardor. From *attenuatus*, a form of Latin *attenuare* (to reduce).

augment (awg ment') *vb.* To *augment* is to increase, fill out. People in menial service jobs can *augment* their salaries with tips. The Women's Lib movement is *augmented* daily as a result of constant media publicity. Melting snow *augments* already swollen rivers in Spring. From Late Latin *augmentum* (increase), based on Latin *augmen* (increase).

augur (aw' gər) *vb.* To *augur* is to foreshadow. An enthusiastic reaction from a first-night audience *augurs* a long run. *Augur* is often followed by *well* or *ill*. Early-morning dark clouds *augur* ill for picnic plans. Common background and interests *augurs* well for a successful marriage. An *augur*, in ancient Rome, was an official who practiced certain rites of observing omens in order to advise the government. His function of divination is known as *augury* (aw' gyə ree) which, by extension, has come to mean "omen" or "indication." A good start is an *augury* of a successful finish.

auspicious (aw spish' əs) *adj.* Anything *auspicious* is favorable and promising. Things that start out under *auspicious* circumstances, like a picnic on a sunny morning, or an inning with the bases loaded and nobody out, have a good chance of winding up successfully; they look rosy. With favorable reviews a play has an *auspicious* beginning, and should have a long and successful run. The augurs of ancient Rome (see *augur*) were officials who interpreted omens such as the flights and feeding of birds. The Latin name for those observing the bird-omens was *auspices* (plural of *auspex*), and that word came from *avis* (bird) and *specere* (to look at). Anything considered favorable by these officials was said to be "under the *auspices*," which, by extension, has come to mean "under the guidance" (of someone). If the omens are good, a situation is considered *auspicious*. The opposite is *inauspicious*, meaning "unfavorable, gloomy, ill-omened."

autonomous (aw tonn' ə məs) *adj.* An independent, self-governing, self-regulating body is said to be *autonomous*. Canada was a colony, then a dominion; it is now *autonomous*. A department of a company which makes its own rules and decisions is *autonomous*. Large conglomerates often buy small corporations with the intention, usually short-lived, of letting them remain wholly *autonomous*. *Autonomy* (aw tonn' ə mee) is the noun: No chapter of a national college fraternity enjoys complete *autonomy*. From Greek *autonomos*, based on *autos* (self) + *nomos* (law).

avuncular (ə vungk' yə lər) *adj.* One who acts like an affectionate uncle is said to be *avuncular*. To be above reproach, a male guardian's relationship to his attractive young female ward should be strictly *avuncular*. Older people are fond of giving younger ones *avuncular* advice, whether or not it is welcome. Life can be pleasant if one is lucky enough to have an *avuncular* boss. Rare indeed is the *avuncular* drill sergeant. From Latin *avunculus* (uncle on the mother's side), from which we also get *uncle*.

awry (ə rye') *adj., adv.* When something is *awry*, it is amiss; it has gone haywire. Despite the most careful attention to detail, plans can go *awry*—or as Robert Burns (1759–1796) would have it: "The best-laid schemes o' mice an' men gang aft agley." When life is going too smoothly, something is sure to go *awry*—a restatement of Murphy's Law. From Middle English *on wry*; *wry* comes from Greek *rhoikos* (crooked).

axiom (ak' see əm) *n.* An *axiom* is a self-evident truth, a truism, a general principle that is universally acknowledged and needs no proof. Some *axioms*: Things equal to the same thing are equal to each other. A straight line is the shortest distance between two points. Men are different from women in more ways than one. Such principles are said to be *axiomatic* (ak see o mat' ik). It is *axiomatic* that two plus two equals four. From Greek *axioma* (something worthy.)

badinage (bad ə nahzh') *n. Badinage* is banter, playful repartee. There are people who refuse to talk seriously and spend their time in idle *badinage*. *Badinage* with an attractive member of the opposite sex can lead to more serious activities. *Badinage* is taken over from the French; the related French verb *badiner* (bah dee nay') means to *trifle*. Alfred de Musset (1810–1857) wrote a comedy in 1834 entitled *On ne badine pas avec l'amour*, meaning, "One doesn't trifle with love," or, more freely, "Don't mess around with love."

bailiwick (bay' lə wik) *n.* One's *bailiwick* is one's field of skill, one's own particular area of expertise. Literally, a *bailiwick* is the district within the jurisdiction of a *bailie* or *bailiff*, whose official duties vary according to locality, but it is most commonly met with in its figurative use: It's best not to tackle problems outside your own *bailiwick*. Knowledge of nuclear physics is far outside most people's *bailiwick*. Something *in your bailiwick* is *up your alley*. From *bailie* plus *wick*, which comes from Latin *vicus* (village, hamlet).

baleful (bale' fəl) *adj.* Anything *baleful* is threatening or destructive. Top sergeants tend to regard recruits with a *baleful* eye. Svengali had a *baleful* influence on Trilby; equally *baleful* was Lord Henry Wotton's influence on Dorian Gray. Muhammad Ali often threatened his opponents with a *baleful* look, and baseball pitchers use the *baleful* eye to intimidate the batter. From Old English *bealofull*.

banal (bə nal', bay' nəl) *adj.* This word describes anything commonplace, hackneyed, or uninspired. Congressmen are given to making *banal* speeches on subjects of national urgency. Writers loathe *banal* reviews of their creative works. A painting of a delightful subject can be ruined by *banal* treatment. Taken over intact from the French.

bastion (bas' chən) *n.* A *bastion* is a stronghold or bulwark. Literally, it describes a projecting section of a fort, but it is used figuratively to denote any stronghold, especially in the moral or abstract sense: The Western world is the *bastion* of democracy. Our court system is the *bastion* of civil liberty. From Italian *bastione*.

bathos (bay' thos—*th* as in *thing*, *s* as in *so*) *n.* Bathos is sentimentality, as opposed to true sentiment. The poetry, or doggerel, on birthday cards wallows in *bathos*. *Pathos* is the real stuff; it evokes true compassion. Plays like *Uncle Tom's Cabin* kept the audience weeping through the medium of unadulterated *bathos*. In *Farewell the Trumpets* (Faber & Faber, London, 1978), James Morris characterized the famous answer to the question "Why do you want to climb Mt. Everest?"—"Because it is there!"—as a case of "supreme *bathos*." From Greek *bathos* (depth).

behemoth (bə hee' məth) *n.* A *behemoth* is a monster, a gigantic creature. "Behold now *behemoth*," were the Lord's words to Job in *Job* 40:15. Some biblical authorities think God was referring to the hippopotamus; others, the elephant. In any event, He was describing an enormous animal, and the word is used that way informally to mean any enormous creature, human or other. The boxing champion Primo Carnera was a *behemoth*. So are scores of professional football players and the Fat Lady at the circus. The word has even been given to inanimate objects, like H-bombs, and to abstractions, like the federal deficit. Cf. another biblical term, *leviathan*.

beleaguer (bə lee' gər) *vb.* To *beleaguer* is to besiege, harass, or beset. Literally, it means "to surround (a fortified town, e.g.) with military forces"; but it is commonly used to mean "harass" in the sense of besetting someone with problems and annoyances. Farmers are often *beleaguered* by the action of pests. Bosses can be *beleaguered* by an entire office staff, or by the demands of clusters of clients clamoring for immediate attention. From prefix *be-* and *leaguer*, an old word for *siege*; *leaguer* is from Dutch *leger* (camp).

bellicose (bel' ə kose—s as in *so*) *adj.* This word describes hostility and belligerence, the attitude of one eager to do battle. In Grade B movies, the prosecutor always opens his case against the hero or heroine with a *bellicose* stance. (The verdict is always *not guilty*.) Flashing eyes and angry postures bespeak a *bellicose* attitude. From Latin *bellicosus*, based on Latin *bellum* (war). Cf. *belligerent*.

belligerent (bə lij' ər ənt) *n., adj.* As a noun, a *belligerent* is a nation at war. Recent history has seen *belligerent* after *belligerent* waste men and resources in useless wars. As an adjective *belligerent* means "hostile, bellicose." Some people go through life frightening others by their aggressive, *belligerent* attitudes. From Latin *belligerans*, a form of *belligerare* (to wage war), based on *bellum*, Latin for war, and *gerens*, a form of *gerere* (to carry on, wage).

bemused (bih myoozd') *adj.* A person *bemused* is puzzled, muddled, preoccupied. Alexander Pope (1688–1744), writing of people who try to write poetry and shouldn't, includes, with "maudlin poetesses" and "rhyming peers," a "parson, much *bemused* by beer." Here, *bemused* takes on the nuance of "addled, befuddled." More commonly, it is a convenient way of describing a state of lingering puzzlement: After reading kit assembly instructions for the third time most people spend a few minutes staring into space with a *bemused* expression. If patients could look up from the couch at their psychoanalysts, they would often witness a *bemused* visage. From prefix *be-* plus Latin *mussare* (to mutter, be at a loss).

bestow (bə stow') *vb.* To *bestow* something is to present or confer it. *Bestow* is commonly followed by *on* or *upon*: Five gold medals were *bestowed* upon Eric Heiden at the 1980 Olympics. Honorary degrees are all too often *bestowed* as awards for financial rather than intellectual endowment. From Middle English *bestowen*.

bibliophile (bib' lee ə file) *n.* A *bibliophile* is a booklover, a collector of books. *Bibliophiles* spend enormous amounts of money collecting first editions. Tycoons who line their shelves with books collected by their interior decorators are *pseudo-bibliophiles*. H. L. Mencken (1880–1956) invented a word for people who "read too much: the *bibliobibuli*," meaning literally, people who get drunk on books. (See *bibulous;* the singular would be *bibliobibulus.*) From two Greek words: *biblios* (book) and *philos* (dear, beloved).

bibulous (bib' yə ləs) *adj.* *Bibulous* people are those addicted to drink. W. C. Fields was *bibulous* in real life and portrayed himself in many films in which the hero was a drinking man. The word comes from the Latin *bibulus* (fond of drinking). All we did was insert the letter *o* in the last syllable, but that small change somehow intensified the meaning from "fond" to "addicted."

blandishment (blan' dish mənt) *n.* This word describes enticing action or speech and is usually used in the plural: In old-fashioned movies, strong men crumpled before the *blandishments* of vamps and sirens. There can be inducements other than action which entice people, like the *blandishments* of life in the tropics. From Latin *blanditia* (flattery, coaxing).

blatant (blay' tənt) *adj.* Anything *blatant* is completely obvious. Erroneous conclusions are sometimes reached on the basis of *blatant* errors. Juries are not always trustworthy; they sometimes base their verdicts on *blatant* misconception of the facts. *Blatant* often indicates an attitude of brazen shamelessness: Some people can stand up and look you in the eye while telling you *blatant* lies. Perhaps from Latin *blatire* (to engage in idle talk), and *blaterare* (to babble). (Is it possible that *blah* comes from either or both of those Latin words?)

bovine (bo′ vine, boe′ vin, boe′ veen) *adj*. Literally, this word means "of the ox family," but it is most commonly used figuratively to mean "dull, stolid, listless, sluggish." Some people just sit around listlessly, never alert; their *bovine* temperament makes it hard for anyone to communicate with them. *Bovine* is just one of a numerous group of *-ine* adjectives referring to animal genera: *accipitrine* (hawks, eagles, etc.); *alcidine* (diving birds: auks, puffins, etc.); *anserine* (geese); *aquiline* (eagles); *asinine* (asses); *buteonine* (short-winged hawks); *caballine* (horses); *canine* (dogs); *cathartine* (vultures); *corvine* (crows); *elephantine* (elephants); *equine* (horses); *feline* (cats); *lacertine* (lizards); *leonine* (lions); *lupine* (wolves); *oscine* (finches, shrikes and other songbirds); *ovine* (sheep); *pavonine* (peacocks); *piscine* (fish); *psittacine* (parrots); *porcine* (pigs); *strigine* (screech-owls); *ursine* (bears); *vulpine* (foxes). *Wolverine*, one might think (and be forgiven for it), belongs in the list. It doesn't. The adjective relating to wolves is *wolfish*. *Wolverine* is a noun describing a type of weasel (the adjective for which is *weaselly*), or, with an upper case *W*, a native of Michigan. For those who may wish to pursue the *-ine* category further, a rhyming dictionary is recommended. *Bovine* comes from Latin *bovis*, a form of *bos* (ox), or *bovillus* (relating to oxen), and the other words in the above list are from other Latin nouns or adjectives. It is likely that the greater part of these *-ine* words would qualify for inclusion in a a list of the *1000 Least Important Words*. But here they are, for good measure.

bravado (brə vah′ doe) *n*. A swaggering show of bold courage is called *bravado*. Bullies are much given to *bravado*. Evel Knievel is a notable practitioner of *bravado*, but he is a poor show when it comes to Idi Amin, whose *bravado*, when he was in power, matched his bulk. The word comes from *bravata*, which is both Italian and Spanish. Its Spanish origin evokes the image of a matador turning his back on the bull with apparent indifference to danger.

brickbat (brik′ bat) *n*. A *brickbat* is a cutting remark, an unkind criticism. The word means literally "a piece of broken brick," thrown as a missile, but it is most commonly used informally and figuratively to describe a caustic comment. A now-famous actress was once described as running the gamut of emotions from A to B. An actor of great renown was criticized as playing the role of king as though he expected somebody else to play the ace; those were *brickbats*. More and more often *brickbats* are hurled at political figures. A *brickbat* is the exact opposite of a *bouquet* in its figurative sense, and is simply an alliterative compound of *brick* and *bat*.

bromide (bro' mide) *n.* Literally, a *bromide* is a chemical compound involving bromine used as a sedative. In common figurative use it denotes a platitude, a commonplace, hackneyed remark, a trite generalization, likewise used as a sedative to soothe someone's nerves. It usually appears in the phrase *old bromide,* like the ones on greeting cards that make you yawn or cringe, depending on your sensibilities. Old-fashioned politicians make speeches almost entirely composed of *old bromides*. Bromine is a very smelly chemical; the name was taken from French *brome*; the French got it, appropriately enough, from Greek *bromos* (stench), and the English added the common chemical suffixes -*ine* for the element and -*ide* for the compound.

brook (brook) *vb.* To *brook* something is to tolerate it, to put up with it. For some reason, this word is almost always used in the negative: People are always *brooking* no interference, refusing to *brook* such conduct, etc. It is not applied to people, but rather to their acts, conduct, or attitudes, and to situations. Strike arbitrators often find it difficult to *brook* a continuation of a long, drawn-out impasse. From Middle English *brouken*.

brouhaha (broo' ha ha, broo ha' ha) *n.* This lively word describes a commotion, uproar, ado. The Abscam disclosures caused a *brouhaha* all over America. In baseball, a *rhubarb* is a type of *brouhaha*. Often there is an implication that the commotion is exaggerated, in view of the minor nature of the incident. Taken over intact from the French; an onomatopoeic invention.

brusque (brusk) *adj.* A manner that is *brusque* is curt, abrupt, and somewhat harsh. People sometimes act *brusquely* in order to present a businesslike image. *Brusque* manners can offend, though they sometimes belie a gentleness one is too shy to reveal. From Italian *brusco* (rough).

bucolic (byoo kol' ək) *adj.* Rustic. Many of those in high places yearn for the *bucolic* life—or so they say in interviews in fan magazines. Most of the commuters rushing home are eager to get out of their pin stripes and embrace a *bucolic* way of life. The French painter Fragonard (1732–1806) is known for paintings of shepherds and shepherdesses against *bucolic* backgrounds. From Latin *bucolicus*, which came from Greek *boukolikos*, which goes back to a Greek word meaning "ox herder."

burgeon (bur' jən) *vb. Burgeoning* is literally the budding and sprouting of plants. In the *Iliad*, Homer writes of "the *burgeoning* wood" that "brings forth leaves." The verb has somehow acquired the implication of "developing suddenly," almost before your eyes. Hamlets near newly established industrial sites *burgeon* into bustling towns. As a result of just the right role, a hitherto obscure actor can *burgeon* into stardom. Unfortunately for hay fever sufferers, when nature *burgeons*, so do allergies. From Middle English *burjon* (bud).

cabal (kə bal') *n.* A *cabal* is a group of plotters, but can also describe the group's intrigues and plots. In a less sinister sense it can mean simply a "clique" or "coterie." Its original use suggests a small group of secret plotters working against the government or authority. One can speak of a *cabal* inside a corporation, whose intrigues are aimed at unseating the president or chairman. The intrigues themselves can be known as a *cabal*. In its more general sense the word can be used to describe a following who trail after a celebrity: Successful writers are often surrounded by a *cabal* of admirers and would-be literary figures. From Middle Latin *cabbala*, based on Hewbrew *qabbalah* (tradition). The original *cabala* was an esoteric rabbinical doctrine which flourished in the Middle Ages, a magical method of interpreting Scripture and predicting the future. Only initiates were allowed to employ the doctrine, hence the "secret group" idea.

cachet (ka shay') *n. Cachet* can be used in a number of ways. It can denote a stamp of approval from one in a high position: The secretary of state put his *cachet* on a plan offered by a subordinate in the State Department. The word can be applied to a feature that imparts prestige: Ownership of a Rolls Royce confers a certain *cachet*, if one is impressed by such things. *Cachet* can mean "prestige" itself: One's position as chairman of the board of a great corporation gives one *cachet*. Familiarity with the classics gives people a definite *cachet* in certain circles. The word was taken over intact from the French, where it means "seal" or "stamp."

cacophony (kə kof' ə nee) *n.* *Cacophony* is strident, discordant noise. Jungle animals fill the air with a *cacophony* of weird sounds. Paris traffic, with its squeaks of brakes and tooting of horns, produces an unbearable *cacophony*. The adjective is *cacophonous* (kə kof' ə nəs). While many teenagers seem to enjoy punk rock, their parents find it merely *cacophonous*. From Greek *kakophonia* (bad sound).

cadaverous (kə dav' ə rəs) *adj.* Anyone *cadaverous* looks haggard and ghastly. The word implies pallor, gauntness, and emaciation. People on hunger strikes look *cadaverous*. Despite their apparent cardiovascular fitness, marathoners toward the end of a race often have a *cadaverous* appearance. From Latin *cadaverosus*, the adjective based on *cadaver*, which we have taken over intact from the Latin as a synonym for *corpse*, which in turn comes from the Latin *corpus* (body).

cadge (kaj) *vb.* People who *cadge* something get it by begging, with the emphasis on imposing on the other fellow's good nature. Hoboes *cadge* food from sympathetic housewives. Devotees of Hare Krishna *cadge* coins by pestering people on the streets. Some people *cadge* by going through the motions of borrowing, with no intention of repaying. From Middle English *caggen*.

cajole (kə jole') *vb.* To *cajole* is to wheedle, to coax by promises and flattery. One can *cajole* something out of somebody or *cajole* somebody into something. Some people are experts at *cajoling* even hardhearted friends into lending them small amounts of money from time to time. Little boys are good at *cajoling* autographs of famous athletes. From French *cajoler* (to wheedle).

callow (kal' owe) *adj.* *Callow* people are immature, or "green." The word is often found in the expression *callow youth*. Aldous Huxley (1894–1963) described some young students as "very young, pink and *callow*." An interesting derivation: the word comes from Middle and Old English *calu*, meaning "bald," a term applied to fledglings, i.e., very young birds, who are bald, i.e., without feathers. The word *fledgling* in turn was applied, figuratively, to inexperienced young people, who aren't bald, but are immature.

calumny (kal' əm nee) *n. Calumny* is slander, smear; the malicious making of false statements in order to damage a reputation. Hamlet tells Ophelia that no one is safe from false accusations: "Be thou as chaste as ice, as pure as snow, thou shalt not escape *calumny.*" And Ben Jonson (1572–1637), in *Volpone*, has this good advice: "*Calumnies* are best answered with silence." The legal profession calls *calumny* "libel" when it is written, and "slander" or "defamation" when it is spoken. To indulge in *calumny* is to *calumniate* (kə lum' nee ate) someone. From Latin *calumnia* (false accusation).

canard (kə nard') *n.* A *canard* is a hoax or false rumor. Reports of great victories, especially when they are issued by Middle Eastern countries at war, are almost always *canards*. Sensational journalism thrives on *canards*. The "discovery" of the Piltdown Man was a monstrous *canard. Canard* is a French word, pronounced in French with the *d* silent, meaning, literally, "duck" (in this sense often seen on menus in the expression *canard à l'orange*), and figuratively, "hoax," as in English.

candor (kan' dər) *n. Candor* is the label of a fine quality in people: frankness, openness, sincerity. *Candor* may displease under certain circumstances, but it is a quality people respect. Juries are impressed by the *candor* of a witness. *Candor* is the opposite of evasiveness, hedging. The related adjective is *candid*, meaning "outspoken, straightforward." People are often asked for their "*candid* opinion" (and usually shrink from giving it). *Candor* was taken intact from Latin, where its literal meaning is "luster, dazzling whiteness," which by extension became "sincerity." The Latin adjective *candidus* underwent the same change; the meaning "shining white" was extended to "honest, straightforward." *Candidates* were so termed because, in Roman times, they customarily wore white robes. (Alas, they are so often anything but "honest, straightforward.")

canon (kan' ən) *n.* A *canon* is a rule or general principle. The practice of law is regulated by an official set of *canons of ethics*. Life in civilized society should be regulated by *canons* of taste and discretion. *Canon law* is church law. In a separate meaning, *canon* is the title of a clergyman serving as an official of a cathedral. From Greek *kanon* (rule).

cant (kant) *n.* *Cant* has a number of meanings. It can be used to describe insincere talk, especially statements of high ideals. We all tire of hearing the repetitious, pious *cant* of the Moral Majority. The word also serves to denote the special argot or jargon of a particular group, class, or profession. Economists' *cant* leaves most people (including other economists) entirely befuddled. Finally, the term is applied to underworld jargon. For example, pickpockets communicate with one another in a *cant* of their own that outsiders can't understand. *Cant* comes from Latin *cantus* (song).

cantankerous (kan tangk' ər əs) *adj.* Stay away from *cantankerous* people: they're bad-tempered, ill-humored, irritable, quarrelsome, grouchy, and generally difficult to deal with and exasperating. Scrooge, with his "Bah! Humbug!" and Cinderella's stepmother are familiar figures who are typically *cantankerous*. Though the word is usually applied to people, it can be used of animals, like *cantankerous* mules, or even inanimate objects, like a *cantankerous* self-starter or a *cantankerous* pump. The word is believed to be descended from a hypothetical predecessor *cantenkerous*, supposed to be a portmanteau combination or running together of *contentious* and *rancorous*.

capitulate (kə pitch' ə late) *vb.* To *capitulate* is to surrender. The Japanese *capitulated* in World War II immediately after the dropping of the atom bomb. The noun is *capitulation* (kə pitch ə lay' shən) and *capitulation* does not necessarily evoke the image of defeated generals: Strong men often *capitulate* after one look at those great big beautiful eyes. From Middle Latin *capitulatus*, a form of *capitulare*.

capricious (kə prish' əs) *adj.* The *capricious* person is impulsive and tends to be erratic. *Caper* is Latin for "goat," and *capri-* is an element in several English words, e.g. *caprice* (ka preece'), meaning "unpredictable switch" or "whim," which reflect the leaping and skipping (*capering*) of goats. Don't rely on *capricious*, whimsical people. A whole nation, or even the whole world, can be made uneasy by a *capricious* head of state. Even on a sunny day, *capricious* winds are a threat to sailing.

captious (kap' shəs) *adj.* *Captious* people are faultfinding and nit-picking. *Captious* critics often overlook the promise shown by young authors. *Captious* questions from the audience can unsettle even experienced speakers. From Latin *captiosus*.

carnal (kar' nəl) *adj*. This word means "sensual," bodily as opposed to spiritual. There are those who care only for *carnal* pleasures, whose *carnal* desires rule their life. *Carnal abuse* (sexual tampering with a child) and *carnal knowledge* (sexual intercourse) are terms in criminal law. From Latin *carnalis* (relating to flesh).

carnivorous (car niv' ər əs) *adj*. *Carnivorous* means "meat-eating." *Carnivorous* animals, like lions and birds of prey, eat meat. *Herbivorous* means "plant-eating." Cattle and elephants, for example, are *herbivorous*. Meat-eating animals are known as *carnivores* (car' nə vores), plant-eating ones are *herbivores* (her' bə vores). *Omnivorous* animals eat both meat and plants and are known as *omnivores* (om' nə vores). Dogs, cats, some birds, and human beings are *omnivorous*. This word has developed a figurative use in the expression *omnivorous reader*: one who reads just about anything that comes his way. All these words come from Latin combinations: *caro*, stem *carn-* (flesh), *herba* (plant) and *omnis* (all) plus *vorare* (to eat greedily, gulp). (From Latin *devorare*, to gulp, we get *devour*.)

carp (karp) *vb*. One who *carps* keeps complaining, finding fault, nit-picking. Constructive criticism is welcome; continual *carping* isn't. *Carping* is synonymous with *caviling* and suggests unreasonable and ill-natured complaining and fussing about minor matters. From Middle English *carpen* (to prate); cf. Icelandic *karpa* (to wrangle).

carrion (kar' ee ən—*a* as in *can*) *n*. This unpleasant word describes dead, decaying flesh, unfit for human consumption. A common sight on country roads is a crowd of crows fighting over *carrion*. *Carrion* is sometimes used as an adjective, describing either the flesh itself or animals that feed on *carrion*. In *Henry VI, Part 2* Shakespeare speaks of "carrion kites and crows." From Latin *caro* (flesh).

castigate (kas' tə gate) *vb*. When you *castigate* someone, you punish him severely. The implication is that the punishment is intended to improve or correct the one punished. The way to improve society is to *castigate* the offenders. The noun is *castigation* (kas tə gay' shən), which may be physical or verbal. The aim of *castigation* should be improvement; not discouragement. From *castigatus*, a form of Latin *castigare* (to punish).

casuistry (kazh' oo iss tree) *n.* This word describes dishonest, specious reasoning. *Casuistry* was the term originally applied to theological reasoning about moral matters, but is now commonly used to describe the fallacious application of general principles to particular situations. No ingenious *casuistry* will ever convince the American public that our defeat in the Vietnam War was some sort of victory. Resort to *casuistry* is the last defense of a man who realizes he is on the losing side of an argument. From Spanish *casuista* (casuist).

cataclysm (kat' ə kliz əm) *n.* A *cataclysm* is a violent upheaval. In geological terminology, a *cataclysm* is a natural disaster that causes changes in the earth's surface. The eruption of Mount St. Helens was a cataclysm of major proportions. Figuratively, the term is applied to a momentous event that affects the social or political order. In that sense, the Russian revolution of 1917 was a *cataclysm* of the first magnitude. (John Reed called it *Ten Days that Shook the World*.) From Greek *kataklysmos* (flood).

catharsis (kə thar' sis) *n.* *Catharsis* is relief from pent-up emotion. The term originally applied to the purging of the emotions, particularly pity and fear, through art, as in the Aristotelian description of the effect of viewing tragedy acted on the stage. *Catharsis* leaves one feeling empty and sad, but spiritually renewed. A psychiatrist's ability to bring a patient's suppressed feelings into the open should result in a complete *catharsis*. After a terrible experience, viewing vivid photographs of the event sometimes brings about a *catharsis* that makes life easier to bear from then on. The adjective is *cathartic* (kə thar' tik). Primal scream therapy is said to be highly *cathartic*. (Whether it is or not, it must be very noisy.) *Cathartic* is also used as a noun meaning "purgative" or "laxative." (The connection is obvious.) From Greek *katharsis* (cleaning).

catholic (kath' ə lik) *adj.* This word, with a lower-case *c*, applies to people (or their views or tastes) who (or which) are broad-minded and have universal sympathies and appreciation—the very opposite of "narrow" in its figurative sense. Be careful when describing someone as *catholic* in outlook to those familiar only with the religious meaning of the word—particularly if the person under discussion is Presbyterian. From Greek *katholikos* (general).

caveat (kav′ ee at, kay′ vee at) *n*. This word, which is Latin for "Let him beware!," is used as a noun meaning "warning." Parents are always issuing *caveats* to their children. Corporate comptrollers and treasurers are fond of *caveats* against reckless spending. "Caveat emptor" is Latin for "Let the buyer beware," a legal principle taken into our law: The seller cannot be held responsible for a defect unless it violates a warranty. "Cave canem" (Latin for "Beware of the dog") was found worked into a mosaic in front of a doorway at Pompeii. These forms are from the Latin *cavere* (to be on one's guard, to beware).

cavil (kav′əl) *vb*. To *cavil* is to quibble, to raise nit-picking, picayune objections; to find fault with, in an irritating manner. One *cavils about* or *at* something. Lawyers are known to *cavil* at the most minor points in lengthy agreements. Most literary and dramatic critics seems to find more pleasure in *caviling* than in praising. From Latin *cavillare* (to jest or joke; by extension, to quibble).

celibacy (sel′ə bə see) *n*. *Celibacy* is bachelorhood, the unmarried state; but it can also apply to abstention from sex, whether one is married or not. Samuel Johnson (1709–1784), in *Rasselas*, wrote: "Marriage has many pains, but *celibacy* has no pleasures." *Celibacy* is sometimes referred to as "single blessedness," by those who are cynical about marriage. *Celibate* (sel′ ə bət or sel′ ə bate) is the adjective. Catholic priests take the *vow of celibacy*. They promise to remain *celibate*. There is a movement among the unmarried public called "the new *celibacy*," which stresses companionship without sex. One gets the feeling this movement will be short-lived. From Latin *caelebs* (unmarried).

champion (cham′ pee ən) *vb*. When you *champion* a person or a cause, you are supporting, defending, arguing in favor of him or it. Southern Democrats *champion* states' rights. Northern liberals *champion* financial support of the arts by the government. It sometimes happens that a high-ranking corporate executive will *champion* a younger colleague's career, which can help a great deal. From Late Latin *campio*, based on Latin *campus* (battlefield); cf. German *Kampf* (struggle, contest).

charlatan (shar′ lə tən) *n*. A *charlatan* is a quack, anyone who claims more skill than he possesses. Make sure a so-called expert is not a *charlatan* before you put yourself in his hands. Some of the people in your life who had better not be *charlatans* are your doctor, your auto mechanic, and your stockbroker. The snake-oil vendors of the Old West were *charlatans*. From Italian *ciarlatano*, based on Italian *ciarlare* (to prate).

chary (chair′ ee) *adj.* This word has two distinct meanings. It can mean "cautious" or "wary": Insecure people can be *chary* of their reputations as experts in their chosen fields. It can also mean "sparing": Literary and dramatic critics seem generally *chary* of granting praise. From Middle English *chary*, *charry* (sorrowful, dear); akin to *care* and *careful*.

chasm (kaz′ əm) *n.* A *chasm* is a deep gap, ravine, or gorge. The Grand Canyon is one of the world's most notable *chasms*. Figuratively, the word is used to denote a deep difference of opinion or attitude: Trade continues despite the political and sociological *chasm* between the United States and Russia. There is a deep *chasm* between civilian and military priorities. From Greek *chasma*.

chicanery (shə kay′ nə ree) *n.* This is a useful word to describe trickery, deception by sophistry, subterfuge, and artful quibbling to obtain an advantage; sharp practice. *Chicanery* is the opposite of straightforwardness. *Chicanery* is the tool of artful lawyers dodging the real issues in a weak case. *Chicanery* is used to sow seeds of doubt in what would otherwise be a clearcut situation. Taken over intact from the French, where it is based upon the noun *chicane* (evasion, quibbling) and the verb *chicaner* (to use tricks, to quibble.)

chide (chide) *vb.* To *chide* someone is to scold him, with the implication that the scolding is on the mild side. One often finds the word paired with the adverb *gently*, which makes it milder yet: A considerate employer will *chide* his secretary gently for being occasionally tardy. Children should be *chided* for not doing their homework. *Chid* is an alternative form to *chided* for the past tense, but its use can cause raised eyebrows. From Middle English *chiden*.

chimera (kə meer′ ə) *n.* A *chimera* is a figment of the imagination, an illusion. The *Chimera* of mythology was a fire-breathing monster, part lion, goat, and serpent. Hence any grotesque monster or horrid creature was called by that name. But its common use, as in the expression to *erect* or *dream up a* *chimera*, is to describe a vain illusion, often a utopian wish-dream. The hope that the establishment of the United Nations would ensure universal peace was a *chimera*.

churlish (chur' lish) *adj*. A *churlish* person is a boor. *Churl* (in the medieval English social order, the lowest caste of freeman) came to mean "peasant" or "rustic," and was then applied to any boorish person. People guilty of *churlish* behavior aren't often invited to dinner parties. *Churlish* conduct can prevent one's advancement not only in society but in professional and business life as well.

cipher (sy' fər) *n*. This word has three distinct meanings. First, it is synonymous with "zero" in numerical parlance: *One* followed by three *ciphers* is one thousand. From that use *cipher* came to signify a person with a minimum of personality, a nonentity. It has happened that one has seen an actor perform in a powerful role and then turn out to be a *cipher* in real life. *Cipher* can also be a synonym for "code," a secret method of communication in writing or otherwise. The breaking of the Japanese *cipher* was one of the greatest Allied achievements in World War II. From Middle Latin *ciphra*, based on Arabic *cifr* (zero).

circuitous (sər kyoo' ə təs) *adj*. Anything *circuitous* is roundabout, indirect. People sometimes arrive late for an appointment because they followed a *circuitous* route. They can also waste a lot of words in a *circuitous* approach to a question. As one might expect, the word is related to *circle*, and that suggests going round and round, whether on the way to a destination or the solution of a problem. From Latin *circuitus* (a going round in a circle).

circumlocution (sur kəm low kyoo' shən) *n*. A *circumlocution* is a roundabout way of phrasing something, the use of more words to express a thought or describe something than are necessary. To say "institution for the education of children" rather than "school" is to use a *circumlocution*. "Male parent" for father is another. From two Latin words: *circum* (around) and *locutus*, a form of *loqui* (to speak).

circumspect (sur' kəm spect) *adj*. A *circumspect* person is watchful, cautious, looks out for pitfalls, looks before he leaps. Clandestine lovers are well advised to be *circumspect*. The noun is *circumspection* (sur kəm spek' shən), a specialty of persons engaged in espionage. Our great revolutionary patriot Samuel Adams (1722–1803), in a 1771 speech, said: "The necessity of the times, more than ever, calls for our utmost *circumspection* . . . ." ('Twas ever thus.) The word comes from two Latin words: *circum* (around) and *spectare* (to observe carefully).

clamorous (klam' ə rəs) *adj*. When people are *clamorous*, they are vociferous and demanding. Voters at town meetings are often *clamorous* in their protests against any proposed increase in property tax. During a long drive, children in the back seat of a car usually become *clamorous* in their request for food, to be there already, to go to the bathroom . . . and sometimes all three at once. From Latin *clamor* (loud shouting), which we have taken over intact as a noun.

clandestine (klan des' tən) *adj*. *Clandestine* is the equivalent of "undercover." *Clandestine* describes acts, usually meetings, arranged very carefully and executed with the utmost secrecy, like the meetings between Romeo and Juliet. Conspirators meet *clandestinely* to hatch their plans. The *clandestine* plottings of the assassins of Julius Caesar went undisclosed for a long time. In *All The President's Men* (Simon & Schuster, 1974) the meetings between Bernstein, Woodward, and their confidential source, Deep Throat, were highly *clandestine*. From Latin *clandestinus*.

claptrap (klap' trap) *n*. This is a word to describe pretentious nonsense, primarily to win praise. Some essays seem learned on the surface, but on closer inspection, turn out to be mere *claptrap*. *Claptrap* is anything contrived to impress, but without substance, like the oratory of demagogues and some evangelists. Derivation uncertain.

cleave (kleev) *vb*. This word has two distinct (and roughly opposite) meanings. It can mean "to split," as in *cleaving* logs or rough diamonds. It can also mean "to cling": long-suffering wives in melodramas of Victorian vintage often *cleave* to the most undeserving of husbands. Despite all those trials and tribulations, Job *cleaved* to his faith. For the past tense, *clove* or *cleft* is now more common. From Middle English *cleven*.

clemency (klem' ən see) *n*. This noun, which denotes mercifulness and leniency, is based upon the adjective *clement* (klem' ənt), a word not in as common use as its opposite *inclement*.

Lawyers often plead for *clemency* for clients who are clearly guilty. Police often feel that judges show too much *clemency* in sentencing criminals, a feeling generally not shared by the criminals. The adjective *clement* comes from Latin *clemens* (gentle, merciful).

cloy (kloy) *vb.* When people or things *cloy*, they become distasteful through excess. Something originally pleasant, like sweetness of disposition or rich food, *cloys* when it is piled on, served up in overabundance. Continual adoration finally *cloys*. Attention is enjoyable, but if assiduously administered, it can *cloy*. *Cloying* is the adjective, meaning "sickeningly sweet," like the heroines of Victorian melodrama, or a diet of rich cakes. From Middle French *encloyer*.

cogent (koe' jənt) *adj.* What is *cogent* is convincing. The word is usually associated with *reason* or *argument*. Judges decide cases in favor of lawyers who present *cogent* arguments. People act when they think there are *cogent* reasons for doing so. It is difficult to find a *cogent* analysis of today's confusing economic trends. From *cogens*, a form of Latin *cogere* (to compel).

cognizant (cog' nə zənt) *n.* To be *cognizant* of something is to be aware of it. It sometimes takes people too long to become *cognizant* of the perilousness of their situation. It takes a first-rate intelligence system to keep the President *cognizant* of what is going on in the world. *Cognizance* (kog' nə zəns) is the noun, meaning "awareness." From *cognitus*, a form of Latin *cognoscere* (to become acquainted with).

collation (ko lay' shən, kə lay' shən) *n.* This word has a number of technical meanings not in common use. One of them is the verification of the numbering of the pages of a book. In ordinary use it means "light meal," with the implication that it is served at some time other than one of the normal mealtimes. Its Latin origin in *conlatus*, a form of *conferre* (to bring or put together) raises the further implication that a *collation* is a meal arranged somewhat impromptu, though the word is not necessarily used that way. Sometimes one stops to visit a friend for a chat, and is agreeably surprised with a pleasant *collation*. (That's a long way from verifying page-numbering.)

colloquy (kol' ə kwee) *n.* *Colloquy* is conversation or dialogue. It is amusing to watch a *colloquy* between two old gossips. The word sometimes implies a degree of formality in the conversational exchange: *Colloquy* between nations is a helpful tool for the avoidance of misunderstanding and strained relations. In this sense, it indicates a high-level conference. From Latin *com*, old form of *cum* (together with) and *loqui* (to talk). Cf. the derivation of **loquacious**.

compendium (kəm pen′ dee əm) *n*. This word denotes a brief, concise treatise on a subject; a summary. Old-fashioned people sometimes keep a *compendium* of physical ailments and medical remedies handy. *Tales from Shakespeare*, by Charles and Mary Lamb, is an early 19th-century *compendium* of the plots of Shakespeare's plays, sometimes known as *Lamb's Tales*. *Compendium* implies that the brief treatment concerns a wide-ranging subject, like a science or history. Taken over intact from Latin, where it means "shortening."

complacent (kəm play′ sənt) *adj. Complacent* people are self-satisfied and quite pleased with themselves. Temporary millionaires are no longer so *complacent* after losing their money in a crash. Do not confuse this word with *complaisant* (obliging). *Complacency* (kəm play′ sən see) is the noun. Charles Lamb (1775–1834), in his essay on *The Behaviour of Married Couples*, wrote: "Nothing is to me more distasteful than that entire *complacency* and satisfaction which beam in the countenances of a newly-married couple." From *complacens*, a form of Latin *complacere* (to please exceedingly).

complaisant (kəm play′ zənt) *adj*. A *complaisant* person is agreeable and obliging. London policemen ("bobbies") are well-known to be *complaisant*. A *complaisant* salesperson is a big help. Do not confuse this word with *complacent* (self-satisfied). From the French *complaisant*, a form of *complaire* (to please).

complement (kom′ plə mənt) *vb*. To *complement* something is to complete it, fill it out, make a necessary addition to it. The addition of period furniture often *complements* a stage set. The purpose of this dictionary is to *complement* your vocabulary. Do not confuse this word with *compliment* (praise). From Latin *complementum* (that which completes), based on the Latin verb *complere* (to complete).

compliant (kəm ply′ ənt) *adj*. A *compliant* person is submissive and yielding. It is easy to do business with a person of *compliant* nature. A *compliant* spouse is a great comfort. Do not confuse this word with *complaisant* or *complacent*. From Italian *complire*, Spanish *cumplir* (to perform what is due).

concomitant (kon kom′ ə tənt) *n., adj.* A *concomitant* is something that accompanies another thing or an event. We must study historical events in the light of their *concomitants*. The appalling death rate on our highways is a *concomitant* of rapid transportation. As an adjective *concomitant* means "accompanying" or "concurrent." Some acts are explainable only through an examination of the *concomitant* circumstances. From Latin *concomitans*, a form of *concomitari* (to accompany).

concrete (kon kreet′) *adj.* Things are *concrete* when they are real, actual (as opposed to *abstract*); specific, particular (as opposed to *general*). A representational painting presents *concrete* subjects; an abstract painting is made of design, rather than things. A *concrete* idea is specific, as opposed to a general idea. Urgent situations require *concrete* proposals. *Concrete* evidence is preferable to circumstantial evidence. The popular expression *hard data* refers to *concrete* facts, not fuzzy thinking. From Latin *concretus*, a form of *concrescere* (to grow together).

conduit (kon′ dwit, kon′ doo it, kon′ dyoo it, kon′ dit) *n.* However this word is pronounced, it is defined in most dictionaries as a channel, whether in the form of a pipe or tube or a natural passage, for the conveyance of liquids, or a protective pipe or tube covering electrical wiring. Latterly, it has come into use in a more abstract sense, descriptive of any means of transmission of anything, such as information or financial benefits. The "leak" is Washington's favorite *conduit* for information to the press and public. Corporations have been described as a "*conduit* for profits." A will, as well as a deed, can serve in law as a *conduit* of title. From Middle Latin *conductus* (pipe channel), based on Latin *conductus*, a form of *conducere* (to connect).

congenital (kən jen′ ə təl) *adj.* This word has two related, but distinct, meanings. It can describe something existing at birth: Hairlip is a *congenital* defect. Another meaning is "by nature": Some people haven't the slightest idea of the proper way to go about things; they're *congenital* idiots! Chimpanzees and mockingbirds are *congenital* mimics. From Latin *congenitus*, based on the prefix *con* (with) and *genitus*, a form of *gignere* (to give birth to).

consensus (kən sen' səs) *n*. A *consensus* is a general agreement or majority view. The word alone expresses the concept of majority opinion, so that it is redundant to use the expression *consensus of opinion*, which one comes across all too often. It is sometimes difficult to achieve a *consensus*, even after the most rigorous debate. The authenticity of an Old Master is better confirmed by a *consensus* of experts rather than the opinion of a single connoisseur. Taken over intact from the Latin.

consortium (kən sor' tee əm, kən sor' she əm) *n*. This is the term for an association, particularly of banks or companies, blending together to combine their capital in an enterprise, often for the purpose of gaining control of an industry. Any association, if of fairly extensive and impressive proportions, may be spoken of as a *consortium*. (OPEC is a glaring and dangerous example.) From Latin *consortium* (partnership).

consummate (kon' sə mate) *vb*.; (kən sum' ət) *adj*. To *consummate* something (note stress on first syllable) is to accomplish it, to bring it to completion. It is often necessary to execute hundreds of documents in order to *consummate* the merger of two large corporations. Marriage is said to be *consummated* only by an act of sexual intercourse. The noun is *consummation* (kon sə may' shən), and means "accomplishment" or "completion," sometimes "fulfillment." "'Tis a *consummation* devoutly to be wish'd," says Hamlet of death, in the famous speech, "To be or not to be." As an adjective, with the second pronunciation, accent on second syllable, *consummate* means complete, top, superb. Heifetz is the *consummate* violinist. Mozart was a *consummate* master of his craft. From Latin *consummatus* (perfect, consummate), based on the verb *consummare* (to bring to perfection).

contentious (kən ten' shəs) *adj*. A *contentious* person is quarrelsome; a *contentious* issue is a controversial one. *Contentious* people are hard to deal with; they seem to enjoy dispute. It is sometimes well to avoid a *contentious* issue in order to prevent acrimonious controversy. The related noun *contention* (kən ten' shən) means "strife." Some ballplayers are well-known for being *contentious*. They are the kind umpires throw out of ballgames. From Latin *contentiosus*.

context (kon' text) *n*. This word has two distinct uses. It can be applied to that part of a statement which affects the meaning of the rest of the statement: It is easy to mistake the meaning of a passage by taking it *out of context*. The *context* in which a word or phrase is used can clear up what would otherwise be ambiguous. *Context* can also refer to the circumstances in which an event occurs. Some acts are comprehensible in the *context* of war. From Latin *contextus* (joining together, connection).

contiguous (kən tig′ yoo əs) *adj.* *Contiguous* means "touching," in the sense of "bordering upon," and is followed by the preposition *to*. Real estate *contiguous* to a main highway is usually more valuable, if zoned for business, and less so, if zoned for residential use. New York and Connecticut are *contiguous* states. Sometimes *contiguous* is used in the sense of "nearby," (though not actually touching): Houses often tremble from the passing of trains along *contiguous* railroad beds. (The context should make it clear whether the word means "actually touching" or "nearby, not far distant.") The word has been used with reference to nearness in time rather than distance, about events immediately preceding or following each other, but this is a rare usage. From Latin *contiguus*, based on *contigi*, a form of *contingere* (to touch): *contingens*, another form of *contigere* (in another meaning —to happen, befall), gave us *contingent*.

contretemps (kon′ trə taw[n]) *n.* A *contretemps* is an unfortunate occurrence, a mischance that results in discomfort, especially embarrassment. This is a word taken over bodily from the French, to be pronounced, if possible, as in French, with the first and third syllables ending in a nasal sound (kong′ trə tawng, with the final *s* and both *g*'s silent). To drop your host's Ming vase while examining it carefully is more than a *contretemps*—it is a disaster. Appearing at a formal reception (that you didn't know was formal) in a plaid business suit would constitute a notable and noticeable *contretemps*.

contrite (kən trite′) *adj.* To be *contrite* is to repent, to be penitent, to suffer from a sense of guilt. In *Recessional*, Rudyard Kipling (1865–1936) wrote of "an humble and a *contrite* heart," hearkening back, perhaps, to Psalm 51:17: "A broken and a *contrite* heart, O God, thou wilt not despise." *Contrition* (kən trih′ shən) is the noun, meaning "remorse." Although Richard Nixon apologized late in the day for his "mishandling" of the Watergate affair, many felt that he was not nearly *contrite* enough. From *contritus*, a form of Latin *conterere* (to wear down, crush).

contumacious (kon tyoo may' shəs) *adj*. To be *contumacious* is to be stubbornly disobedient. A *contumacious* witness may be held guilty of contempt of court. It is difficult to deal with a *contumacious* subordinate. Mules are typically *contumacious*; and to those given to anthropomorphizing, so are jalopies, crab grass, and unruly hair. From *contumacis*, a form of Latin *contumax* (stubborn, defiant).

conundrum (kə nun' drəm) *n*. A *conundrum* is a puzzle or riddle. This word applies especially to the type of riddle with an answer based on a play on words. Why didn't the Israelites starve in the desert? Because of the sand which is there (sandwiches— get it?). Figuratively, the word is used to characterize a problem hard to solve: The question of an individual's technical domicile has been a legal *conundrum* for years. Derivation unknown.

co-opt (ko opt') *vb*. This word is most commonly used in the sense of "preempt": Conservatives have *co-opted* abortion as a political issue. In a slightly stronger sense, *co-opt* can be used to mean "commandeer": The navy *co-opted* every vessel available. Literally, when someone is *co-opted*, he is elected or appointed as a member of a group by those who are already members. If a committee, for instance, was permitted to add three more members by majority vote, they would, in doing so, be *co-opting* the new members. From Latin *cooptare* (to elect).

copious (koe' pee əs) *adj*. Anything *copious* is plentiful, abundant. The consumption of *copious* amounts of food and wine is a sure sign of a good dinner party. *Copious* examples help to clarify the meaning of a word. The word also describes things that produce a plentiful yield, like a *copious* harvest, or *copious* springs. From Latin *copiosus*.

corollary (kor' ə lerr ee) *n*. A *corollary* is a natural consequence or the inevitable result of something. Jealousy has been described as a "normal *corollary* of love." When Polonius said to his son Laertes in *Hamlet* (act I, scene 3):

> This above all, to thine own self be true,
> And it must follow, as the night the day,
> Thou canst not then be false to any man,

he was stating a *corollary*—a consequence that followed as inevitably as the night follows the day. From Late Latin *corollarium*, which in Latin meant "gift" or "gratuity."

corporeal (kor pore' ee əl) *adj*. Anything *corporeal* is physical, material, as opposed to spiritual. The psychiatrist takes care of your emotional ills; the general practitioner attends to your *corporeal* ailments. The word can also mean "tangible," as in the legal term *tangible personal property*. The opposite word, *incorporeal*, means "intangible." In *Hamlet* (act III, scene 4), Hamlet speaks to his father's ghost, which the queen cannot see. She is alarmed that he "with the *incorporal* air does hold discourse." (*Incorporal* was Shakespeare's spelling of *incorporeal*.) *Corporeal* and *incorporeal*, as well as *corporal* (as in *corporal* punishment, for example), all come from *corporis*, a form of the noun *corpus*, Latin for *body*, from which we also get *corpse* and *corps*, and other words.

correlate (kor' ə late) *vb*. To *correlate* things is to connect them in a systematic relationship: Congress must *correlate* the findings of the various committees investigating a single subject in order to reach intelligent conclusions. The word can also be used to describe the bringing together of various activities and organizing them for the most effective action: Generals must *correlate* the activities of the air force and the tank corps. This verb is an example of "back formation": It was formed from the noun *correlation*, which comes from Middle Latin *correlatio*.

coruscate (kor' ə skate) *vb*. To *coruscate* is to sparkle, either physically or abstractly. A richly laid table in Buckingham Palace gleams with coruscating gold and silver. Aldous Huxley (1894–1963) wrote of "an ornate style that *coruscated* with verbal epigrams." The drama critic Brooks Atkinson described playwright Christopher Fry as "*coruscating* on thin ice." From *coruscatus*, a form of Latin *coruscare* (to flash).

cosset (kos' it) *vb*. When you *cosset* someone you are pampering and coddling him. People who are *cosseted* from birth often turn out to be self-centered. When teachers *cosset* teacher's pets, the rest of the class can become annoyed. From Old English *cossetung* (kissing); akin to German *küssen* (to kiss).

coterie (koe' tə ree) *n*. A *coterie* is a clique, a select group, intimate and exclusive and united by a common interest or purpose. Every successful movie star is surrounded by a *coterie* of admirers who hope to benefit by the association. In that sentence the word has a somewhat derogatory implication, like *clique*, but the word is of general application and can be applied to any group united by common aim, like the Southern Democrats in Congress or the Young Republicans. Taken over intact from the French.

craven (kray' vən) *adj. Craven* is a highly uncomplimentary term for "cowardly," "faint-hearted" to a contemptible degree, "cringing." *Craven* people run up the white flag without even considering resistance. *Hamlet* (act IV, scene 4), thinking himself a coward, soliloquized about his "*craven* scruple," i.e., a scruple that in itself stamped him a coward. From Middle English *cravant* (overthrown).

craw (kraw) *n.* This term applies to a bird's crop or an animal's stomach, but it is used frequently and figuratively in the expression *stick in one's craw*, meaning "be intolerable." When something *sticks in your craw*, you simply can't stand it. Constant whiners can drive one crazy; they *stick in one's craw*. Those beautifully populated television commericals that promise everything from eternal youth to instant success *stick in the craws* of sensitive viewers. From Middle English *crawe*.

credible (kred' ə bəl) *adj.* What is *credible* is believable, convincing. The word can be applied to a report or statement or to the person making it. The *New York Times* can be relied upon for *credible* reporting. A *credible* witness is a great asset in court trials. Do not confuse *credible* with *creditable* (kred' ə tə bəl), meaning "deserving of praise": The rescue at Entebbe was a highly *creditable* achievement; or with *credulous* (krej' ə ləs), meaning "gullible": Some people are *credulous* enough to believe that conjurors are actually capable of real magic. From Latin *credibilis*, based on *credere* (to trust). *Credulous* is from Latin *credulus*.

creditable (kred' ə tə bəl). *adj.* See **credible**.

credulous (krej' ə ləs). *adj.* See **credible**.

crestfallen (krest' faw lən) *adj.* When you are *crestfallen*, you are disappointed and dejected. Students are *crestfallen* when their term papers are returned to them with poor grades. Think of the poor struggling author, *crestfallen* as he accumulates rejection slips. Brooklyn Dodger fans of old often had good reason to feel *crestfallen*. Today's Mets fans have inherited the mantle (would that it were Mickey!). The *crest* is from Latin *crista* (crest of an animal).

culpable (kulp' ə bəl) *adj.* *Culpable* behavior is blameworthy. Many avoidable accidents are the result of *culpable* disregard of hazardous road conditions. From Latin *culpabalis*, based on *culpa*, Latin for "fault," "guilt," as in "Mea culpa, mea culpa, mea maxima culpa," from the *Confiteor* ("I confess," said at the beginning of the general confession as part of the Mass).

curmudgeon (kur muj' ən) *n.* This term can be applied to anyone quick to anger, to complain, to bark. *Curmudgeons* have the opposite of sunny dispositions, and are hard to get along with. Harold Ickes, a tough character in Franklin D. Roosevelt's cabinet, was known as The Old *Curmudgeon*. Scrooge was an outstanding *curmudgeon*. The derivation is unknown, except that the *cur-* may be from the word *cur*, in the sense of a "low person."

cursory (kur' sə ree) *adj.* A *cursory* look or inspection is a hasty, superficial one, done without attention to details, the opposite of *thorough*. *Cursory* inspection of cars coming off the assembly line is what is responsible for those expensive recalls. When you read a book in a *cursory* fashion, you're just dipping into it and may be overlooking the subtleties. From Late Latin *cursorius*, based on Latin *cursor* (runner), related to *cursus* (running), which is also a form of *currere* (to run). The Roman poet Lucretius (99–55 B.C.), explaining the continuity of life on the planet, wrote of the succession of the generations, who, like *cursores* (runners), hand on the torch of life.

curt (kurt) *adj.* To be *curt* is to be rudely abrupt. We can't help being *curt* at times with those with whom we do not wish to engage in long conversation, like door-to-door salesmen, telephone solicitors, children pleading to stay up long past their bedtime, and strangers on trains who would just love to talk, while one wants to read. Top sergeants issue *curt* orders. A soft answer turneth away wrath; a *curt* one causeth it. From Latin *curtus* (shortened), which suggests rebuff.

cynosure (sy' nə shoor, sin' ə shoor) *n.* This word describes the center of attraction, and is usually found in the expression *cynosure of all eyes*. When Marilyn Monroe entered a room she was the *cynosure of all eyes*. In *L'Allegro*, John Milton (1608–1674) wrote of "some beauty...the *cynosure* of neighboring eyes." When the British were courting the Grand Sharif Hussein of Mecca, an Arab leader, in their fight against the Turks in World War I, they addressed him in long, flowery terms which went on for eight lines of print, climaxing in "the *cynosure* of all devout Believers." From Latin *Cynosura*, based on Greek *Kynosoura*, literally *kynos* (dog's) plus *oura* (tail). Because of the shape, the constellation Ursa Minor was given the name *Kynosoura* by the Greeks, *Cynosura* by the Romans. The tip end of the constellation is the Pole Star, which guides mariners, and is the "observed of all observers." Hence *cynosure*, the center of attention.

dalliance (dal' ee əns) *n*. To engage in *dalliance* is to dawdle. *Dalliance* sometimes means merely "time-wasting," but its commonest use is in the phrase *amorous dalliance*, which means "flirtation," and *dalliance* all by itself usually has that implication. *Dalliance* is great fun, but can lead to complications. The verb is to *dally* (to trifle, play, sport), and here, too, the implication is clearly amorous. From Middle English *daliaunce*, and Low German *dallen* (to talk foolishly).

daub (dawb) *vb*. To *daub* is to smear, or to coat (something) with soft adhesive matter. Some contemporary abstractions look as though they have been *daubed* with paint while the painter kept his eyes firmly shut. Lips should never be carelessly *daubed* with lipstick—the result can be frightful. From Middle English *dauben*, based on Latin *dealbare* (to plaster).

dauntless (dawnt' lis) *adj*. *Dauntless* people are fearless. In adventure stories, the *dauntless* few always face hordes of savages coolly. In war stories we read of *dauntless* captains who lead their companies into no man's land without the slightest regard for their own safety. All those wonderful movie heroes, like Errol Flynn and John Wayne, were nothing if not *dauntless*. From Latin *domitare* (to tame) plus *less*. There are those to whom this word appears to have a Victorian tinge; its use nonetheless is recommended.

dearth (durth) *n*. *Dearth* is scarcity. It is a negative word and describes the lack of something. There is a *dearth* of good news in the newspapers these days. From the way things are going there appears to be a *dearth* of talent in the field of economics. The *dearth* of food in parts of the Third World is a blot on the escutcheon of developed countries. From Middle English *derthe*.

debacle (day bah' kəl, də bak' əl) *n*. *Debacle* is a sudden collapse, a disastrous breakdown. We are all familiar with General Custer's *debacle* on the Little Big Horn. *The Charge of the Light Brigade* is another example. The Crash of 1929 was a financial *debacle*. For the Ford Motor Company the Edsel was a *debacle*. The Bay of Pigs was both a military and political *debacle*. The word was taken over intact (except for the accents) from French *débâcle*, literally, a "breaking up" (as of an ice jam), but figuratively, a "collapse," as in English.

debase (də base') *vb*. To *debase* is to lower (someone or something) in quality, rank, worth, etc. Inflation has *debased* the value of the dollar. Some people feel *debased* by taking a menial job. Voltaire (1694–1778), in *Oedipe*, (act I, scene 4) wrote: "Virtue *debases* itself in justifying itself." From prefix *de-* plus Late Latin *bassus* (low).

debilitate (dih bil' ə tate) *vb*. To *debilitate* is to weaken, whether the object is a person or thing. A bout of the flu will *debilitate* the sufferer for a considerable period. Inflation has *debilitated* the purchasing power of the currencies of the world in various degrees. *Debilitation* (dih bil ə tay' shən) is the act of weakening: Military success is at times the result of the *debilitation* of enemy forces through hunger and cold. *Debility* (dih bil' ə tee) is the state of being weak, i.e., weakness, the result of *debilitation*. The *debility* of an enemy force will prevent a counterattack. *Debilitate* is from Latin *debilitatus*, a form of *debilitare* (to weaken); *debility* is from Latin *debilitas* (weakness); both are based on the adjective *debilis* (weak).

debunk (dee bungk') *vb*. When you *debunk* something (usually a statement or claim) you show it up as false or exaggerated and strip it of its pretensions. There were those who had the courage to *debunk* certain generals' claims of success in Vietnam. Jingoism should be *debunked* at every opportunity. From prefix *de-* plus *bunk*, short for *bunkum*, which came from an episode in Congress: After a particularly eloquent, angry speech made by Congressman Walker to the sixteenth Congress (1819–1821), he was asked to explain his outburst. He answered that he was not speaking to the House, but to Buncombe, the county in North Carolina that he represented. Naturally, he pronounced Buncombe "bunk'm," and the word gained currency as insincere speechmaking and eventually, as humbug generally. Hence *debunk*, to *take the bunk out* of something.

decimate (des' ə mate) *vb*. To *decimate* is to destroy a large proportion or number (of a group). Time and again, plague has *decimated* the earth's population. Successive earthquakes have *decimated* whole sections of Italy and Iran. Originally, *decimate* applied to the killing of every tenth man of a group (like a regiment or a village) chosen by lot, as punishment for an offense like sabotage or insurrection. The word comes from Latin *decimus* (tenth), from which we also get *decimal*.

déclassé (day klə say') *adj*. Anyone or anything *déclassé* is of inferior class or quality. Loud clothes and rough manners stamp people as definitely *déclassé*. This word is borrowed from the French where it means "come down in the world." It can have that meaning in English as well. A neighborhood that has deteriorated (for instance, by going commercial in spots) can be said to be *déclassé*. The term can be applied to people as well, as in the case of an executive who, through adverse circumstances, becomes *déclassé* to the point of working as a night watchman.

decorous (dek' ə rəs) *adj*. One who is *decorous* or behaves in a *decorous* manner can be said to be well-mannered, seemly, observant of the proprieties. We like to believe well-brought-up people are as *decorous* alone as they are in public. The noun is *decorum* (də kor' əm), meaning "dignity of behavior, observance of the proprieties." Finishing schools teach the art of maintaining *decorum* on all occasions. We read in the papers that teachers in our public schools have a hard time maintaining *decorum* in the classroom. The adjective is from Latin *decorus*, the noun from Latin *decorum*.

decorum (dee kor' əm) *n*. See **decorous**.

decry (dee kry') *vb*. When you *decry* something you disparage it, call attention to its defects. Politicians out of office regularly *decry* the state of the nation. Drama critics habitually *decry* the state of the American theatre, particularly in comparison with the British. Senior citizens with little else to do spend a great deal of their time *decrying* just about everything. Do not confuse *decry* with *descry* (dee skry'), which means "to discern, catch sight of." From French *décrier*.

deduce (dee dyoos') *vb*. To *deduce* something is to draw a conclusion from given data. Sherlock Holmes *deduced* amazingly accurate conclusions from the subtlest clues. Sir Isaac Newton (1642–1727) wrote in a 1675 letter: "Whatever is not *deduced* from the phenomena is to be called a hypothesis,..." What you *deduce* is called a *deduction*. When Sherlock *deduced* something, he arrived at a *deduction*; but do not confuse *deduce* with *deduct* (which means merely "to subtract"), even though the noun related to both words is the same. From Latin *deducere* (to lead down, derive); *deduct* and *deduction* are both from *deductus*, a form of *deducere*.

deem (deem) *vb*. What is *deemed* is believed, judged, considered. Our government *deems* it unwise to engage in unilateral disarmament. It is *deemed* unsafe to render an opinion without a full investigation. Nelson Algren (b. 1909) *deems* it unwise to "play poker with a stranger named 'Doc'," or to "eat at a place named 'Mom's'," or to "go to bed with a woman who has more troubles than you have." From Middle English *demen*.

deferential (def ə ren' shəl) *adj*. To be *deferential* is to act respectfully. This meaning is derived from one of the meanings of the verb *to defer* (dee fur'), which signifies yielding in matters of judgment or opinion. When judges enter courtrooms, all present are expected to arise in a *deferential* attitude. Children should act *deferentially* to their elders—a practice which, alas, seems well on its way to obsolescence. *Deference* (def' ə rəns) is the noun, commonly found in the phrase *due deference*, especially in the expression *with all due deference* (which usually implies no deference at all, in the same way that *with all due respect* means the opposite of its literal meaning, implying the absence of the slightest trace of respect). From Latin *deferens*, a form of *deferre* (to hand over).

definitive (də fin' ə tiv) *adj*. Anything *definitive* is authoritative, the last word on the subject. A *definitive* work on the subject is a final, unchallengeable authority. A *definitive* edition is one that closes the book, so to speak, on further questioning. Ralph Kirkpatrick's edition of Bach's *Goldberg Variations* is the *definitive* one. Edward Lockspeiser has written the *definitive* biography of Claude Debussy. *Definitive* can also take on the meaning of "final," in the sense of "conclusive": When the other chap tells you that such and such is his *definitive* offer, that is supposed to mean that he will not consider any counteroffers. (It usually means, "keep trying; come again; what's your best offer?") Do not confuse *definitive* with *definite*. From Latin *definitivus*.

delectation (dee lək tay' shən) *n.* *Delectation* is delight and enjoyment. Expensive restaurants catering to the middle class are prone to offer "sumptuous meals and exciting entertainment for your *delectation*." (This is all too often an exaggeration.) A related adjective is *delectable* (dee lek' tə bəl), meaning "delightful, highly enjoyable," as in a *delectable dinner*, a *delectable anecdote*. Elderly gentlemen in old-fashioned novels often tend to regard pretty young females as "*delectable* young ladies," implying a note of unfulfillable yearning. *Delectation* is from Latin *delectatio*, *delectable* from Latin *delectabilis*.

deleterious (del ə teer' ee əs) *adj.* What is *deleterious* is harmful, injurious. By itself, it commonly means "injurious to health": Cigarettes contain *deleterious* substances. A lawsuit can be based on the presence of *deleterious* matter in canned food. In context, the injuriousness implied is of a more general nature. Excessive eating or drinking produces *deleterious* effects. (Weight Watchers and AA to the rescue!) Parents often worry that their youngsters who travel widely may be exposed to *deleterious* influences. From New Latin *deleterius*, based on Greek *deleterios* and Latin *deletrix* (something destructive).

demonic (dee mon' ik) *adj.* This word is used to describe anything that is like a demon, or as though possessed or activated by a demon. One can speak of *demonic* glee, *demonic* laughter, *demonic* energy. Dr. Jekyll worked *demonically* in his laboratory, forgetful of the world outside. Carl Gustav Jung (1875–1961), a pioneer in psychiatry, writing of the unconscious, described it as "not only bestial ... and *demonic*, but ... spiritual and ... divine." From Late Latin *daemonicus*, based on Greek *daimonikos*.

denigrate (den' ə grate) *vb.* Anyone or anything *denigrated* is defamed; his or its reputation is blackened. To *denigrate* a person or thing is to speak disparagingly of the subject matter; sneering is part of the act. After praising an author's first publication, critics often *denigrate* his later works. The press is quick to *denigrate* the floundering of a new administration. Cynics *deni-*

grate the virtues of patriotism. Cf. *deprecate*. "Churchmen [have through the ages] delighted in *denigrating* womanhood as the source of the human race's downfall," according to Francis X. Murphy in "Of Sex and the Catholic Church" (*Atlantic Monthly*, February 1981). From *denigratus*, a form of Latin *denigrare* (to blacken), which is based on Latin *niger* (black, which gives us *Negro* and an unfortunate variant).

denizen (den' ə zən) *n.* *Denizens* are inhabitants, residents. Tigers, lions, elephants and other *denizens* of the jungle are engaged in a constant search for water. Moby Dick was a *denizen* of the deep. People are justifiably afraid of finding themselves among the *denizens* of the more disreputable sections of big cities. From Middle English *denisein*, based on Latin *de intus* (from within).

deprecate (dep' rə kate) *vb.* To *deprecate* is to express disapproval, to belittle. Philistines *deprecate* the value of a classical education. Snobs *deprecate* the virtues of an honest rustic upbringing. *Deprecate* is milder than *denigrate*, and synonymous with *depreciate* used in that sense. Do not confuse with *depredate* (plunder). From Latin *deprecatus*, a form of *deprecare* (to deprecate).

deracinate (dee ras' ə nate) *vb.* To *deracinate* is to uproot. This word can be used both literally and figuratively. It is well to *deracinate* the weeds before you plant the seeds for the new garden. In the figurative use, to *deracinate* is to separate a person from his native culture and environment. The refugees, although safe in their new environment, could not help but feel *deracinated*. From the French *déraciner*, based on French prefix *dé-* plus *racine* (root); all from Latin *radicis*, a form of *radix* (root), from which we get *radical*, *radish*, etc.

derelict (derr' ə likt) *n., adj.* This word can be used as a noun or an adjective and has at least two meanings as each. As an adjective, it can mean "abandoned": A *derelict* ship or house or patch of ground is one abandoned by the owner and allowed to fall into ruin. Ingenious people can buy a *derelict* farmhouse and convert it into a charming cottage. *Derelict* has another entirely different meaning as an adjective: "neglectful of duty." People who are *derelict* in the position for which they have been hired soon get the pink slip. Who was the *derelict* blacksmith responsible for the "want of a nail" for which the kingdom was lost?

Derelict, as a noun, implies something abandoned by its owner, like a ship, beached and left standing and falling apart. In a separate sense, it means "vagrant" or "bum." After years of hard drinking, a man can lose job and family and wind up a *derelict* on Skid Row. *Dereliction* (derr ə lik' shən) is deliberate failure to perform one's assigned task, and is usually found in the expression *dereliction of duty*, which often results in a dishonorable discharge. From Latin *derelictus*, a form of *derelinquere* (to forsake).

deride (dee ride') *vb.* To *deride* is to scoff at or mock someone or something. When you *deride* someone, you laugh at him, ridicule him. Hippies *deride* convention. The *-rid-* in both *deride* and *ridicule* comes from Latin *ridere* (to laugh). "Laughing friends *deride*/Tears I cannot hide...." is a lover's plaint in the song *Smoke Gets in Your Eyes*, from the 1933 Broadway musical *Roberta*. *Risus* is a form of *ridere*, and gives us *derisive* (də rye' səv), which describes the state you are in when you are *deriding* someone: The *derisive* snicker of a smart aleck is one of the most infuriating sounds in the world.

derisive (də rye' siv) *adj.* See **deride**.

derogatory (dee rog' ə tor ee) *adj.* Anything *derogatory* is disparaging and belittling. *Derogatory* remarks can damage a reputation. The old saying about "sticks and stones" just isn't true. Cf. *denigrate* and *deprecate*. The related verb *derogate* (derr' ə gate) means "to detract," and is usually followed by the preposition *from*: When President Truman relieved General MacArthur of his command, he drastically *derogated* from the general's authority. From Latin *derogatus*, a form of *derogare* (to detract from).

descry (dee skry') *vb.* When you *descry* something, you make it out, catch sight of it. The implication is that the thing *descried* is far away: The ship's lookout who, peering through the mist, finally *descries* land, cries out his discovery in tones of excited glee. Do not confuse *descry* with *decry* (to disparage—a very different state of affairs). From Middle English *descrier* (to proclaim).

desecrate (des'ə krate) *vb.* To *desecrate* something is to treat it irreverently, to profane and defile it. To *desecrate* a sacred or hallowed place is to violate its sanctity. Grave-robbers *desecrate* cemeteries. Nixon and his cronies *desecrated* the White House. Demagogues, quoting (and misquoting) Abraham Lincoln and other great figures of our proud past, *desecrate* their memories. This word was concocted on the model of *consecrate*, its opposite, which was derived from Latin *consecratus*, a form of *consecrare* (to consecrate).

desiccate (des' ǝ kate) *vb*. When something is *desiccated*, it is dried up. Months without rain *desiccate* farmlands. Timber can be *desiccated* by placing it in ovens that heat the air around it. In the food line, *desiccated* means "dehydrated" as applied to soups, milk, etc. *Desiccated* is also used figuratively to mean "dried up" in the sense of "dull, listless," as in *a desiccated old maid*, *desiccated prose*, a *desiccated style* in any of the arts. Note the one *s* and two *c*'s: *desiccare* is Latin for "to dry thoroughly," and in turn comes from the Latin prefix *de-* plus *siccus* (dry), from which we get the French *sec*, a word familiar in the world of wine. The immediate derivation is from *desiccatus*, a form of *desiccare*.

desuetude (des' wǝ tood) *n*. *Desuetude* is disuse; the state of no longer being used. Antique dealers are redecorating old merry-go-round horses that have fallen into *desuetude*. People in retirement all too often allow their once fertile brains to grow feeble through *desuetude*. Certain laws, as the result of *desuetude*, are now being ignored. President Grover Cleveland (1837–1908), speaking of long unused laws, spoke of their twenty years of "innocuous *desuetude*." From Latin *desuetudo*.

desultory (des' ǝl tor ee) *adj*. This word describes anything fitful and lacking in steadiness. People get nowhere through occasional and *desultory* attempts to find a job. It is important to make a program and keep to it; *desultory* efforts will not succeed. The current war between Iran and Iraq has been characterized not by fixed battles, but only by *desultory* fire from both sides. An interesting derivation, from Latin *desultor* (literally, a circus rider who jumps from one horse to another; figuratively, an inconstant person).

detrimental (deh trǝ ment' ǝl) *adj*. Anything *detrimental* is harmful, injurious. By now we are all familiar with the fact that smoking may be *detrimental* to health. Unjust laws and obsolete taboos are *detrimental* to society. From Latin *detrimentum* (loss, damage).

detritus (dee try' tǝs) *n. Detritus* is debris, waste matter. In deep forests, the ground is covered with the *detritus* of fallen leaves and branches. When a river dries up, it reveals the *detritus* left behind from the erosion of its stony banks. *Detritus* would also apply to the charred timbers, twisted metal and ashes left behind after a fire. The term may be applied to society, as in the *detritus* left behind after a ravaging war—the starving refugees, the wandering survivors. From *detritus*, derived from Latin *detritus*, a form of *deterere* (to rub away).

dexterous, dextrous (dek' stǝ rǝs, dek' strǝs) *adj.* A *dexterous* person is skillful and clever. Its specific application is to manual skills, *dexterity* (dek sterr' ǝ tee), but it is used in a more general way to describe any form of skill or adroitness. Research and full preparation in a lawsuit are essential, but without *dexterous* handling before a jury all those efforts may come to naught. *Dexter* is Latin for "right," in the sense of "on the right hand," and by extension "skillful." See *adroit,* and the discussion of right- and left-handed in that entry.

diaphanous (dye af' ǝ nǝs) *adj.* What is *diaphanous* is sheer, almost transparent. Women can be seductive in *diaphanous* gowns. The most ordinary scenes can seem romantic in a *diaphanous* mist. As applied to feminine apparel, a rather vulgar synonym is *see-through;* even worse is *peekaboo;* but, whatever the adjective, the result can be quite effective. From Greek *diaphanes* (transparent), based on the verb *diaphainein* (to show through).

diatribe (dye' ǝ tribe) *n.* A *diatribe* is a bitter attack in words. In the heat of an election campaign the mutual *diatribes* of the candidates become less and less effective and sometimes downright offensive to the listeners. Legal arguments can be more effective with subtlety than with *diatribes.* From Greek *diatribe* (discourse), based on the verb *diatribein* (to rub away). The "rub" concept persists in the fact that those who resort to *diatribes* are "rubbing it in."

dichotomy (dye kot' ǝ mee) *n. Dichotomy* is a division into two parts, generally for the purpose of differentiation between two contrasting concepts, as in the *dichotomy* between theory and practice, between logical action and impulse, between theoretical communism and its practical workings. Many law-abiding persons of deep religious conviction are troubled by the *dichotomy* between the limitations of church law and the relative permissiveness of civil law. Died-in-the-wool fundamentalists go through life unconcerned with the *dichotomy* between Genesis and Darwin. From Greek *dichotomia*.

didactic (dye dak' tik) *adj.* *Didactic* activity is instructive, intended to teach. *Didactic* writing may help your education but usually doesn't lift your emotions. *Didactic* often covers the situation where the communication is overburdened with instructions and explanations: One often has to plough through *didactic* literature quite strenuously in order to get the point. Propagandistic theatre is usually too *didactic* to be entertaining. From Greek *didaktikos*.

diffident (dif' ə dənt) *adj.* A *diffident* person is shy and lacking in self-confidence. Young lawyers feel *diffident* when facing a judge and jury for the first time. *Diffident* is the opposite of *brash* New teachers are *diffident* on the first day of school. The noun is *diffidence* (dif' ə dəns): *Diffidence* is what makes it so difficult for young men to start a conversation with attractive young women they'd love to get to know. From *diffidens*, a form of Latin *diffidere* (to lack confidence).

digress (də gres', dye gres') *vb.* To *digress* is to depart temporarily from the main topic. Lecturers sometimes *digress* for a moment to tell the audience about a funny thing that happened on the way to the hall. Some people *digress* so often that their audience loses sight of the main topic. The act itself is called *digression* (də gresh' ən or dye gresh' ən). Thomas Huxley (1825–1895) criticized people who waded into scientific matters beyond their depth for distracting their hearers "from the real point of issue by eloquent digressions . . ." From *digressus*, a form of Latin *digredi* (to depart).

dilettante (dil' ə tont) *n.* This word describes a dabbler, one who takes up an activity, particularly in the arts, for his own amusement rather than seriously, and goes into it in a rather superficial way. Some people seem cut out almost from birth to be serious musicians; others may be talented but are content to remain *dilettantes*. Churchill, speaking in Canada on December 30, 1941 about the war effort, said, "There is no room now for the *dilettante*, the weakling, the shirker, or the sluggard . . ." Taken over intact from the Italian.

diminution (dim ə nyoo' shən) *n. Diminution* is a lessening, a decrease. Arteriosclerosis causes a *diminution* of memory function. Old age causes a gradual *diminution* of the hearing faculty. Inflation causes *diminution* of our spending power. From Latin *diminutio*.

disaffection (dis ə fek' shən) *n. Disaffection* is disloyalty, with the implication that loyalty once felt no longer exists. The unreasonable demands of a foreman often result in *disaffection* among the rank and file. People who experience *disaffection* are said to be *disaffected*. After hearing some of the White House tapes, even Nixon's most vociferous supporters became *disaffected*. From Latin prefix *dis-* (as a negative) plus Latin *adfectio*, or *affectio* (favorable state of mind, goodwill, from which we get *affection*).

disconsolate (dis kon' sə lit) *adj.* A person who is *disconsolate* is hopelessly unhappy. Bereavement leaves some people *disconsolate* no matter how hard friends try to cheer them up. To be *disconsolate*, in this sense, is to be inconsolable. *Disconsolate* sometimes takes on the somewhat less intense meaning of "gloomy": Markets are depressed by industry's *disconsolate* prospects. From Latin prefix *dis-* (as a negative) plus *consolatus*, a form of Latin *consolari* (to console).

discursive (dih skur' siv) *adj.* Anything *discursive* rambles from subject to subject. Some treatises are so *discursive* that it is hard to keep the main topic in mind. The word comes from Middle Latin *discursivus*, which was based on Latin *discursus*, a form of the verb *discurrere* (to run to and fro). *Discursion* (dih skur' zhən) is the little-used noun. The author (an attorney) once complained to a judge about his opponent's "*ex*cursions into *discursion*" and was told by the judge that such frivolity was an "*in*cursion" into the solemnity of the court.

disdain (dis dane') *vb.* To *disdain* something is to scorn and despise it, to look upon it with contempt or to think it beneath one's dignity. Thinking people *disdain* TV commercials that use pretty girls instead of informative data to sell their products. Gourmets *disdain* the products of the fast-food chains. One can *disdain* to reply to an insulting note. Some observations are so absurdly irrelevant that one should *disdain* to comment on them. The adjective describing the attitude of a *disdaining* person is *disdainful*, synonymous with *scornful*. Those Abscam congressmen should have been more *disdainful* about accepting those "Arab" bribes. From Latin prefix *dis-* (as a negative) plus *dignare* (to consider worthy).

disingenuous (dis ən jen' yoo əs) *adj.* A *disingenuous* person or act is an insincere one. A *disingenuous* person tries to appear *ingenuous*, i.e., to act innocent and sincere in order to achieve an ulterior end. A suggestion, apparently made for your benefit, that is really motivated by the speaker's own self-interest, may be characterized as *disingenuous*. *Disingenuous* remarks lack candor or frankness. The spanking parent who tells the wailing child, "This hurts me more than it hurts you," or, "This is only for your own good," would appear to be guilty of a *disingenuous* characterization of the situation. For derivation see **ingenuous**.

disparate (dis' pər ət, də spar' ət —*spar* as in sparrow) *adj.* What is *disparate* is distinctly different in kind. Einstein engaged in activities as *disparate* as formulating the Theory of Relativity and playing the fiddle. The *disparate* ideas of some husbands and wives reveal that they come from different worlds. From *disparatus*, a form of Latin *disparare* (to separate).

dissemble (dih sem' bəl) *vb.* To *dissemble* is to give a false appearance. It can take an object: Some people work long hours to make a good impression and *dissemble* their lack of experience. However, the word is generally used by itself and in that usage is synonymous with *dissimulate*, in the sense of "acting hypocritically," while concealing one's true motives and thoughts. It would be nice always to be able to tell the truth, but in this hard world we must often *dissemble*. Basically from Latin *dissimulare* (to disguise, conceal), influenced by French *sembler* (to seem, appear) and *dissemblable* (dissimilar). See *dissimulate*.

dissertation (dis ər tay' shən) *n.* A *dissertation* is a formal essay or discourse, especially a treatise required for the degree of Ph.D. There are those who take years to complete their Ph.D. *dissertations*. The word is at times used ironically, to characterize a long-winded treatment of a subject: Sometimes you ask a simple question and have to endure a *dissertation* on the subject. From Latin *dissertatio*, based on *dissertatus*, a form of *dissertare* (to discuss, argue).

dissimulate (dih sim' yə late) *vb.* When you *dissimulate* something you disguise it, hide it under a false exterior. A skillful politician must learn to *dissimulate* his true feelings on a given issue so as not to disaffect a particular audience. Con men *dissimulate* their true motives, often posing as protectors of the interests of the poor. Used by itself (without an object), to *dissimulate* is to conceal one's thoughts, feelings, motives, generally through the use of hypocritical words or acts. A practiced double-spy must *dissimulate* at every moment. Cf. *dissemble*. Do not confuse *dissimulate with simulate*. To *simulate* is to pretend, to make a showing of (something): People with only a smattering of knowledge in a given field all too often *simulate* great expertise. We are familiar with the use of *simulated* on television, when models are used, especially in news about space activities. *Dissimulate* is from Latin *dissimulatus*, a form of *dissimulare* (to disguise, conceal); *simulate* is from Latin *simulatus*, a form of *simulare* (to pretend).

dissolute (dis' ə loot) *adj.* A *dissolute* person has no morals and is shamelessly uninhibited by any rules of conduct. The word can also mean "dissipated," to describe those who indulge in unbridled pleasure without moral restraint. In *The Rake's Progress*, William Hogarth (1697–1764), in a series of paintings and engravings, depicted the ruin and downfall of a *dissolute* person. *Dissolute* is a very strong word of condemnation. When St. Augustine went to Carthage, he found it a "cauldron of *dissolute* loves." In *King Henry IV, Part I* (act I, scene 2) Shakespeare wrote of " . . . a purse of gold most resolutely snatched on Monday night and most *dissolutely* spent on Tuesday morning." From Latin *dissolutus*, a form of *dissolvere* (to break up). The form *dissolutus*, literally *broken up*, came to mean "profligate, dissolute."

distraught (dih strawt') *adj.* When you are *distraught* you are greatly upset, deeply troubled. People become *distraught* by bereavement, financial disaster, and other calamities. The American public was *distraught* with shock and grief following the assassination of President Kennedy. Henry Wadsworth Longfellow (1807–1882), in his poem *The Three Silences of Molinos*, described the Spanish monk as " . . . *distraught* with dreams and visions." Do not confuse *distraught* with *distracted* in the sense of "having one's attention *diverted*"—although *distracted* can also be used as synonymous with *distraught*. Both are from Latin *distractus*, a form of *distrahere* (to pull to pieces).

doff (dof) *vb.* When you *doff* your hat or any other article of clothing, you take it off. A man should *doff* his hat on entering a church. *Doff* is a contraction of *do off*, and is a rather formal and elegant word to describe the removal of clothing. Men used to *doff* their hats on entering an elevator if there were ladies present, especially in hotels and department stores, but this custom has gone out of fashion. *Doff* can be used to mean "lay aside, get rid of," referring to things other than apparel: *Doff* those silly ideas and get down to practical planning! This is a fairly rare usage. Cf. *don*.

dogged (dog' əd) *adj*. *Dogged* means "persistent," "determined," "stubbornly tenacious." People try to attain success through *dogged* efforts. There are those who, despite logical arguments on the other side, stick to their opinions with *dogged* conviction. People, as well as efforts or convictions, can be described as *dogged*: *Dogged* students often wind up first in their class. Though the word derives from the concept of trailing with dogs, note that it is pronounced differently from the past tense of *to dog*, meaning "to hound," "keep after," which is pronounced as one syllable: *dogd*.

doggerel (daw' gə rəl) *n*. This is the word to describe trivial, poor verse. Limericks are written in *doggerel*. So are many epigrams:

> *Candy is dandy*
> *But liquor is quicker.*
> or
> *I'm a poet*
> *And I don't know it.*

Cf. *dog Latin* (false Latin); *doggerel* comes from *dog* plus the pejorative ending *-rel*.

dogmatic (dog mat' ək) *adj*. *Dogmatic* is opinionated and describes the asserting of opinions in an arrogant manner with an air of authority. A *dogmatic* person expresses an opinion as though it were a proven and universally accepted fact, permitting of no possible contrary belief. You can't argue with *dogmatic* people; they think they're infallible. The noun is *dogmatism* (dog' mə tiz əm): unjustified positiveness in matters of opinion. Sir William Osler (1849–1919), the great Canadian-born physician and philosopher-writer, said, "The greater the ignorance, the greater the *dogmatism*." From Latin *dogma*, based on Greek *dogma* (a philosophical doctrine; literally, that which one thinks is true).

doleful (dole' fəl) *adj.* Anything *doleful* is mournful and sorrowful. You can tell from a person's *doleful* expression that he has experienced a great loss or is in serious trouble. Pessimists always see the *doleful* side of any situation. From Latin *dolor* (sorrow).

dolt (dolt —*o* as in *go*) *n.* A *dolt* is a blockhead or nitwit. *Doltish* means "stupid." *Dolts*, in a word, are numbskulls. Simon Bolivar (1783–1830), the liberator of South America, is alleged to have said satirically, "The three greatest *dolts* in the world are Jesus Christ, Don Quixote, and I." From *dold*, a form of Middle English *dollen* (to dull).

don (don) *vb.* To *don* an article of clothing is to put it on. Cf. *doff*: just as *doff* is a contraction of *do off*, *don* is a contraction of *do on*. A commuter, returning from a sweaty day in the city, *doffs* his business suit, *dons* a sport shirt and slacks, and looks like a different person. *Donning* formal evening clothes once in a while gives people a great lift.

dormant (dor' mənt) *adj.* Anything *dormant* is temporarily inactive, in abeyance. Problems may lie *dormant* for years, but eventually have to be faced. People sometimes enthusiastically map out a program and then let it remain *dormant* for an extended period. *Dormant* can be applied to concrete things as well, like a *dormant* volcano, or *dormant* germs, which, unfortunately, can become active under certain stimuli. *Dormant* is a form of the French verb *dormir* (to sleep), and means, literally, "sleeping."

dossier (dos' ee ay) *n.* A *dossier* is a record; literally, an accumulation of documents containing data relating to someone or something, but used loosely to mean "record," in the sense of background information. Before people are hired, prospective employers like to examine the applicants' *dossiers*. Sometimes a considerable *dossier* exists, which explains what otherwise might seem an inexplicable occurrence. Taken over intact from the French, where it is pronounced *daw syay'*.

doughty (dow' tee—*ow* as in *how*) *adj.* A *doughty* person is stout-hearted, resolute, unafraid. Our movie and television heroes, rough, tough, and *doughty*, always win against incredible odds. *The Three Musketeers* and its sequels, by Alexandre Dumas (1802–1870), recount the valorous exploits of the *doughty* trio, Athos, Porthos, and Aramis. *Doughty* deeds have always won a fair lady. Robert Cunninghame-Graham (1735–1797) wrote:

> If *doughty* deeds my lady please,
> Right soon I'll mount my steed,

Doughty was taken over intact from Middle English; akin to German *tüchtig* (fit, able).

dour (doo' ər) *adj.* A *dour* person looks severe and stern. The words can take on the shades of "harsh, sullen, forbidding," like those unrelenting fathers in Victorian novels. A *dour* visage is said to be a characteristic of many Scots. *Dour* manners inhibit attempts to establish friendly relations. The Puritans are usually depicted as a *dour* lot. From Latin *durus* (hard), from which we also get words like *durable* and *duress*.

doyen (doy' en, dwa yen') *n.* The *doyen* is the senior member (in the sense of leading representative) or dean of a group. The British ambassador is considered the *doyen* of the diplomatic corps in Washington. *Doyen* is often interchangeable with *dean*: Justice Cardozo was the *doyen* (or dean) of jurists. *Doyen* can also apply to an especially skilled or knowledgeable person who is outstanding in his field: Oppenheimer was the *doyen* of atomic physicists. The word is taken over from the French, where it is the equivalent of *senior* or *oldest member* of a group.

draconian (dray koe' nee ən) *adj.* This word expresses the concept of extreme harshness or severity and is most often found in the term *draconian measures*, describing harsh laws or procedures, the kind beloved of dictators. Hitler's racial laws were an extreme example of *draconian measures*. The word comes from *Draco*, an Athenian lawgiver who flourished around 620 B.C. and was responsible for laws that were strict to the point of cruelty. The word is sometimes capitalized, as alluding to *Draco*, and is not to be confused with *draconic* (drə kon' ik) which means "dragonlike."

droll (drole) *adj.* *Droll* people and things are oddly amusing. *Droll* people make you laugh by whimsical, eccentric conduct or words. *Droll* situations can sometimes be embarrassing. The word comes from its French equivalent: *drôle*. Daladier (1884–1970), the French premier, characterized the early stage of World War II as "une drôle de guerre" (an odd sort of war). (The phrase became, in English, "the phony war.") What *droll* people do is called *drollery* (dro' lə ree), and that was the profession of court jesters.

dudgeon (duj' ən) *n. Dudgeon* is resentment and indignation, and is practically always found in the expression *in high dudgeon*, meaning "very resentful and full of indignation." Its most common use is to describe an indignant exit. *He* (or *she*) *left in high dudgeon* suggests the image of a deeply offended diplomat or dowager, hustling out with feathers ruffled. (Has anyone ever left anywhere in low dudgeon?) Derivation unknown.

duplicity (dyoo plis' ə tee) *n.* This word expresses deceitfulness, double-dealing, bad faith. It describes the acts of one who pretends to feel one way and acts the opposite way, and cheats. Double agents are masters and prime examples of *duplicity*. *Duplicity* involves betrayal. The *duplicity* of the participants in the TV quiz show *The $64,000 Question* shocked the public when it was exposed. To "take a dive" in the boxing ring is a glaring example of *duplicity*. From Late Latin *duplicitas*.

ebullient (ih bul' yənt—*u* as in *but* or *put*) *adj.* An *ebullient* person is high-spirited, exuberant. The prospect of being reunited with their loved ones after a long separation puts people into an *ebullient* mood. The noun is *ebullience* (ih bul' yəntz). *Ebullience* usually follows the completion of final exams or the accomplishment of an onerous task. From Latin *ebulliens*, a form of *ebullire* (to boil up). Though one sometimes hears that "the market is *boiling*," the *-bull-* in *ebullient* has nothing to do, etymologically, with the *bull* in the *bull market*.

eclectic (ek lek' tik) *adj.* Anything or anyone *eclectic* is selective, choosing from various sources. An *eclectic* person will choose the best from various sources in order to form his tastes or arrive at his opinions. The result may also be said to be *eclectic*. Some people refuse to follow one philosophical system, and are *eclectic* in forming their own. Architecture drawing on elements from a number of styles can present a pleasing *eclectic* result. From Greek *eklektikos* (selective).

edify (ed' ə fy) *vb.*; **edifying** (ed' ə fy ing) *adj.*; **edification** (ed ə fə kay' shən) *n.* These words, though related, serve somewhat different purposes. *Edify* has two distinct senses: to "instruct," and to "uplift." *Edifying* as an adjective reflects the *uplifting* aspect: The sight of a beautiful cathedral is *edifying*. The reading of fine poetry is inspiring and *edifying*. Most of what you see on TV these days is hardly *edifying*. *Edification*, the noun, reflects the *instructing* or *enlightening* aspect: Will you explain that argument further, please, for the audience's *edification*? From Middle English *edifien*, based on Latin *aedificare* (to build).

effective (ih fek' təv) *adj*. See **efficacious**.

effectual (ih fek' choo əl) *adj*. See **efficacious**.

effectuate (ih fek' choo ate) *vb*. To *effectuate* something is to bring it about, make it happen, bring it to pass. Our country must exert its best efforts to *effectuate* a resolution of the complicated question of Palestinian autonomy. Arbitration rather than litigation is an efficient method of *effectuating* settlement of multi-party controversies. From Middle Latin *effectuatus*, a form of *effectuare* (to bring to pass).

efficacious (ef ə kay' shəs) *adj*. What is *efficacious* is productive of the desired result. The word is not always interchangeable with *effective*, and never with *effectual* or *efficient*. *Efficacious* is used where a specific result is attained: Aspirin is *efficacious* in bringing down body temperature. Concentrated study is *effectual* in producing good examination grades. *Effective* has a number of uses: (1) In situations where something is helpful in producing an *effect*: This machine will do the trick; it's quite *effective*. (2) In situations where something *goes into effect*: This statute is *effective* as of Jan. 1, 1982. (3) Where something is actual (as opposed to apparent): Many have voiced agreement, but the *effective* membership isn't over 200. (4) Where something or somebody is impressive or striking: Conviction contributes to the making of an *effective* speech. The painting of a landscape is really *effective* when it makes you feel you're there. *Effectual* covers the concept of answering the purpose: A machine may not be the most *efficient* one but can still be *effectual*. The negative, *ineffectual*, is perhaps more often heard than *effectual*. It is generally used as a pejorative describing people who get nowhere, "losers," the Casper Milquetoasts of the world. It is a term often applied to nonachievers. *Efficient* describes a method, machine, substance or person producing a result with the least waste: The gadget using the least amount of energy is the most *efficient* one. *Efficacious* is from Latin *efficacis*, a form of *efficax*; *effective* is from Latin *effectivus* (practical); *effectual* is from Late Latin *effectualis*; *efficient* is from Latin *efficiens*, a form of *efficere* (to produce). All these words eventually go back to the Latin verb *facere* (to do, to make).

efficient (ih fish' ənt). *adj*. See **efficacious**.

efflorescence (ef lə res' əns) *n*. An *efflorescence* is a flowering or blossoming, but is more often used figuratively: Beethoven's later works were the *efflorescence* of his art. The Age of Pericles was the *efflorescence* of Greek culture. *Efflorescence* is used to describe the growth and development of one's art or the blossoming of a culture or civilization. From Latin *efflorescens*, a form of Latin *efflorescere* (to blossom).

effrontery (ih frun' tə ree) *n*. This word describes impudent boldness, shameless audacity. How can one have the *effrontery* to pester an exhausted athlete for his autograph as he is running off the field to avoid the onslaughts of the spectators? Some people will stop at nothing, and have the *effrontery* to ask perfect strangers for a loan. There are budding playwrights who, after one mild success, have the *effrontery* to couple themselves with William Shakespeare. From French *effronterie*, which comes from Old French *esfront* (shameless), going back to Latin *ad frontem* (at the face), from which we got *affront*, a word somewhat related to *effrontery*.

effulgent (ih ful' jənt—*u* as in *but*) *adj*. The *effulgent* beauty of the Mona Lisa makes the other paintings near it seem drab by comparison. Oscar Wilde's *effulgent* wit shines throughout his plays. From Latin *effulgens*, a form of *effulgere* (to glitter).

egregious (ih gree' jəs) *adj*. This is an intensely pejorative adjective, applied to things that are exceptionally, glaringly bad. As things turned out, our involvement in Vietnam was an *egregious* mistake. The Nixon tapes revealed one *egregious* plan after another to obstruct justice. "Between you and I" is an *egregious* solecism. *Egregious* has an interesting derivation and development: It comes from a Latin phrase *e grege*, ("out of the herd," or "flock"), i.e., "out of the (common) herd," "exceptional" in a positive sense, and that was its original sense in English: "outstanding." Somehow, in the course of time, it came to mean the exact opposite: "outstandingly bad."

egress (ee' gres) *n*. An *egress* is an exit, and like *exit*, covers both the act and the means of going out of a place, i.e., the exit that is made or the exit through which it is made. P.T. Barnum put up a sign reading, "THIS WAY TO THE EGRESS," to expedite the quick and willing departure of otherwise lingering spectators. Few knew the meaning of *egress*, and the crowd thought the arrow pointed to the exhibit of another exotic animal. Every public place should be provided with ample means of *egress*. The *egress* of a space capsule from orbit is fraught with danger. From Latin *egressus* (departure).

elegy (el' ə jee) *n*. An *elegy* is a mournful poem. The most famous one is the *Elegy Written in a Country Churchyard*, commonly known as *Gray's Elegy*, by Thomas Gray (1716–1771). The term can also apply to a musical composition in a melancholy vein, like Ravel's *Pavane for a Dead Princess*. Do not confuse *elegy* with *eulogy*. The adjective is *elegiac* (el ə jy' ək), as used in phrases like *an elegiac poem about death, an elegiac lament for lost youth*. From Latin *elegia*, taken from Greek *elegeia*.

elicit (ih lis' ət) *vb*. To *elicit* something is to draw it out, in the way in which persistent questioning by the police results in a disclosure. A sad face often *elicits* compassion. It may take years for psychoanalysis to *elicit* the deep-seated core of the neurosis. Do not confuse *elicit* with *illicit*. From Latin *elicitus*, a form of *elicere* (to entice out).

elide (ih lide') *vb*. To *elide* is to omit, and the word is most often applied to the omission of one or more letters, whether in pronunciation or in writing, as in *can't* for *cannot*, *you're* for *you are*, etc. The noun for the phenomenon is *elision* (ee lizh' ən). *Elide* can also apply to the omission or cutting out of things other than letters: In cutting a production of *Hamlet* in order to shorten time of performance, producers sometimes *elide* an entire scene. The deletion of the expletives in the Nixon tapes is an example of editorial *elision*, and many think intentional *elision* explains the famous 18½-minute gap. The verb is from Latin *elidere* (to strike out); the noun is from *elisus*, a form of *elidere*.

elucidate (ih loos' ə date) *vb*. To *elucidate* something is to make it clear or lucid, to throw light upon it. Footnotes are intended to *elucidate* the text. Forthright answers can *elucidate* uncharacteristic behavior. *Elucidation* (ə loos ə day' shən) is enlightenment. From Latin *elucidatus*, a form of *elucidare* (to enlighten), based on *lucis*, a form of the noun *lux*, meaning "light," from which we get *lucid*.

emblazon (em blay' zən) *vb.* To *emblazon* is to adorn richly, deck in brilliant colors. The term was used originally to describe the decoration of anything with heraldic ornaments. At Christmas time we *emblazon* our houses with varied and beautiful decorations. The word is sometimes used to mean "proclaim" or "extol": On the death of a monarch it is customary for his subjects to *emblazon* his accomplishments and honor his memory throughout the land. From prefix *em-* plus Middle French *blason* (buckler, round shield).

emend (ee mend') *vb.* To *emend* is to correct or edit. A careful editor will *emend* a text to meet the needs of the particular readership. Do not confuse *emend* with *amend* (ə mend'), which implies the making of minor alterations, in a somewhat less sweeping way, and is also used in connection with the changing of a law or proposed law amendment. From Latin *emendare* (to correct, based on prefix *e-* (away from) plus *mendum* (mistake).

emeritus (ih merr' ə təs) *adj.* This word applies to a person who has retired while retaining his honorary title and is usually found in the expression *professor emeritus*. A man who has not taught for years might continue to be addressed as Professor So-and-So, whereas in reality he is *emeritus*. This word which is a form of Latin *emerere* (to earn by service), developed as a Latin noun meaning "veteran" in the military sense.

emote (ih mote') *vb.* One who *emotes* is acting emotionally. The American public *emoted* when they first viewed the released Iranian hostages. *Emote* is sometimes used pejoratively, to indicate theatrical behavior. Hollywood queens *emote* off the screen as well as on. *Emote* is an example of a "back formation," from the noun *emotion*, which is from Latin *emotus*, a form of Latin *emovere*, (to move out).

empirical (em peer' ə kəl) *adj.* An *empirical* judgment or opinion is one based on observation and experience, as opposed to theory. After the working out of a theory, it is often well to get it confirmed *empirically*. *Empirical* implies trial-and-error procedures. The U.S. Food and Drug Administration requires *empirical* proof of the safety and validity of a new medicine. From Greek *empeirikos* (experienced); an *empiricus*, in Latin, is an unscientific doctor—the dangerous trial-and-error type.

emulate (em′ yə late) *vb.* To *emulate* is to imitate, with the implication of an attempt to equal or surpass. It is common for ambitious children to *emulate* their fathers and teachers. The word sometimes takes on the implication of successful rivalry: New York now *emulates* Paris and Rome as a fashion center. Thorstein Veblen (1857–1929), the economist and sociologist who made "conspicuous consumption" a catchword, spoke of "the propensity for *emulation*," which we often speak of as "keeping up with the Joneses." From Latin *aemulatus*, a form of *aemulari* (to rival).

encomium (en koe′ mee əm) *n.* *Encomium* is high praise. The word implies a certain degree of formality, as in an official speech or situation. Our returning hostages from Iran were greeted with an *encomium* from the president. A victorious general usually receives an *encomium* from the head of state. From Greek *enkomion*.

endemic (en dem′ ik) *adj.* Anything *endemic* is characteristic, peculiar to a particular place, race, nation, sect. This word is used, for example, of diseases that flourish regularly in certain parts of the world: Dysentery is *endemic* to India, Egypt, and to much of the rest of the Third World. Not only illnesses, but also customs and folkways can be said to be *endemic* to a particular place or sect: Community singing is *endemic* to Wales. Vendettas are *endemic* to Sicily. From New Latin *endemicus*, based on Greek *endemos*; note the *demos* (people), from which we get *democracy*.

enervate (en′ ər vate) *vb.* To *enervate* someone is to weaken him and lessen his vitality. The heat and humidity of tropical countries often *enervate* their people. Graft and corruption can *enervate* an entire country. From Latin *enervatus*, a form of *enervare* (literally, to remove the sinews—*nervi*, in Latin, from which we get *nerves*—from someone). The early anatomists appear to have confused nerves and sinews.

enigmatic (en ig mat′ ik) *adj.* *Enigmatic* people and things are puzzling and obscure. Mona Lisa's smile is often described as *enigmatic*, concealing secret thoughts, like the woman in Elizabeth Pym's *Excellent Women* (E. P. Dutton, N.Y., 1952), who looked "as if she saw and thought more than she would ever reveal." The word can describe things other than smiles: The circumstances of the disappearance of many missing persons are *enigmatic*. From Latin *aenigmatis*, a form of *aenigma*; taken intact into Latin from Greek *aenigma* (riddle). The noun is *enigma*, a puzzle or mystery. In 1939, Churchill called Russia " . . . a riddle wrapped in a mystery inside an *enigma*."

enmity (en' mə tee) *n*. *Enmity* is hostility, antagonism. *Enmity* all too often develops among heirs as they struggle over the division of an estate. Germany's traditional *enmity* with England and France motivated World War II. From Latin *inimicus* (enemy), based on negative prefix *in-* and *amicus* (friend), from which we get *amicable*.

ennui (ahn wee') *n*. *Ennui* is boredom. It is a word taken bodily from the French, and expresses world-weariness and emptiness of feeling, often felt by the "man who has everything." Once people make money, enough to buy all the things they have dreamt of, they are often beset by *ennui*. After you have once seen a smooth professional performance of a play, an inept amateur performance will fill you with painful *ennui*.

entity (en' tə tee) *n*. This word, often a rather elevated synonym for "thing," covers anything having a distinct existence. A corporation is an *entity*, distinct from its stockholders. Arnold Bennett (1867–1931) called the train a "luxurious complete *entity*." All the planets make a single solar system, but each one is an *entity*. From Middle Latin *entitas*.

enure (en yoor') *vb*. See **inure**.

envisage (en viz' əj) *vb*. To *envisage* something is to visualize something or imagine it. Some people can tell a story so vividly that one is able to *envisage* the landscape and the characters. *Envisage* can also imply *foresee*: Based on current developments, it is easy to *envisage* a world in which electronics will control almost every aspect of our lives. From French *envisager*.

ephemeral (ih fem' ə rəl) *adj*. What is *ephemeral* is short-lived, soon over and done with. Beset with the problems of adulthood one tends to look back with nostalgia at the *ephemeral* blessings of childhood. What is more *ephemeral* than yesterday's TV listings? In his *Meditations*, the Roman emperor-philosopher Marcus Aurelius (A.D. 121–180) said: "All is *ephemeral*—fame and the famous as well." From Greek *ephemeros* (short-lived). Latin took over the related word *ephemeris* (diary) intact from the Greek. Those momentous diary entries soon fade; their importance is *ephemeral*.

epicure (ep′ə kyoor) *n.* An *epicure* is a gourmet, a fastidious diner who understands and lays great stress upon the refinements of cooking and relishes the best of food and drink. The adjective *epicurean* (ep ə kyoo ree′ ən) is often mistakenly taken as describing high living and riotous luxury. Far from it; that is a corruption of the teaching of Epicurus (341–270 B.C.), a Greek philosopher who maintained that pleasure was the highest good, but that it came from *modest* living, which led to calm of mind and body. In *Antony and Cleopatra* (act II, scene 1), Shakespeare speaks of "*Epicurean* cooks" who sharpen Antony's appetite with "cloyless" (i.e., *uncloying*—see *cloy*) sauces. Do not apply *epicure* to those who too fondly love their food and drink without discrimination.

epigram (ep′ ə gram) *n.* *Epigrams* are witticisms, witty sayings, wisecracks, tersely expressed, often in verse. Samuel Taylor Coleridge (1772–1834) defined it this way in 1802, echoing Polonius, in Shakespeare's *Hamlet*, who says, " . . . brevity is the soul of wit":

What is an Epigram? *A dwarfish whole,*
Its body brevity, and wit its soul.

Epigram applies particularly to a brief satirical poem, usually ending with a terse, witty observation, or, as W. H. Fowler put it (Modern English Usage, Oxford), "with a sting in its tail." Sir John Harrington (1561–1612), a favorite of Queen Elizabeth I, wrote:

Treason doth never prosper; what's the reason?
For if it prosper, none dare call it treason.

And there is Dorothy Parker's

Men seldom make passes
At girls who wear glasses.

And Oscar Wilde's

> *The only people who think about money as much as*
> *the rich are the poor.*

From Latin *epigramma*, taken over intact from the Greek.

epitaph (ep' ə taf) *n*. An *epitaph* is, literally, a tomb inscription, but the word is used more generally to cover any written praise of one who has passed on. Churchill used it that way in a 1944 speech: "'Not in vain' may be the pride of those who survived and the *epitaph* of those who fell." Hamlet says (act II, scene 2): "After your death, you were better have a bad *epitaph* than their ill report while you live." Do not confuse *epitaph* with *epithet*. From Latin *epitaphium*, based on Greek *epitaphion* (over a tomb).

epithet (ep' ə thet - *th* as in *thing*) *n*. An *epithet* is a descriptive word or phrase, often one that has become identified with a famous character, real or fictional. In *Richard the Lion-Hearted*, *Lion-Hearted* is the *epithet*, and, even standing alone, would identify Richard I (1157–1199) of England. *The Obscure* is the *epithet* in *Jude the Obscure*, the novel by Thomas Hardy (1840–1928). The phrase *man's best friend* is an *epithet* for *dog*. *The Almighty* and *The Eternal* are *epithets* for *God*. Do not confuse *epithet* with *epigram*. From Latin *epitheton*, taken over from the Greek, where it means "something added."

epitome (ih pit' ə mee) *n*. The *epitome* of something is its embodiment, its typical representation. Florence Nightingale is the *epitome* of heroism and compassion. In this sense, *epitome* is synonymous with *personification*. Most television commercials are the *epitome* of mediocrity. James Morris (*Farewell the Trumpets*, Faber & Faber, London, 1978) called the Viceroy's palace in New Delhi "...a stone *epitome* of British authority in India." Taken over intact from the Greek via Latin.

equable (ek' wə bəl) *adj*. *Equable* people are even-tempered, unvarying. People with *equable* temperaments are easy to get along with. New Zealand is noted for its *equable* climate. Do not confuse *equable* with *equitable* (fair, just). From Latin *aequabilis*.

equanimity (eh kwə nim' ə tee) *n*. *Equanimity* is composure, calmness of temperament. Both Sir William Osler (1849–1919), the Canadian-born physician and philosopher-writer, and

Reinhold Niebuhr (1892–1971), the U.S. theologian and philos-opher, preached the importance of "cultivating *equanimity*." William Ralph Inge (1860–1954), the "gloomy dean" of St. Paul's Cathedral, London, taught us to "accept with proud *equanimity* the misfortunes of life." From Latin *aequanimitas*.

equitable (ek' wə tə bəl) *adj.* What is *equitable* is fair and just. The goal of any arbitration is to reach an *equitable* settle-ment. Under our system of justice, every person is entitled to *equitable* treatment in our courts. Do not confuse *equitable* with *equable* (even-tempered, unvarying). From Latin *aequitas* (fair-ness, justice).

equivocal (ih kwiv' ə kəl) *adj.* This word can mean either "un-certain, undetermined," or "questionable," depending upon the context. When someone doesn't know how to react, he assumes an *equivocal* attitude (i.e., an uncertain attitude). If someone acts disloyally and can no longer be trusted, he can be said to have exhibited an *equivocal* character (i.e., an untrustworthy, questionable one). A related verb is *equivocate* (ih kwiv' ə kate), meaning "to hedge," in order to avoid committing oneself. You can't get a straight answer from people who *equivocate*: "Well, I guess so, but on the other hand...." "I am in earnest—I will not *equivocate*...!" said William Lloyd Garrison (1805–1879), restating his position against slavery. *Equivocal* is from Late Latin *aequivocus* (ambiguous); *equivocate* is from Middle Latin *aequivocatus*, a form of *aequivocare* (to equivocate).

errant (err' ənt) *adj.* *Errant* has two distinct meanings. It can describe conduct that amounts to misbehaving: It is wise for a parent to discipline his *errant* child. Teachers must learn to control their *errant* pupils. It can also mean "wandering aimless-ly," as in *an errant stream*, *an errant breeze*, and in this use *errant* is a gentle, poetic word. Do not confuse *errant* with *erratic* (ə rat' ik), which means "eccentric, queer." *Errant* comes from Latin *errans*, a form of *errare* (to wander); *erratic* from Latin *erraticus*, based on *erratus*, another form of *errare*.

ersatz (ur' zahts—*ur* as in *burden*) *adj.* This word applies to anything that is synthetic, artificial, substitute; not the genuine article; something else, generally of inferior quality. In Europe, during World War II, you couldn't get real coffee; all they served was *ersatz*, burnt cereal mixed with chicory. When people are looking for honest-to-goodness suede, they won't accept some *ersatz* man-made material. *Ersatz* can be used as a noun, describing anything artificial used as a substitute for a natural product. The word is taken over bodily from the German, where it means "substitute."

erudite (err' yoo dite, err' oo dite—*oo* as in *look*) *adj.* Erudite means "learned" (learn' əd), "scholarly." It is a fortunate thing to study under a group of *erudite* teachers. The writings of Cicero (106–43 B.C.), on friendship, old age, etc., are erudite studies of those subjects. Addison (1672–1719) and Steele (1672–1729) collaborated on a series of *erudite* essays. *Erudition* (err yoo dish' ən, err oo dish' ən) is the noun, meaning "learning." *Erudite* comes from Latin *eruditus*, a form of *erudire* (to instruct); *erudition* from Latin *eruditio*.

eschew (es choo') *vb.* To *eschew* something is to shun or avoid it. The avoiding is not casual, but determined. The Book of Common Prayer tells us to "Eschew evil, and do good." Vegetarians *eschew* flesh, fish, and fowl. Don't run the *-sch-* together; es choo. From Middle English *eschewen*. *Scheowe* was early Middle English from which we get *shy*, and there is a connection between *eschewing* and *staying shy* of something.

esoteric (es ə terr' ik) *adj.* This adjective covers anything obscure, far out, beyond the grasp of most people. The word can apply to ideas, works of art, doctrines, systems of thought, philosophies, and the like. Picasso's later paintings, Salvador Dali's surrealist work, and much of today's serious music are largely *esoteric*. People fall asleep in church during *esoteric* sermons. The word comes from Greek *esoterikos* (inner); anything *esoteric* is "inside stuff," meaningful only to the few. *Esoterica*, a plural noun denoting things that are understood by or meant for a select few, is taken over intact from the Greek, via New Latin.

ethereal (ih theer' ee əl—*th* as in *thing*) *adj.* What is *ethereal* is light, delicate, airy. Charles William Beebe (1877–1962), the ornithologist (authority on birds), described one species as the "smallest, most *ethereal* and daintiest of birds." One can speak of ethereal, heavenly music. Some people radiate *ethereal* beauty, as though not of this world. The word is from Latin *aethereus*, which came from Greek *aitherios*, based on *aither*; the *ether-* in *ethereal* is not the chemical ether, but the ether supposedly occupying the upper regions of space.

etymology (et ə mol' ə jee) *n.* This word is used to mean "derivation," in the sense of the specific derivation of a particular word: The *etymology* of the word *etymology* is two Greek words: *etymos* (true) and *logos* (word). The etymology of *demijohn* (a large bottle with a short neck) has nothing to do with demi- (half): it comes from *Dame Jeanne*, a mythological French lady of that name, who must have had a large bottom and a short neck. *Etymology* is also used to denote the study of word origins in general. In that sense, *etymology* is sometimes an exact science, at others guesswork. Do not confuse *etymology* with another word that closely resembles it: *entomology* (ent ə mol' ə jee), the study of insects, from Greek *entomon* (insect); or, as some people say: "*Etymology* is about words; *entomology* is about ents."

eulogy (yoo' lə jee) *n. Eulogy* can mean either a specific speech or writing in praise of a person (usually deceased) or thing, as in a *flowery eulogy* that keeps a funeral service going for hours, or "praise" generally. When a seemingly impossible job is well done, it is deserving of the highest *eulogy*. The verb is *eulogize* (yoo' lə jize). Corporations sometimes *eulogize* a retiring chairman's past accomplishments in high-flown polysyllables. From Greek and Late Latin *eulogia* (praise).

euphemism (yoo' fə miz əm) *n.* This is the term applied to a mild or indirect word or phrase substituted for one considered too harsh or indelicate. Examples: to *pass away, go to meet one's Maker, give up the ghost, go to one's eternal rest,* for *die; underprivileged* for *poor; minority* for *black* or *Hispanic.* The word can apply to either a specific case, or the general practice of resorting to such substitutes. *Euphemism* is one of the tools of political oratory. The practice was satirized by Moliere (1622–1673) in his play *Les Precieuses Ridicules*, about the linguistic affectations used by the pretentious literary women of seventeenth-century France, who specialized in *euphemism. Euphemistic* (yoo fə mis' tik) is the adjective. Virginia Woolf (1882–1941) wrote about "... those comfortably padded lunatic asylums which are known, *euphemistically*, as the stately homes of England." Do not confuse *euphemism* with *euphony* (yoo' fə nee): see *euphonious. Euphemism* is from Greek *euphemismos* (use of words of good omen).

euphonious (yoo foe' nee əs) *adj.* This pleasant-sounding word means just that: "pleasant-sounding." People not particularly attractive physically can seem so because of their *euphonious* way of speaking. The delicate, *euphonious* sounds made by a harpsichord are a delight to the ear. The noun is *euphony* (yoo′ fə nee), meaning "agreeableness of sound" generally, often applied to words: The *euphony* of Robert Burns's poetry sometimes obscures its serious meaning. From Greek *euphonia*.

euphoric (yoo for′ ik) *adj.* Euphoric expresses the mood of a person enjoying an exaggerated feeling of well-being. Its slang equivalent is "high." Usually, the word implies that the feeling is unjustified by the circumstances, or is entirely without a basis in reality. Not realizing that Dunkirk was a sorry defeat rather than a glorious victory, the British were *euphoric* when the retreat was completed. The deadliness of opium is hidden by the *euphoric* mood it generates. *Euphoria* (yoo for′ ee ə) is the noun. The general *euphoria* when the American hostages were released in Iran obscured the fact that the whole thing should never have happened in the first place. From Greek *euphoria* (state of well-being).

exacerbate (ig zas′ ər bate) *vb.* To *exacerbate* a situation is to worsen it, to aggravate it, in the sense of increasing its bitterness. A clumsy nurse's ministrations serve only to *exacerbate* the pain of the patient. Harsh words can only *exacerbate* bitter feelings. Inept handling *exacerbates* any situation. The *-acerb-* part of the word is found also in *acerbic*. We get *exacerbate* from Latin *exacerbatus*, a form of *exacerbare* (to exasperate, embitter).

excoriate (ik skore′ ee ate) *vb.* When you *excoriate* someone, you upbraid him scathingly, reprimand him harshly. Literally and physically, the word means "to flay," i.e., to strip the skin off (someone). Like *flay*, its common use is the figurative one, to describe merciless reprimand. Top sergeants are famous for *excoriating* raw recruits. After imposing sentence, judges sometimes *excoriate* the convicted criminal for the heinousness of his offense. People, in relating proudly how they tore into an offender, sometimes say, "I skinned him alive." They might as well have used *excoriate*, which comes from Latin *excoriatus*, a form of *excoriare* (to skin).

excrement (ek′ skrə mənt) *n.* Excrement is feces. Like the Latin word it comes from, *excrementum*, it is broad enough to describe any bodily waste, but it almost always refers to fecal matter. The captured I.R.A. terrorists went on a hunger strike and smeared their own *excrement* on the walls of their cells.

exculpate (ek' skull pate, ik skull' pate) *vb.* To *exculpate* someone is to free him from blame. *Exculpate* is synonymous with *exonerate*. After an accident on the highway, the police usually charge one driver with an offense and *exculpate* the other. The noun is *exculpation* (ek skull pay' shən). There are instances in the annals of crime where, after a conviction and imprisonment, a third party admits his guilt and brings about the *exculpation* of the one wrongly accused. The faithful husband, who really had to work late at the office, pleads with his jealous wife for *exculpation*. From Latin *exculpatus*, a form of *exculpare* (to free from blame). See *culpable*, for an explanation of the -*culpa*-component.

execrable (ek' sə krə bəl) *adj.* Anyone or anything *execrable* is detestable, abominable, hateful. The Nazis were guilty of *execrable* acts against defenseless people. To betray one's comrades is *execrable* beyond words. Uriah Heep, the villainous clerk in *David Copperfield*, is the prototype of an *execrable* person. John Wesley (1703–1791), the evangelist who founded Methodism, wrote of "that *execrable* sum of all villainies, commonly called the slave trade." There is a related verb: to *execrate* (ek' sə krate), with two meanings. It can mean "to detest": Partisans of either the extreme right or the extreme left *execrate* all who do not share in their beliefs. It can also mean "to curse": People who bring about their own misfortunes often *execrate* others for having caused their downfall. *Execrable* is from Latin *exsecrabilis*; *execrate* is from Latin *exsecratus*, a form of *exsecrari* (to curse).

exegesis (ek sə jee' səs) *n.* This word, taken over intact from the Greek, means "interpretation," especially of Scripture, but applicable generally. The plural is *exegeses*. There have been several *exegeses* of *Finnegans Wake*—by James Joyce (1882–1941)—most of which need an *exegesis* of their own. Most people cannot follow the most painstaking attempt at an *exegesis* of the Theory of Relativity. Robert Hillyer (1895–1961), the American poet (and the author's English teacher at Harvard, 1923–24), wrote, in a letter to Robert Frost (1874–1963):

> Blest be thy name, O Vogue, that canst embalm
> A minor poet with a potted palm.
> Make me immortal in thy exegesis—
> Or failing that, at least a Doctor's thesis.

exemplary (ig zem′ plə ree, eg′ zəm plə ree) *adj*. *Exemplary* acts are commendable; they set a high standard, an example worth imitating. *Exemplary* conduct sets an *example* for others. The *exemplary* behavior of the people of London during the Blitz is a glorious chapter in English history. *Exemplary* has a special meaning in law: "serving as an example." *Exemplary damages*, when awarded, are in excess of actual damages suffered, and are imposed as an *example*. An *exemplary penalty* serves the same purpose. The Latin source, *exemplaris*, means "serving as a copy."

exhort (ig zort′) *vb*. To *exhort* someone is to urge him, to advise him with great emphasis. Churchill *exhorted* his fellow Britons to sneer at Hitler's arrogance. Foremen *exhort* their workers to give their all for the good of the company. From Latin *exhortari* (to urge). The noun, *exhortation* (eg zor tay′ shən) is from Latin *exhortatio*.

exigency (ek′ sə jən see) *n*. *Exigency* is urgency. When the enemy attacks, there is sufficient *exigency* to justify calling out the troops. The plural is used in the sense of "urgent needs, demands": The *exigencies* of party politics require voting as a bloc, despite one's occasional differences as an individual. The *exigencies* of the recent drought required extreme steps for the conservation of water. *Exigent* (ek′ sə jənt) is the adjective: An *exigent* situation requires immediate attention and action; an *exigent* person won't take no for an answer. *Exigency* is from Middle Latin *exigentia*; *exigent* is from Latin *exigens*, a form of *exigere* (to demand).

exonerate (ig zon′ ə rate) *vb*. To *exonerate* someone is to free him from blame. *Exonerate* is synonymous with *exculpate*. The production of a watertight alibi is the best way to be *exonerated* of complicity in a crime. We get *exonerate* from Latin *exoneratus*, a form of *exonerare* (to disburden), which is based on Latin *ex* (from) and *onere*, a form of the noun *onus* (burden, charge).

exorcise (ek′ sor size) *vb*. One can *exorcise* (i.e., expel) an evil spirit from a person by prayer or religious rites: The clergy are said to be expert in *exorcising* demons; or one can *exorcise* (i.e. free) a person or place from evil spirits or influences: Sometimes, despite strenuous efforts, it is impossible to exorcise a house from a feeling of doom. From Late Latin *exorcizare*, based on Greek *exorkizein* (to cause someone to swear an oath).

expatiate (ik spay' shee ate) *vb*. When you *expatiate* upon a subject, you are dwelling upon it at great length, going into it in great detail. Those who wish to impress others with the importance of an issue sometimes wear them out by *expatiating* on the theme at too great a length. Politicians should point out their own accomplishments rather than *expatiate* on the other fellow's shortcomings. From Latin *exspatiatus*, a form of *exspatiari* (to walk about, wander, deviate).

expiate (ek' spee ate) *vb*. To *expiate* one's guilt, misdeeds, or sins is to atone or make amends for them. Ehrlichman threw himself into the doings of good deeds in order to *expiate* his guilt for past misdeeds as President Nixon's aide. St. Francis of Assisi *expiated* his sinful youth by renouncing worldly pleasures and devoting himself to religion. From Latin *expiatus*, a form of *expiare* (to atone for).

expostulate (ik spos' chə late) *vb*. To *expostulate* is to argue vigorously with someone in order to talk him out of doing something or to remonstrate against something he has done. Parents often *expostulate* with their children about the evils of marijuana, sleeping late, long hair, loud rock, etc. Republican and Democratic legislators spend a good deal of time *expostulating* in principle about legislation proposed by the other side. It is futile to *expostulate* with an obstinate person. From Latin *expostulatus*, a form of *expostulare* (to demand urgently).

expropriate (eks pro' pree ate) *vb*. When you take something away without the owner's consent, you *expropriate* it. It has become routine for governments of Third World nations to *expropriate* business firms owned by aliens. *Expropriate* can apply to ideas as well as tangible property: It is wrong to *expropriate* somebody else's ideas and put them into the suggestion box as your own. From Middle Latin *expropriatus*, a form of *expropriare*.

expunge (ik spunj') *vb*. Anything *expunged* is wiped out, erased, deleted. It happens sometimes that in editing his rough draft, an author *expunges* some of the best passages. When a judge rules that certain testimony is irrelevant, he can order it *expunged* from the record. Certain parts of the Nixon tapes, particularly the famous 18½-minute gap, would appear to have been *expunged*. From Latin *expungere*.

extempore (ik stem' pə ree) *adj.*, *adv.* Anything that is, or happens, *extempore* is impromptu, done on the spur of the moment. Public figures giving press conferences must become skillful in answering questions from the audience *extempore*. A related adjective is *extemporaneous* (ik stem pə ray' nee əs), meaning "impromptu, unrehearsed." Student actors in improvisation courses put on *extemporaneous* performances. President Truman's *extemporaneous* sidewalk speeches were his best. From Latin *ex tempore* (literally, out of the time; freely, at the moment). *Extemporaneous* is from Late Latin *extemporaneus* (on the spur of the moment).

extenuate (ik sten' yoo ate) *vb.* To *extenuate* is to lessen the seriousness of an offense, or someone's guilt, or to make it seem less serious. *Extenuating circumstances* is a common phrase, to describe surrounding facts that partially excuse an offense or a fault. In a prosecution for robbery, the judge may take into account the absence of a weapon, and a first offender's poverty and need, as *extenuating circumstances* in passing sentence. It is commonly said that youth *extenuates* a crime. Patrick Henry (1736–1799) used *extenuate* to mean "underestimate" in his famous "liberty or death" speech: "It is vain, sir, to *extenuate* the matter." From Latin *extenuatus*, a form of *extenuare* (to reduce, diminish).

extirpate (ek' stər pate) *vb.* To *extirpate* something is to root it out, destroy it utterly, eradicate it, exterminate it. Smallpox has been practically *extirpated* in the civilized world. The conquering Spaniards tried to *extirpate* the practice of human sacrifice from Aztec culture. From Latin *exstirpatus*, a form of *exstirpare* (to tear up by the roots), based on the prefix *ex-* (from) plus *stirpe*, a form of *stirps* (root).

extrapolate (ik strap' ə late) *vb.* To *extrapolate* is to make a future estimate based on past data. The *Farmer's Almanac* extrapolates next year's weather from the study of past records. Speculators *extrapolate* the future action of stocks from past performance. Sometimes the word has the meaning of "conjecture" or "predict": Political analysts *extrapolate* the public's reaction to a proposal, for example, disarmament, from a study of the attitudes expressed on related issues in the past. This word was formed by imitation of another word, *interpolatus* (discussed under *interpolate*), by putting together the Latin *extra* (outside, beyond) and *-polatus*, a component of *interpolatus*, a form of *interpolare* (to polish up, and by extension, to falsify).

exuberant (ig zoo′ bə rənt) *adj.* Anyone who is *exuberant* is in high spirits, full of enthusiasm. Friends or relations who have been away for years usually receive an *exuberant* welcome when they return. Sailing high against the wind on a sparkling sunny day makes people feel *exuberant* (unless they're seasick). Sweeping views of the countryside make hikers *exuberant*. The word can also have the meaning of "lavish, profuse": In the tropics, the trees are covered with *exuberant* foliage, the ground with *exuberant* vegetation. That is not its common use in English, although it is derived from Latin *exuberans*, a form of *exuberare* (to grow thickly, to abound).

facet (fas′ ət) *n.* A careful lawyer will examine every *facet* of a situation, and a careful jeweler will examine every *facet* of a gem, because *facet*, in its figurative sense, means "aspect" or "phase" or "angle" of a situation, and in its literal sense, one of the many polished "faces" of a gem. A diamond, for instance, has sixty-four *facets*. Just as one shouldn't make a decision without considering every *facet* of the problem, one shouldn't buy a diamond without having a qualified expert examine every *facet* of the stone. The word comes from French *facette*, (little face). The French word *face* comes from Latin *facies*.

facile (fas′ əl) *adj.* A public speaker should be *facile*, able to act and perform with ease. A *facile* speaker can face any audience impromptu, without notes. A good pianist has *facile* fingers, which fly over the keys with the greatest of ease. Something managed with ease is said to be *facile*, like a *facile* victory, one easily won. There is a danger, however, in using this word, because it can imply superficiality. People sometimes reach a *facile* solution of a problem, but it doesn't stand the test of time. One must be sure that the context makes it clear whether *facile* is being used as a compliment or a pejorative. This word was taken over bodily (except for the pronunciation: fah seel′) from the French, meaning "easy," and they got it from the Latin *facilis*, the opposite of *difficilis*, from which we get *difficult*.

facilitate (fə sil′ tate) *vb*. Look at *facile* for the origin of this word, which means to "make easy, help along." Planning ahead always *facilitates* any task. Travel agents *facilitate* those journeys abroad that are otherwise complicated by all sorts of red tape. The Romans had the word *facilitas* (easiness) from which we get *facility* (fə sil′ ə tee), meaning "aptitude, ease of performance."

fallacious (fə lay′ shəs) *adj*. A *fallacious* argument is one that is unsound and misleading. It is based upon a *fallacy* (fal′ ə see), an erroneous or mistaken belief based, in turn, upon unsound reasoning. It was *fallacious* to believe that the sun revolved around the earth. This mistaken belief was founded upon the *fallacy* that we stood still while all the heavenly bodies moved. The testimony of eyewitnesses, though sincere, is often *fallacious*, because people tend to see not what happens, but what they want to see. The arguments that raged, and still rage, against the Darwinian theory of evolution were and are *fallacious*, based on dogma and against scientific evidence. We get *fallacious* from Late Latin *fallaciosus* (deceptive), which came from Latin *fallacia* (deceit)

fallow (fal′ owe) *adj*. Land left plowed but unseeded is said to be *fallow*. From that literal meaning, we get the metaphorical (see *metaphor*) meanings "dormant, inactive, unproductive." After the harvest, a farmer may leave his land *fallow* for a season or two. By neglecting books and staring at the television screen for hours on end, a person can leave his mind *fallow*. You might run across *fallow* in an entirely different sense: "pale yellow, dun." This seemingly unconnected meaning must have something to do with the color of unplowed land. A certain species of deer is called "fallow deer." There is an anonymous old poem entitled *The Three Ravens* that contains the lines:

Down there came a fallow *doe,*
As great with young as she might go.

The Middle English word *falwe* gave us *fallow*. Since the word, in its figurative sense, is somewhat pejorative, it might be well to avoid using it as a color. Incidentally, the deer in that poem was far from unproductive.

falter (fall′ tər) *vb*. To *falter* is to waver, vacillate. It also means "to stumble, totter," and sometimes "to give way." Its usual meanings are "waver" and "stumble": His courage never *faltered*, even in the face of overwhelming odds. Seasoned soldiers do not *falter* in the face of duty. In a more physical sense: The old woman *faltered* as she climbed the steep hill with her heavy burden. Middle English had *faltren*; in Icelandic, *faltrast* means "to be uncertain."

farrago (fə rah' go, fə ray' go) *n*. This musical-sounding word is taken over without change from the Latin, where its literal meaning is "mash" (mixed cattle fodder) and figurative sense is any "mixture" or "medley." These days, it can be said that most packaged foods contain a *farrago* of chemical preservatives. In other words, a *farrago* is a *hodgepodge* or *mishmash*. It is an interesting word to use figuratively, in a sentence like, "His presentation was nothing more than a *farrago* of outworn concepts and trite phrases." *Mishmash* and *medley* aren't bad words to use; synonyms are *olio* (a word beloved of crossword-puzzle makers— from *olla*, Spanish for *stewpot*) and *gallimaufry* (gal ə maw' free), a highly literary word used principally to impress the bourgeoisie (from, it is believed, Middle French *galimafree*); but *farrago* is recommended as a suitable variation on the theme.

fatuous (fat' choo əs) *adj*. *Fatuous* means "inane" or "foolish," with a strong implication of complacency (see *complacent*) and smug self-satisfaction. Young swains tend to gaze upon their beloveds with the most *fatuous* expressions. Bejeweled ladies at sumptuous dinner parties are often given to making *fatuous* remarks. So do chairpersons of obscure organizations when introducing equally obscure speakers. There is nothing wrong with the good old word *silly*, which comes from Middle English *sely* or *silly*, meaning "happy" or "innocent," but *fatuous*, from Latin *fatuus* (silly), is an expressive replacement, having, as it does, the added coloration of *smug* and the implication of "stupid."

feasible (fee' zə bəl) *adj*. This is a "can do" word. *Feasible* describes something that can be accomplished, a goal that is not beyond wild dreams, something *workable*. Our trips to the moon, once strictly science fiction, turned out to be *feasible*. The word can have the tinge of *suitable* as well, as when people search for a *feasible* route to the mountaintop. Another shade of meaning is "plausible, likely." The police will release a suspect who comes up with a *feasible* alibi or other explanation. But its main use is to denote something *practicable*, something demonstrably *doable*. It is a good word with which to lighten the workload of *viable*, a currently much overworked vogue word. It comes from Middle English *feseable*, which, through various stages, goes all the way back to Latin *facere* (to do).

feckless (fek' ləs) *adj.* A *feckless* person is untrustworthy because he is incompetent, feeble, or irresponsible, lazy without spirit or energy, or all of these unpleasant things. One is irritated by a novice's *feckless*, fumbling attempts to get the car going. Don't trust a *feckless* person with any responsibilities. *Feck* is a word out of the dialect of Scotland and the North of England meaning "effect" or "value." Hence, *feckless* speaks for itself.

fecund (fee' kənd, feh' kənd) *adj.* Anything or anyone *fecund* is *productive*, *fertile*. *Fecund* parents produce offspring, usually in quantity; *fecund* trees produce blossoms and fruit; *fecund* minds produce a variety of ideas, innovations, inventions. Johann Sebastian Bach (1685–1750), with all that massive body of music to his credit, was *fecund* in more ways than one: he had twenty children. Thomas Alva Edison (1847–1931) had a most *fecund* mind: he produced over one thousand inventions. Crabgrass is one of the most *fecund* of weeds: each plant produces about half a million seeds. The Latin source, *fecundus* (fruitful), gave us this useful word.

feisty (fye' stee) *adj.* If you are *feisty*, you are full of spirit, lively, ready for anything. Presidents often have their hands full dealing with *feisty* new congressmen. Students get into a *feisty* mood once exams are over. *Feisty* can imply something more than spirit: It can mean "short-tempered and quarrelsome." Often, you can't feel safe with *feisty* people because you never know when they're going to turn on you. The word has a very humble origin: In certain American dialects a *fiest* is an ill-tempered mutt. Feisty is a picturesque word, but colloquial, not to be used in formal contexts.

felicitate (fə lis' ə tate) *vb.* I *felicitate* you on having bought this book in order to improve your vocabulary. When you *felicitate* someone, you are *congratulating* him. You *felicitate* someone on achieving his Ph. D., or on his daughter's marriage. The act is called *felicitation* (fə lis ə tay' shən), a word often used in the plural: "My *felicitations* on your election to the Senate!" *Felicitare* means "to make happy" in Late Latin; it was based on Latin *felicitas* (success, good fortune). Note the different approach in *felicitous*, where *felicity* is also discussed.

felicitous (fə lis' ə təs) *adj*. This word, stemming from the Latin noun *felicitas* (success, good fortune), applies to things, concrete or abstract, that are well-suited, appropriate, well-chosen, like *felicitous* remarks or the *felicitous* jokes with which a talented public speaker puts his audience at ease. A well-chosen gift might be called *felicitous*. The noun *felicity* (fə lis' ə tee) is *not* a synonym of *felicitousness* (appropriateness), but means "great happiness," as in *marital felicity*, a blessed state worth striving for and worthy of fervent *felicitations* (see *felicitate*).

felicity (fə lis' ə tee). *n*. See **felicitous**.

feral (fih' rəl, feh' rəl) *adj*. An untamed animal that has escaped from a zoo or a circus is often referred to as "feral," meaning "wild or savage." Animals that have been domesticated and then get loose usually revert to a *feral state*. "We were surrounded by growling, *feral* denizens of the forest" is right out of a boys' adventure story. *Feral* can be applied to human animals as well, when they are cruel to the point of savagery. The word may be used in place of *uncivilized*. It comes from Late Latin *feralis*, which in turn came from Latin *ferus* (wild).

ferret (ferr' it) *vb*. Usually followed by *out*. When you rummage around and eventually find something, you have *ferreted* it out. It sometimes takes a good deal of investigation to *ferret* out the real facts of a situation and a lot of *ferreting* to find bargains at a flea market. The verb is taken from the noun *ferret*, an animal that can be domesticated and trained to smell and drive out rabbits and rats. The word has an interesting derivation, from Vulgar Latin *furritus* (small thief), which was based on *fur*, the Latin word for *thief*, from which (through Latin *furtivus*) we get our word *furtive*. *Ferret-faced* is often used to describe a person with pinched features and shifty (*furtive*) eyes.

festoon (feh stoon') *n*., *vb*. A *festoon* is a chain of flowers or ribbons hung in a loop as a decoration. To *festoon* something is, literally, to decorate it with *festoons*. Buildings are *festooned* on important occasions like coronations or jubilees or welcome-home parades. Corridors and rooms are *festooned* for parties and celebrations. The verb can be used figuratively (and picturesquely) as a vivid description of situations where something or someone is adorned or surrounded in a smothering sort of way. When you visit someone in his hospital room, his bed may be *festooned* with feeding tubes. Cities all over the world, these days, swarm with Japanese tourists *festooned* with camera straps and equipment. During Christmas shopping season, people bump into each other *festooned* with parcels. We get this word from the French *feston*, which was in turn based on the Italian *festone* (decoration for a feast; *feast* is *festa* in Italian, which gave rise to *festone*).

fetid, foetid (fet' id, fee' tid) *adj*. An adjective to describe a very unpleasant state of affairs. It means "stinking," or, more delicately, "malodorous," and comes from the Latin *fetidus*. It is an apt description for a room recently vacated by a conference of cigar-smoking tycoons, or a musty, unventilated cave inhabited by a hermit short of soap and water. The word can also be applied, figuratively, to hateful or odious people. *Bad smell* has long been associated with hatefulness: cf. "stinker" as an intense pejorative.

fey (fay) *adj*. *Fey* people may be amusing but somewhat difficult to deal with. They are eccentric, in a whimsical way, unworldly, appear to be a little bit "touched," and tend to behave irresponsibly. The word *fey* was originally applied to anyone believed to be conscious of impending doom, even death. It probably acquired its meaning as a result of confusion with the word *fay*, an uncommon synonym of *fairy*. Some may be old enough to remember Zasu Pitts of silent movie fame, whose typical role was the *fey* character who never knew what to do with her hands. Goldie Hawn is a more up-to-date example of the *fey* character, a bit on the zany side and fairly unpredictable. *Fey* people seem to be preoccupied with what's going on in their own private world. *Fey* is Middle English, based on Old English *faege* (doomed to die); akin to Icelandic *feigr* (doomed).

fiasco (fee ass' ko) *n*. A *fiasco* is a total and humiliating failure. Most of us know what it is to make elaborate preparations for an event, only to have it end in a total flop, i.e., a *fiasco*. When invitations to a party are sent out bearing the wrong address and nobody shows up, that is a *fiasco*. The same is true of an officer who finds out, too late, that he has marched his troops twenty miles in the wrong direction. *Fiasco* is an Italian word meaning, literally, "straw-covered wine bottle," and figuratively, "disastrous failure." The connection between the two meanings is lost in history. From Italian *fiasco* in its literal meaning we get *flask*.

fiat (fy′ ət) *n.* A *fiat* is a decree, and comes directly form the Latin *fiat*, which means "Let it be done." Despots rule by *fiat*, unhindered by parliaments. Less technically, a *fiat* is an order, whether issued under authority or arbitrarily, like some of those laid down by the big boss in a company or a political party. Modern sociologists agree that appropriate criminal punishment should be determined scientifically and not by police or judicial *fiat*. In a more abstract way, it has been said that moral actions are determined by *fiats* of conscience. This is a fairly literary word, too much so, perhaps, to be applied to the rules laid down to henpecked husbands.

fiduciary (fih doo′ she er ee) *n., adj.* This word applies to a person or firm handling assets of a third party, like a trustee, executor, guardian or anyone else in a position of trust. The connection between the owner and the one entrusted with the assets is called a *fiduciary relationship*. A guardian who, for instance, spends his ward's money on his own pursuits is said to "violate the *fiduciary* relationship," or "exceed his *fiduciary* capacity." The Latin origin, *fiduciarius*, means "entrusted."

figurative (fig′ yə rə tiv) *adj.* The *figurative* use of a word or phrase involves a *figure* of speech (we get *figurative* from *figure*), especially a metaphor; something other than the literal use of the term. When you say, "He's a tiger when he's mad," or "Her boss is a real tiger," you are speaking *figuratively*. No real tiger is involved. Other examples: We arrived neck and neck; my heart raced a mile a minute; we won by a mile. The concept is an old one: the word *figurativus* exists in Late Latin, based upon Latin *figuratus*, a form of *figurare* (to form, shape).

finite (fy′ nite) *adj.* Anything *finite* has limits, is limited in some way, whether in time, space, numerically, or otherwise. *Finite* is the opposite of *infinite* (in′ fən ət). Man's imagination can conceive the Infinite, but his powers are *finite*. *Finite* resources hamper the accomplishment of great, idealistic objectives. All machines have *finite* capacities; the concept of perpetual motion is an illusion. From Latin *finitus*, a form of *finire* (to limit, to end) from which we also derive *finish*.

flaccid (flak′ sid) *adj.* Raggedy Ann and Andy have *flaccid* arms and legs; they are limp and flabby. That is the literal meaning of *flaccid*. Figuratively, the word means "weak, ineffectual, unimpressive:" *Flaccid* leadership can bring a country to depression and despair. *Flaccid* reasoning at a trial will make no impression on His Honor. The Latin adjective *flaccidus* gave us this useful, though often mispronounced word.

flagellate (flaj' ə late) *vb*. To *flagellate* is to whip or flog. We have heard of religious fanatics who *flagellate* themselves as part of their rites. Figuratively, the word is used in the sense of punish, especially with severe criticism, as when drama critics *flagellate* a playwright for allegedly flippant treatment of what they consider a serious subject. The word can also be used in the sense of "driving" or "urging" someone or oneself, for instance, to fulfill his duty. People *flagellate* themselves (in this sense) to meet a deadline. The word comes from Latin *flagellatus*, a form of the verb *flagellare* (to whip).

flamboyant (flam boy' ənt) *adj*. *Flamboyant* describes anyone or anything outstandingly showy or striking. People who get rich overnight often dress *flamboyantly*, in loud colors and extravagant designs; actors who "ham it up" and "chew the scenery" are said to have a *flamboyant* style. International playboys addicted to fast women and fast cars have a *flamboyant* life style. The word, taken intact from the French, is a form of the verb *flamboyer* (to flame, flare up).

flatulent (flatch' ə lənt) *adj*. A word that describes an unpleasant condition, meaning "suffering from gas" or "causing gas" (in the digestive tract). A heavy meal often makes one *flatulent*. Beans are one of the most *flatulent* of foods. The condition of the sufferer is called *flatulence* (flatch' ə ləns). The late English music-hall artist Gracie Fields sang a song about *flatulence* called "Wind Around My Heart." The word is also used figuratively to describe writing that is bombastic, pompous, turgid, and overwritten. The *flatulent* prose of most political orators is outrageous and usually soporific. (The idea is that the prose consists mostly of wind.) These words come from New Latin *flatulentus*, based on the Latin noun *flatus* (a blowing).

flay (flay) *vb*. A most unpleasant word, synonymous with excoriate, in both its literal and figurative meanings. To *flay* is to strip off the skin, hide or any outer covering (usually) of a living creature; in other words, to skin alive. Certain savages *flay* newly captured wild boars. Worse still, some tribes are said to *flay* their human captives (alive, that is). Most distressing. In the figurative sense, to *flay* means "to criticize scathingly." Critics *flay* performing artists for listless performances, or creative artists for dull writing, painting, music, etc. The word comes from Middle English *flen* and is akin to Icelandic *fla* (pronounced *flay*).

fledgling (flej' ling). *adj.* See **callow.**

flippant (flip' ənt) *adj.* A term applied to anything frivolous or disrespectful, not to be taken seriously, often shortened to *flip*, which is a *flippant* abbreviation of *flippant.* The Book of Proverbs (XV. 1) tells us that a soft answer turneth away wrath. A *flip* one often turns it on. *Flippant* is a pejorative, a disparaging word suggestive of a somewhat flighty, disrespectful attitude towards the subject matter or the person addressed, or both. Even mildly patriotic people are made unhappy by *flippant* remarks about Old Glory. The derivation is uncertain; probably related to the verb *flip* (to toss or jerk something, like a coin or a playing card).

flout (flout) *vb* To *flout* is to scorn, mock, scoff at, disdain, in the way the Beat Generation *flouted* the accepted rules of social conduct. President Truman, in his *Memoirs*, reacting to General MacArthur's statement on Korea, wrote: "This was a challenge to the authority not only of the President .... It also *flouted* the policy of the United Nations .... I was deeply shocked." Do not confuse *flout* with *flaunt*, which means to "show off, display ostentatiously," as in the slogan, "If you've got it, flaunt it!" Many people, unfortunately, *flout* the distinction, and flaunt their *flouting.* According to some sources, including Philip Howard, the English linguist, this confusion resulted from a solecism of Edward Heath when he was Prime Minister. Whether or not that is the case, we are told that the word *flout* comes from Middle English *flouten* (to play the flute). And if the connection seems remote, we are referred to the Dutch verb *fluiten*, which means "to play the flute," but also "to jeer."

foible (foy' bəl) *n.* A word that comes from the French word *faible*, meaning "weak." It describes a minor, relatively harmless weakness in a person's character, and is especially appropriate when that character is otherwise a strong one. Even great men have their *foibles*, the way idols have feet of clay. There is a famous line in *The Art of Poetry* by the Roman poet Horace (65–8 B.C.): " .... If great Homer nods for a moment (i.e., slips up), I wince." Hannah More (1745–1853), the English writer, wrote: "Half our misery from our *foibles* springs." Somewhat akin to peccadillo (a minor offense, a trivial fault), but *foible* refers more to the general character of a person, while *peccadillo* applies rather to a specific small offense, actually committed.

foment (foe ment') *vb.* Foment means to "instigate, promote," in the sense of "get (something) moving or going," and is usually applied in an unfavorable way. The S.D.S. (Students for a Democratic Society, a left-wing group) *fomented* a great deal of unrest and even rioting at universities in the 1960s and 1970s. Guerrillas often attempt to *foment* rebellion in the countrysides of unsettled countries. This meaning developed from the original use of the word: to apply warm or medicated water, or a warm poultice, to a part of the body. *Fomentum* is the Latin for *poultice*, based in turn on the Latin verb *fovere* (to warm or keep warm). If you "keep things warm," you keep them hopping, as it were, and it is easy to see how the figurative, now current meaning developed. Do not confuse *foment* with *ferment*, which has a figurative meaning: "to seethe" (with excitement or agitation). A group among whom agitators have *fomented* unrest can, however, be said to be *in ferment*.

font (font) *n.* A *font* is a church basin, usually of stone, for holding baptism water, a holy water receptacle. But the word is often used figuratively to mean "source" or "fountainhead." A learned work can be said to be a *font* of information on a subject. The word, however, has another entirely distinct meaning: "set of type" (of uniform size and style). Boldface, roman, italics, etc., are *fonts*. "Wrong font" is indicated by proofreaders with the symbol *wf*, to show that a character is of the wrong size or style. There are two derivations: the holy water basin comes from Latin *fontis*, a form of *fons* (fountain); the style of print from Vulgar Latin *funditus* (a pouring or casting), based on Latin *fundere* (to pour; type was formed by pouring lead into molds).

foray (for' ay) *n.*, *vb.* A *foray* is a sudden raid, usually to take plunder; *to foray* is to make such a raid. In adventure stories, savages often make *forays* on the hero's camp during the dark of night. *Foray* is also used in a figurative sense: Companies often make *forays* on their competitors to get hold of personnel with knowhow. *Foray* can be used as a verb: In jungle country, small groups of soldiers sometimes *foray* deep behind enemy lines. *Foray* was formed by "back formation" from *forayer* (marauder, plunderer), which in turn is from Middle English *forray*. The word is related to *forage*, which originally meant "fodder," or the "search for fodder."

force majeure (force mah zhoor') *n.*, *adj.* This is a term taken over bodily from the French, meaning "superior force"; in other words, an unforeseeable, uncontrollable event that makes it impossible to perform one's obligations (under a contract) and exempts him, in most cases, from liability for failure to live up to his agreement. *Force majeure* is commonly known as "an act of God" (who gets blamed for everything). The term covers things like floods and other natural catastrophes, as well as strikes, riots, wars, and all sorts of unpleasant happenings. Many contracts contain a clause exempting one from liability for failure to perform a service or deliver merchandise when such failure is caused by an "act of God" or *force majeure*.

forensic (fə ren' sik) *adj.* This word describes things having to do with the law and the courts. Expert medical witnesses engage in *forensic medicine*, the application of their medical knowledge to legal questions. Those more or less unintelligible psychiatrists on the witness stand (half of whom say that the accused was sane while the other half swear that he was as crazy as a bedbug) are practicing *forensic psychiatry*. *Forensic* comes from the Latin adjective *forensis* (relating to the *forum*, the open square where, among other things, judicial business was conducted.)

formidable (for' mə də bəl) *adj.* A *formidable* person or thing is one to be feared or dreaded. To the layman, the lawyer on the other side always appears *formidable* (he says all those disagreeable, nasty things and seems so sure of himself). *Formidable* things and people are *intimidating*, like a six-and-a-half-footer or a precipitous mountain that blocks the way. *Formidable* can mean "awe-inspiring," when speaking of a musician's *formidable* technique, or a great expert's *formidable* knowledge of his subject. This versatile word has yet another shade of meaning: "powerful," as when politicians speak of facing *formidable* opposition. The French use "Formidable!" all the time, the way we use "Terrific!" It all comes from the Latin adjective *formidabilis*, based on the verb *formidare* (to dread).

fortuitous (for tyoo' ə təs) *adj.* A *fortuitous* meeting or event is one that happens *by chance*. *Fortuitous* means "accidental" and relates to happenings that are not prearranged, but are the result purely of happenstance. Probably as a result of confusion with the word *fortunate* through similarity of sound, fortuitous can mean "fortunate" or "lucky," but it ought to be reserved for chance happenings, like *fortuitous encounters*. Circumstances can be both fortuitous *and* fortunate, like a lucky accidental meeting, a fortuitous encounter with someone you've been trying to find for a long time. The original meaning is made clear from the derivation of the word from Latin *fortuitus*, an adjective based on *forte*, Latin for "by chance."

founder (found' ər) *vb*. When a ship *founders*, it's all over: to *founder*, when it comes to ships, is to *sink*; and a foundering ship is headed for Davey Jones's locker. When plans *founder*, it's likewise all over: plans that *founder* fail, fizzle out, like Robert Burns's "... best laid schemes o'mice an' men'" which "gang aft a-gley." Thus, many companies *founder* for lack of capital. When a beast is said to *founder*, as on a stony hill, it is stumbling, and must be helped along. To *founder*, applied to animals, can also mean "to become ill by overeating." Whether it is sinking, or fizzling out, or stumbling, *foundering* is an unfortunate activity, to be strenuously avoided, if possible. *Foundren*, in Middle English, meant "to plunge" (to the bottom), and that usage came from the Latin noun *fundus* (bottom).

fractious (frak' shəs) *adj*. A *fractious* person is peevish and irritable. A *fractious* boss can make the life of the entire office staff miserable. When the start of a sports event is delayed, the crowd can become quite *fractious*, not only in the sense of "irritable" but in another sense of *fractious*: *unruly*. People can become unruly because they are irritated by something or other, but there are those who are just plain unruly for reasons of their own. They, too, are spoken of as *fractious*: It is difficult to get *fractious* oxen to submit to the yoke. Teachers have trouble managing *fractious* children. *Fractious* people, then, are *hard to manage*. Being *fractious* must have something to do with the concept of *breaking*, because the word comes from Late Latin *fractio*, based on Latin *fractus*, a form of *frangere* (to break, shatter).

fruition (froo ish' ən) *n*. *Fruition* is fulfillment, attainment, realization, results achieved. When after years of planning, we landed men on the moon, all that effort *came to fruition*. When an inventor's concept is reduced to patent, then prototype, then a marketable product, all his hard work has been *brought to* *fruition*. The word is related to *fruit*, which is the tangible result of years of work and waiting, from the planting of the seed to the picking. It comes from Late Latin *fruitio*, based in turn on *fruitus*, a form of the Latin verb *frui* (to enjoy, have the benefit of).

fulminate (ful' mə nate—*u* as in *put*) *vb*. Usually followed by *against* to *fulminate* is to send forth denunciations and condemnation. Public officials observe the custom of *fulminating* against crime in the streets. Missionaries (old style) used to *fulminate* against the practices of the natives, like eating one another and going bra-less. The noun is *fulmination* (ful mo nay' shən), meaning "shouted denunciation." Most campaign speeches are devoid of affirmative programs and are nothing more than a stream of *fulminations* against the opposition. *Fulminatus* is a form of the Latin verb *fulminare* (to lighten—from *fulmen*, a thunderbolt). To *fulminate* can be said to be the equivalent of *thundering* against whatever the orator is against.

fulsome (full' səm) *adj*. Anything, be it praise or language or ostentatious display, can be said to be *fulsome*, which means, in general, "offensively excessive." It is quite sickening to observe the *fulsome* praise with which underlings seek to butter up their superiors. The *fulsome* quantity and richness of the food at some dinner parties can take away one's appetite. The "nouveaux riches" too often display themselves in *fulsome* array. The commonest use of this word is in the phrase *fulsome praise*, which is exaggerated and insincere and smacks of the sycophant or toady. From Middle English *fulsom* (foul, disgusting).

furtive (fur' tiv) *adj*. *Furtive* describes the qualities of *stealth*, *slyness*, *shiftiness*, *sneakiness*. Guilty, frightened men enter a room and look around with *furtive* glances. One's *furtive* manner can make him look guilty. This word is discussed under the entry *ferret*. *Fur* (nothing to do with animal skins) is Latin for *thief*. *Furtivus* has the literal meaning, in Latin, of "stolen," from which it came to mean "concealed" and eventually "furtive." Unlicensed street vendors, on the lookout for the police, often have a *furtive* look about them.

fusillade (fyoo' sə lade) *n*. Technically, a *fusillade* is a military term signifying a "simultaneous discharge of arms," the sort of bombardment the enemy keeps up from across the river in war stories. It has a figurative meaning, however, which is rather expressive, as when the President's news conference is characterized by a *fusillade* of questions from the reporters. The word gives just the right explosive atmosphere. *Fusil* is French for *gun*, and the French use *fusillade* the same way as we do in English.

gadfly (gad' fly) *n*. A *gadfly* is a species of fly that annoys cattle. The word is commonly used figuratively, to mean any "pest" or anyone who annoys people by continual carping, or persistently pesters others with schemes, demands for action, etc. There are certain legislators whose main function is to act as *gadflies* to their colleagues. *Gadfly* tactics in the office may improve efficiency, but usually make the *gadfly* pretty unpopular. *Gad* means "cattle goad," from the Scandinavian; *gaddr* is Icelandic for "spike."

garrulous (gar' ə ləs, gar' yə ləs—*a* as in *at*) *adj*. A *garrulous* person is talkative and keeps rambling on, usually about trivial matters. *Garrulous* players at the next table are anathema to serious bridge players. When a *garrulous* friend returns from a trip, it is often difficult to stay awake while he recounts his adventures. From Latin *garrulus*.

gauche (goshe—*o* as in *go*) *adj*. *Gauche* people are crude, uncouth, and awkward, lacking in social grace and insensitive. *Gauche* may be applied to conduct as well to people. One's social life can be severely limited as a result of one's *gauche* manners. For an explanation of the origin of *gauche*, see *adroit*.

generic (jə nerr' ik) *adj*. What is *generic* is general, common, in the sense of "applicable to a whole class." Thus, the word *building* is a *generic* name for any structure, whether a single residence, an apartment house, or an office building. Similarly, *crime* is *generic* for any breach of the penal code, all the way from illegal loitering to rape or murder. A special use covers the case of trademarks that have lost their legal protection through widespread use, like *aspirin*, *vaseline*, *victrola*, etc. These were once protected trademarks, but have now become *generic*, and denote a type of product rather than a particular make. Companies often keep a staff of lawyers busy to protect their trademarks and prevent this from happening. Another special use occurs in the field of medications: In a drugstore, when offered a trademarked proprietary product, one can ask for its *generic* equivalent; i.e., an untrademarked product that is identical, and normally costs substantially less. We get this word from Latin *generis*, a form of *genus* (kind, type).

genesis (jen' ə səs) *n*. The *genesis* of anything is its origin or source. We're all familiar with *Genesis* as the title of the First Book of the Old Testament. (Some of us may think the Big Bang was the *genesis* of it all.) Hemingway's experiences during the Spanish Civil War were the *genesis* of *For Whom the Bell Tolls*. Night-long exposure to the bitter cold may be the *genesis* of later ill health. Taken over intact from the Greek.

genre (zhon' rə) *n*. A *genre* is an artistic style. Lyric poetry is a *genre* of literature that does not often appeal to the general readership. Contemporary atonal music is a *genre* that takes a great deal of getting used to. *Genre*, particularly applied to painting, has the special meaning of "scenes of everyday life." Most people like *genre* paintings because they tell a story in realistic terms. Taken over intact from the French (kind, type), derived in turn from Latin *generis*, a form of *genus*, with the same meaning.

gentry (jen' tree) *n*. This word describes upper-class people (well-born and well-bred). It is the *gentry* who attend polo games and yacht races, rather than baseball and football games. The British speak of the *landed gentry*, i.e., the land-owning class just below the nobility. Another use is to describe the people of any particular class or group: the newspaper *gentry*; the boxing *gentry*. From Old French *genterie*.

germane (jər mane') *adj*. What is *germane* to a subject is relevant, pertinent. Many people, in discussion, tend to wander off into all sorts of bypaths, hardly *germane* to the main topic. When examining counsel asks a witness a question that is not *germane* to any of the issues in the case, it should be objected to as irrelevant, incompetent, and immaterial. This word has an interesting derivation, from Latin *germanus* (born of the same parents).

googol (goo' gəl) *n*. You may never come across this term and it won't be counted as one of the "Thousand," although, as you will see, it is related to 1,000. A *googol* is an astronomical number, the largest that can be expressed in words, used primarily to measure the unimaginable distances of outer space. Technically, a *googol* is the digit 1 (one) followed by 100 zeros, also expressed as 10^{100}, or 10 to the 100th power. In contrast, the more familiar trillion, or 1,000 billion, now the measure of our national debt, is 1 (one) followed by a mere twelve zeros—a trifle. Though the author hasn't heard it used that way, the *googol* may become useful if the inflationary tendencies of our age continue, and it may come in handy when an exasperated parent has to say to a persistent child: "If I've told you once, I've told you a *googol* times—the answer is no!" *Googol* was coined by the American mathematician Edward Kasner (1878—1955), either arbitrarily or from the prattling of a very young child, or even from Barney Google with his goo-goo-googley eyes.

gormandize (gor' mən dize) *vb.* To *gormandize* is to eat gluttonously. *Gourmand* is sometimes used where *gourmet* should be. A *gourmand*, sometimes spelled *gormand*, is a person who simply likes his food; a *gourmet* is a connoisseur of good food. The emphasis in *gourmand* is quantity and excessive feeding; in *gourmet*, it is good taste and knowing selectivity, as well as interest in the preparation and serving of food. *Gormandize* applies only to gluttons. If we can believe those old Victorian menus, our forefathers *gormandized* regularly every day as if they hadn't eaten for weeks. *Gourmand* and *gourmet* are both taken over intact from the French. *Gormandize* is from French *gourmandise*.

gossamer (goss' ə mər) *n.* Technically, *gossamer* is the filmy cobweb left by spiders on grass or bushes, but it is commonly used as a noun or adjective, somewhat poetically, to describe any thin, delicate fabric. Ballerinas look delightful in those *gossamer* tutus. Hummingbirds have tiny wings like *gossamer*. "A trip to the moon on *gossamer* wings" is "just one of those things." *The Gossamer Albatross* is the name given to the 70-pound solar-powered aircraft that crossed the English Channel in the summer of 1981. The origin of the word is in doubt. There is a legend that *gossamer* was the delicate thread that came from the raveling of the Virgin Mary's winding-sheet, which fell on her ascension; the raveling material was "God's seam" and that became *gossamer*. More likely, the source is Middle English *gossomer* (goose-summer—an early name for *Indian summer*, when geese are supposed to be plentiful). Other possibilities: *God's summer*, *gaze à Marie* (gauze of Mary). Take your choice.

grandiloquence (gran dil' ə kwənts) *n. Grandiloquence* is the term applied to high-flown, bombastic speech. Fourth-of-July speakers often have an unfortunate tendency to indulge in *grandiloquence*. Simple, direct sermons are best; *grandiloquence* often leaves the congregation cold. The adjective is *grandiloquent* (gran dil' ə kwənt), meaning "pompous, bombastic." A *grandiloquent* summary to a sophisticated jury often defeats its own purpose. An example of *grandiloquence*: "When promulgating your esoteric cogitations, or articulating your superficial sentimentalities, or amiable, philosophical or psychological observations, beware of platitudinous ponderosity. Let your conversational communications show lucidity and intelligibility without rodomontade, voracious vivacity or jejune bafflement. Seduluously avoid all polysyllabic profundity, pompous propensity or psittacistic vacuity, observable or apparent." (In other words, keep it simple.) *Grandiloquence* is a noun derived from the Latin adjective *grandiloquus*, which was based on the Latin words *grandis* (great, large) and *loqui* (to speak).

gratuitous (gra too' ə təs, gra tyoo' ə təs) *adj.* *Gratuitous* can mean either "given free of charge" or "uncalled for, unprovoked." It is too bad that many museums have had to abandon their *gratuitous* entrance policies. In the second sense: Sometimes, without your having said a word, the other fellow makes a *gratuitous* remark that hurts you to the quick. In this sense the word is often used in the phrase *gratuitous insult*. From Latin *gratuitus*, which also had both meanings. Cf. *gratuity*.

gratuity (grə too' ə tee, grə tyoo' ə tee) *n.* This term covers anything given voluntarily, i.e., not legally required, like a tip or gift over and above the regular price for something or payment due for services. The most common form of *gratuity* is a tip. When you stay a while at a friend's who has a household staff, you are expected to leave *gratuities* for them. See *gratuitous*, for a related word. *Gratuity* is from Latin *gratuitus* (done or given without pay), based on *gratus* (pleasing, agreeable) a form of which, *gratum*, means "favor."

gravamen (grə vay' mən) *n.* The *gravamen* of an accusation (especially in the law) is its material part. In an armed robbery case, the *gravamen* of the charge is the carrying of a loaded revolver. In some cases, where the breach of contract is late delivery, the perishability of the merchandise is the *gravamen* of the lawsuit. Generally speaking, the *gravamen* is that issue that *weighs* most heavily in an accusation or legal action. The word comes from Late Latin and is based on Latin *gravare* (to load, weigh down).

gregarious (grə gair' ee əs) *adj*. A *gregarious* person is sociable, fond of company, a good mixer. Some people are loners; others are *gregarious*. *Gregarious* people like to go out a lot and be part of a group. *Gregarious* was derived from Latin *gregarius* (belonging to a herd or flock), which is based on *gregis* a form of *grex* (herd, flock).

guise (gize—*g* as in *go*) *n*. *Guise* has a number of uses; semblance, assumed appearance, style of dress. The characters in the paintings of Fragonard (1732–1806) usually appear in the *guise* of shepherds and shepherdesses. Here, *guise* is used in the sense of "style of dress," but it is more commonly used to mean "semblance": Confidence men steer their victims wrong under the *guise* of friendly advice. Lots of bad advice is given to trusting innocents under the *guise* of expertise. The word comes from Middle English.

habituate (hə bich' oo ate) *vb*. To *habituate* someone to something is to get him accustomed to it, used to it, gradually get him to accept it as normal, as a matter of course. After a while, wealth *habituates* the fortunate owners to a luxurious lifestyle. Authority too often *habituates* people to expect instant obedience as a matter of course. There are several related words: *habit, habitual, habitude,* among others. A *habitude* (hab' ə tood, hab' ə tyood—*oo* as in *boot*) is one's usual condition or character. Those brought up in a happy, warm household are usually endowed with a sound emotional *habitude*. Simple, rustic people are more apt to show a *habitude* of courtesy and kindness than harried city dwellers. *Habituate* is from Late Latin *habituatus* (conditioned), a form of *habituare*, based on Latin *habitus* (condition, character).

hackneyed (hak' need) *adj*. *Hackneyed* words and phrases are trite, made stale from overuse. *Hackneyed* expressions are the tools of unimaginative writers. Examples: *in the last analysis*; *beyond the shadow of a doubt*; *without let or hindrance*. In his *Dictionary of Modern English Usage* (Oxford University Press, Oxford, 1926), H. W. Fowler (1859–1933) writes, under the heading *Hackneyed Phrases*: "... when they suggest themselves (to a writer) it is because what he is writing is bad stuff, or it would not need such help. Let him see to the substance of his cake instead of decorating with sugarplums." There are two schools of thought about the derivation of *hackney*: one, that it comes from Old French *haquenée* (an ambling horse), the name given to ordinary horses as opposed to war-horses; the other that *hackeney* is a Middle English word and a special use of the place name *Hackney*, once a town near London, now one of its boroughs. *Hack* in British usage is the name given to a horse kept for common hire and, by extension, to one that is old and worn out. A *hack* writer creates dull, trite prose. You are free to choose your own derivation; whatever it is, avoid *hackneyed* language.

halcyon (hal' see ən) *adj.* What is *halcyon* is carefree and happy. The word can mean "tranquil, peaceful," as in *halcyon weather*, but it usually evokes the image of past joyous, carefree times. How sweet to recall the *halcyon* days of youth! The word is derived from Greek *halkyon*, a variant of *alkyon* (kingfisher). The original *Halkyon* was a mythical bird alleged to have the power of calming the sea while it nested on its waters.

harbinger (har' bin jər) *n.* Someone or something that signals the approach of things to come is a *harbinger*. A *harbinger* may be called a "forerunner." Crocuses are a *harbinger* of spring. There is in fact a small early-blooming North American herb known as *harbinger-of-spring*. The enthusiasm of audiences in the early stages of an actor's career is a *harbinger* of long-term success. From Middle English *herbenger* (host).

harridan (har' ə dən—*a* as in *as*) *n.* This is a forceful word for a scolding hag, an ill-tempered old woman. It evokes the images of the opening scenes of *Macbeth*. The Queen of Hearts in *Alice in Wonderland* is a fine prototype. Katharina, in *The Taming of the Shrew*, does a great deal of scolding but is too young to be called a *harridan*. The word is from the French *haridelle* (jade).

hedonist (hee' də nist) *n.* A *hedonist* is one who believes that pleasure is the chief aim in life and lives that way. The doctrine is called *hedonism* (hee' də niz əm). *Hedonists* are strictly self-centered. The social manners of the last days of the Roman Empire were dictated by the *hedonists*. *Hedonism* contributed to the downfall of the aristocrats of the French revolution. From Greek *hedone* (pleasure).

hegemony (hə jem′ ə nee) *n*. This word is used to denote dominant influence, especially of one nation or state over others. When Hitler proclaimed, "Tomorrow the world," he was seeking world *hegemony*. The U.S.S.R has *hegemony* over a number of satellite states. This word comes from Greek *hegemonia* (supremacy).

hegira (hə jye′ rə, hej′ ə rə) *n*. A *hegira* is a journey to a pleasanter place. "Thank God it's Friday!" cry the commuters, rejoicing in their weekly *hegira* from the teeming cities to the peaceful countryside. In the twenties, many American intellectuals made a *hegira* to the more enlightened cities of Europe. The original *hegira* was Muhammad's flight from Mecca to Medina in 622 A.D. to escape persecution. And, occasionally, the word was used to imply a flight from danger to security, but that aspect is generally absent in modern usage.

heinous (hay′ nəs) *adj*. This strong word should not be weakened by overuse. Save it to mean "excessively evil, positively hateful." Treason is a *heinous* offense. The Nazi policy of genocide was a *heinous* chapter of German history. What could have been more *heinous* than the sin of Judas? Anything *heinous* is about as bad as possible, foul and abominable. From Middle French *heineus*; cf. French *haine* (hatred).

herbivorous (hur biv′ ə rəs) *adj*. See **carnivorous**.

hermaphrodite (hur maf′ rə dite) *n*. A *hermaphrodite* is a living organism with both male and female organs of sex. The adjective *hermaphrodite* or *hermaphroditic* (hur maf rə dit′ ik) means "bisexual." In Greek mythology, Hermaphroditus was the son of the god Hermes and the goddess Aphrodite, and became merged in body with the nymph Salmacis, thus becoming both man and woman.

heterogeneous (het ə rə jee′ nee əs) *adj*.; **homogeneous** (ho mə jee′ nee əs) *adj*. *Hetero-* and *homo-* are prefixes derived from the Greek words *heteros* and *homos* meaning "different" and "same," respectively; *genos* is Greek for *kind* or *type*. Thus *heterogeneous* means "composed of different kinds," and *homogeneous* means "composed of the same kind." They are antonyms. The Greeks had the words *heterogenes* and *homogenes*; the endings became *-eus* in Middle Latin. Though there are *homogeneous* ethnic groups in various parts of America, its people at large are *heterogeneous*, composed of many different racial types. Some discos cater to a *heterogeneous* throng of artists, business tycoons, and hangers-on—a motley crew, a mixed bag.

heuristic (hyoo ris' tik) *adj.* This term is applied to teaching methods and systems, and means "helping to learn," encouraging (students) to find out for themselves. *Heuristic* teaching methods involve trial-and-error procedures to find solutions, somewhat akin to the Socratic method of teaching by means of question and answer. The word comes from New Latin *heuristicus*, based on Greek *heuriskein* (to find out).

hiatus (hie ay' təs) *n.* A *hiatus* is a gap. The word is synonymous with *lacuna*. The 18½-minute gap in one of the Nixon tapes caused quite a stir in its day; it was a notable *hiatus*. A *hiatus* may be abstract as well as physical: There is often a wide *hiatus* between theory and practice. *Hiatus* applies as well in any case where there is a break in a sequence, as in the case of two, four, six, ten, twelve.... The word was taken over bodily from the Latin where it means "opening."

hie (hye) *vb.* To *hie* is to hasten. This word evokes a pleasant nostalgic atmosphere. Once off the ship, a sailor will often *hie* to meet his lady love. One can simply *hie*, or *hie oneself*. *Hie* yourself down to the voting booth! A poem by Louise Chandler Moulton (1835–1908), *Arcady*, starts: "I *hied* me off to Arcady." From Middle English *hien*, based on Greek *kiein* (to go).

homily (hom' ə lee) *n.* A *homily* is a sermon, a moralizing talk, usually with the implication of tedious length and dullness. Polonius's long speech to his departing son, Laertes, in *Hamlet*, is a *homily*. Reformers are fond of delivering *homilies* to condemned criminals. From Greek *homilia*. According to the author's *English English* (Verbatim, Essex, CT, 1980) the British slang equivalent is *pi-jaw* (*pi-* is short for *pious*, and *-jaw* is slang for *talking to*), "one of those lectures or sermons delivered by a school teacher or scout leader on a 'man-to-man' basis...."

homogeneous (ho mə jee' nee əs) *adj.* See **heterogeneous**.

honorarium (on ə rare' ee əm) *n.* Literally, an *honorarium* is a voluntary payment for services when there is no legal obligation to pay. It is a more or less euphemistic substitute for *fee*. A club will sometimes give an invited speaker an *honorarium* for giving a talk at its weekly meeting. Royalty will sometimes bestow an *honorarium* upon a physician or other professional. A visiting American clergyman who preached the sermon at St. Paul's Cathedral, London, on an anniversary of its founding, was given two bottles of sherry as an *honorarium*. We get the word from the Latin adjective *honorarius* (done or given as an honor).

hubris (hyoo' bris) *n.* Hubris is arrogance, insolent pride (the kind that goeth before a fall). *Hubris* is the opposite of *modesty*. No matter how successful your career, be careful to avoid *hubris*. It is proper to be proud of your accomplishments, but not to give way to *hubris*. *Hubris* is a Greek word taken over intact, and one of the common sins in Greek tragedy.

hyperbole (hye pur' bə lee) *n.* Hyperbole is exaggeration, intentionally used as a figure of speech. *We won by a mile; I waited an eternity; I'd give a million bucks to see his face when he finds out*—these are all examples of *hyperbole*, extravagant assertions that are not intended to be taken literally. Taken over intact from the Greek.

hypothesis (hie poth' ə sis) *n.* A *hypothesis* is a supposition or theory used to explain an occurrence in the absence of actual proof. The plural is *hypotheses*. A *hypothesis* is used as a starting point for further investigation that will either support it or disprove it. The word is often found in the expression *working hypothesis*, a conjecture for the time being, until real proof can be established. The Big Bang theory of the origin of the universe, as we know it, is still only a *hypothesis*. The adjective is *hypothetical* (hye pə thet' ə kəl), meaning "unsupported by truth." The verb is *hypothesize* (hye poth' ə size), meaning "to assume without proof." *Hypothesis* was taken over intact from the Greek.

iconoclast (eye kon' ə klast) *n.* One who challenges accepted beliefs is an *iconoclast*. The word comes from two Greek words, *eikon* (image, idol) and *klastes* (breaker), so that literally an *iconoclast* is an "image-breaker." Most modern scientists are *iconoclasts* where religious beliefs are concerned. Darwin was an *iconoclast*, putting forth his theory of evolution in opposition to Genesis. The adjective is *iconoclastic* (eye kon ə klas' tək). An *iconoclastic* attitude toward the institution of marriage is widespread among today's youth.

idyllic (eye dil′ ǝk) *adj.* Anything *idyllic* is happily peaceful or charmingly romantic. One delights in recalling the peace and quiet enjoyed during the *idyllic* month in the country. Nothing is more *idyllic* than the first stages of a budding romance. Jean Fragonard (1732–1806), the French painter, gave the world his *idyllic* landscapes peopled with shepherds and shepherdesses. *Idyllic* is the adjective form of the noun *idyll* (eye′ dǝl), a poem or prose piece about pastoral scenes or sweet charming happenings. Among the most famous of them are *Idylls of the King* by Tennyson (1809–1892), poems about the legend of King Arthur. *Idyll* comes from the Latin *idyllium*, taken from Greek *eidyllion* (short pastoral poem).

ignominy (ig′ nǝ min ee) *n.* This word applies to either the disgrace resulting from a shameful act or the dishonorable conduct itself. Oscar Wilde (1854–1900) suffered the *ignominy* of a notorious trial and a prison sentence. No decent man would practice the *ignominy* of abandoning ship before the women and children were saved. The adjective is *ignominious* (ig nǝ min′ ee ǝs), meaning "shameful, humiliating." At the first sight of real opposition, a bully will beat an *ignominious* retreat. The noun and adjective are from Latin *ignominia* and *ignominiosus* respectively.

illicit (ih lis′ ǝt) *adj.* Illicit means "unlawful." During the Civil War the protection of runaway slaves was *illicit*. Prohibition made the sale of intoxicating liquor *illicit*. The word has more the flavor of "forbidden" than "unlawful" in the phrase *illicit love*, a favorite topic of Edwardian novels. One rarely sees the antonym *licit* (lawful), which comes from the Latin *licitus*, a form of *licere* (to be allowed). *Illicit* is from Latin *illicitus*; the *il-* is a negative prefix, as in *illogical* or *illiterate*.

illusory (il loo′ sǝr ee) *adj.* This word describes things that are deceptive, that cause a false impression, an illusion. People have the *illusory* impression that money puts an end to all troubles. The "peace in our time" announced by Neville Chamberlain was *illusory* indeed; so was the "light at the end of the tunnel" so often announced during the Vietnam War. From Late Latin *illusorius*, based on Latin *illusus*, a form of *illudere* (to mock, deceive).

imbibe (im bibe') *vb*. To *imbibe* is to drink. Englishmen *imbibe* enormous quantities of tea. The verb can be used figuratively in the sense of "*drink in, absorb*." It is to be hoped that students will *imbibe* knowledge and ideas by paying attention to their college courses. Instead of rushing headlong through the countryside, travelers should try to *imbibe* the beauty of the scenery. When used without an object, *intoxicating liquor* is understood: It is not good to *imbibe* too freely. From Latin *imbibere* (to drink in) based on prefix *im-* plus *bibere* (to drink).

imbroglio (im brole' yo) *n*. This word has several meanings: "confused situation," as in an *imbroglio* at an airfield to which many flights have been diverted because of fog; "bitter misunderstanding": Because of language difficulties, Russo-American discussions sometimes end up in an *imbroglio*; "violent disagreement": Committee members sometimes become involved in an *imbroglio* over the proper use of funds. The word was taken over intact from the Italian, where it means "entanglement." A closely related word is *embroilment*, which, however, comes from a different source: Middle French *embrouiller*, based on prefix *em-* plus *brouiller* (to mix).

immemorial (im mə mor' ee əl) *adj*. This word describes things that extend back beyond memory. They can be intangible things, like folkways that have existed from time *immemorial*, or great trees like those mentioned in "moan of doves in *immemorial* elms" by Tennyson (1804–1892). This lovely, haunting word comes from Late Latin *immemorialis*.

immutable (ih myoo' tə bəl) *adj*. What is *immutable* is unchangeable, like the *immutable* laws of nature, or like human nature that everybody says "you can't change." When a really stubborn person makes up his mind, his opinion becomes fixed and *immutable*. Rudyard Kipling (1865–1936), in *Plain Tales from the Hills*, used the description "as *immutable* as the hills." We get *immutable* from the Latin *immutabilis*; *mutare* is the Latin verb for to "change," from which we get the *mut-* in *immutable* and other English words: *commute, mutation*, etc.

impassive (im pas' iv) *adj*. *Impassive* people neither feel nor show emotion. It is disconcerting to recount a hair-raising adventure and have your listener just sit there *impassively*. Experienced soldiers are *impassive* in the face of danger. From Latin prefix *im-* plus Latin *passivus* (submissive).

impecunious (im pə kyoo' nee əs) *adj. Impecunious* describes the unfortunate state of being penniless. (It was Abe Lincoln who is alleged to have said that money in itself is not all that important, but its absence can be mighty inconvenient.) The novels of Horatio Alger (1834–1899) featured honest, *impecunious* youths who invariably rose to fame and fortune. This word is derived from Latin prefix *im-* plus Latin *pecuniosus* (wealthy), which is based on *pecunia* (money, wealth). Cf. *pecuniary*.

impede (im peed') *vb.* To *impede* is to hinder. Steep hills *impede* a hiker's progress. Financial or domestic problems *impede* concentration on one's office work. *Impede* is derived from Latin *impedire* (literally, to entangle the feet). Note the *-ped* , from Latin *pedis*, a form of *pes* (foot), which we also see in *pedal, pedestrian*, etc.

imperious (im peer' ee əs) *adj.* An *imperious* person is domineering, bossy, dictatorial. You can't argue with an *imperious* office manager *Imperious* manners make people unapproachable and rule out suggestions. This word is from Latin *imperiosus* (commanding, tyrannical), based on Latin *imperium* (command, sovereignty), which gave us related words like *imperial* and *empire*.

imperturbable (im pər tur' bə bəl) *adj.* An *imperturbable* person is calm, not easily excited, impassive, unlikely to be easily disconcerted. Buddha is always represented as serene and *imperturbable*. People who have arrived tend to surround themselves with an aura of *imperturbable* self-possession. *Unflappable* is a (mostly British) synonym for this word, and *imperturbability* and unflappability are desirable traits in a leader. *Imperturbable* is much more often used than its positive opposite, *perturbable*. (This phenomenon is discussed at some length under *inscrutable*.) From Late Latin *imperturbabilis*, based on Latin negative prefix *in-* plus *perturbare* (to disturb utterly, throw into confusion).

implacable (im plak' ə bəl) *adj. Implacable* people are relentless and cannot be pacified. The tragic losses at Verdun in World War I were shared by the *implacable* adversaries, France and Germany. Pleas for mercy to *implacable* judges fall on deaf ears. From Latin *implacabilis*.

implement (im' plə ment) *vb.* To *implement* something (a plan, a promise) is to put it into effect, to carry it out. Once a plan is agreed upon, you have to take the necessary steps to carry it out. One should avoid making promises that can't be *implemented*. From Late Latin *implementum* (filling up), based on Latin *implere* (to fill up).

implicate (im' plə kate) *vb.* When you *implicate* someone in a crime or a conspiracy, you involve him in it, or show him to be involved. People who turn state's evidence *implicate* their collaborators in the crime. The noun *implication* (im plə kay' shən) can refer to the state of being *implicated*, but is almost always used to mean "something implied," something to be inferred from something else: When a person keeps evading the issue, he raises the *implication* that he is trying to conceal something. Innuendo creates *implications*. A common use is seen in a sentence like "I resent that *implication*!" *Implicate* comes from Latin *implicatus*, a form of *implicare* (to entwine, entangle; figuratively, to involve). *Imply* comes from the same Latin verb. *Implicate* is almost always used in an unfavorable sense.

implicit (im plis' ət) *adj.* This word has two distinct uses. It can mean "implied, taken for granted": Honest performance by all parties is *implicit* in every agreement. *Implicit* can also mean "unquestioning, absolute": In a successful partnership, the partners must have *implicit* trust in one another. The armed forces expect *implicit* obedience from all personnel. Rightly or wrongly, inventors alway have *implicit* faith in their inventions. From Latin *implicitus*, a form of *implicare* (to entwine, entangle). (*Implicitus* is a variant form of *implicatus*, which gave us *implicate*.)

imponderable (im pon' dər ə bəl) *n.* Anything difficult to estimate is *imponderable*. Weather is often an *imponderable* factor in planning the day's activities. The word is more often used as a noun: The very existence of the human race is fraught with the *imponderables* of the nuclear age. The word comes form Middle Latin *imponderabilis*, based on Latin *ponderare* (literally, to weigh; by extension, to weigh mentally, i.e., to ponder). The verb *ponder* itself means "to consider thoughtfully," with the implication that no matter how deeply you *ponder* something *imponderable*, you can't predict the probabilities. Thus, *an imponderable* is a matter that cannot be determined by decision.

importunate (im por' chə nət). See **importune**.

importune (im por tyoon', im por' chən) *vb*. When you *importune* someone, you are pressing him urgently and requesting something of him persistently. Government officials have to get used to being *importuned* by all sorts of special interests. Cyrano de Bergerac is a famous example of an *importuning* suitor (to be sure, on another's behalf). Thomas Gray (1716–1771) wrote the following lines in a poem entitled *On His Own Character*:

> *Too poor for a bribe, and too proud to* importune,
> *He had not the method of making a fortune.*

The related adjective is *importunate* (im por' chə nət) meaning "persistent in making requests." Parents are often annoyed by their children's *importunate* cries for attention. The poet Louise Imogen Guiney (1861–1920), in *The Wild Ride*, wrote of hearing, "All night, from their stalls, the *importunate* panting and neighing [of the invisible horses]." From Latin *importunus* (assertive, inconsiderate).

impugn (im pyoon') *vb*. To *impugn* something is to challenge it, to call it in question, to discredit it. Suspicious people are all too prone to *impugn* the other fellow's motives. In olden times, men were quick to *impugn* one another's honor and offer to duel. Senator Joe McCarthy was always ready to *impugn* the loyalty and patriotism of honorable Americans. From Latin *impugnare* (to attack), based on *pugna* (battle), from which we get *pugnacious*. Do not confuse *impugn* with *impute* (to attribute, ascribe).

impute (im pyoot') *vb*. When you attribute or ascribe a result or quality to anything or anybody, you are *imputing* it. *Impute* often implies unjust accusation: People sometimes *impute* the cause of a disaster to those who have had nothing to do with it. But good things as well as bad may be *imputed*: People who really succeed through their own efforts are sometimes too prone to be modest and to impute their success to luck. The ancients *imputed* both good fortune and bad to the gods. Actors speak lines written for them and audiences often *impute* to them greater intelligence or wit than they possess. From Latin *imputare* (to *impute*), based on *putare* (to think, to believe). Do not confuse *impute* with *impugn* (to challenge, call in question).

inauspicious (in aw spish' əs) *adj*. See **auspicious**.

incarnate (in kar' nət) *adj*. *Incarnate* means "personified." Sir Galahad is a prime example of virtue *incarnate*. Hitler was evil *incarnate*. Job, in the Bible, was patience *incarnate*. *Incarnate* expresses the concept of embodiment. The biographer James Parton (1822–1891), in *The Life of Andrew Jackson*, called him "the most American of Americans—an embodied Declaration of Independence—The Fourth of July *incarnate*." From the Latin prefix *in*- and *carnis*, a form or *caro* (flesh), which gave rise to Late Latin *incarnatus* (made flesh). The related noun, *incarnation* (in kar nay' shen) means "embodiment." The astronauts are the *incarnation* of courage. An accomplished ballerina is the *incarnation* of grace.

inchoate (in koe' it) *adj*. Things just begun, undeveloped and unorganized, can be described as *inchoate*. New organizations are prone to remain in an *inchoate* state until a firm hand takes over. When one has not organized his argument, his presentation all too often turns out to be an *inchoate* jumble of generalizations. From Latin *incohatus*, a form of *incohare* (to begin). (Note the spelling of *inchoate*; *inchoatus* was a variant of *incohatus*.)

incipient (in sip' ee ənt) *adj*. Anything *incipient* is just beginning, in an initial stage of development. *Incipient* can apply to anything hatching or brewing, all the way from a scratchy throat to a romance. People feel limp and listless during the *incipient* stages of a fever. A suddenly darkening sky usually signals an *incipient* storm. From Latin *incipiens*, a form of *incipere* (to begin).

inclement (in klem' ənt) *adj*. *Inclement* means "harsh, severe." *Inclement* weather is bitter weather, and that is the way this word is used for the most part. Applied to people, it means "cruel, without mercy," but this is not a common use. *Clement* means the exact opposite, whether it describes people or the weather, but it is a word not in common use. From Latin *inclemens*.

incognito (in kog nee' toe, in kog' nə toe) *n*., *adj*., *adv*. The usual use of *incognito* is as an adverb in the expression *traveling incognito*: Famous movie and television stars are so pestered by fans that they often resort to *traveling incognito*, under an assumed name, and in disguise. The assumed identity is also known as *an incognito*. Dark glasses, wigs, and false names do not always manage to preserve one's *incognito*. From Latin *incognitus* (unrecognized).

incongruous (in kong' groo əs) *adj.* Things that are *incongruous* are out of keeping with one another. The old clothes worn by Howard Hughes were *incongruous* with his immense wealth. Some music is unpleasantly contrived from an *incongruous* mixture of musical styles. John Tyndall, the English physicist (1820–1893), wrote of superstition as "*incongruous* with intelligence." From Latin *incongruus* (inconsistent).

increment (in' krə mənt) *n.* An *increment* is an increase, growth or gain, something added. The improvement in the value of your stock and the accumulated dividends are *increments*. Newborn lambs are an *increment* to the flock. A raise in salary is an *increment*. An unwanted increase in your weight is, physically speaking, an *increment*, but it is the kind of gain most people consider a loss. From Latin *incrementum*.

incredulous (in krej' ə ləs) *adj. Incredulous* people are skeptical, inclined not to believe. *Incredulous* people cramp your style when you attempt to recount your adventures. A surprisingly large number of people were *incredulous* about our moon landings, insisting that the films were special effects created in the studio. The noun is *incredulity* (in krə dyoo' lə tee). Galileo's conclusion about the earth revolving about the sun was at first met with smiles of *incredulity* and later with prosecution for heresy. Do not confuse *incredulous* with *incredible* (unbelievable). From Latin *incredulus*, based on the Latin negative prefix *in-* and *credere* (to believe). See also **credible**.

incubus (in' kyə bəs) *n.* See **incumbent**.

inculcate (in kul' kate) *vb.* To *inculcate* is to teach by persistent urging, to implant (ideas, habits) through constant admonition. It is a good idea to *inculcate* steady habits in young people. One can *inculcate* something (a habit, a virtue, an idea) *in* a person, or *inculcate* the person *with* an idea, etc.: Good teachers *inculcate* their pupils with a thirst for knowledge. From *inculcatus*, a form of Latin *inculcare* (to impress upon).

incumbent (in kum' bənt) *n., adj. Incumbent*, as an adjective, usually followed by *on* or *upon*, means "obligatory." The duty of providing for the young is *incumbent* upon their parents. It is *incumbent* upon the state to educate the youth at least through the secondary levels. As an adjective, *incumbent* has another quite distinct meaning: "holding office," as in *the incumbent mayor*, *the incumbent chairman*. By itself, as a noun, it means "office-holder": The *incumbent* knew he was going to lose the next election. The *incumbent* was challenged by a younger, more vigorous candidate. From Latin *incumbens*, a form of *incumbere* (to lie upon). A related Latin verb with the same meaning, *incubare*, gave us the intriguing, if not often used, word *incubus* (in′ kyə bəs), which was the term applied to a male demon believed, in olden days, to swoop down on sleeping women and have sexual intercourse with them in their sleep. (This must have been a convenient explanation of otherwise unexplainable pregnancy.) *Incubus* has come to mean "nightmare," whether literally or figuratively. Thus it may be said that the constant burdens of state become a leader's *incubus*. See also the discussion of *succubus*, the converse of *incubus*, under *succumb*.

indecorous (in dek′ ə rəs) *adj*. The opposite of **decorous**.

indigenous (in dij′ ə nəs) *adj*. *Indigenous* means "native," in the sense of "characteristic, inherent." *Indigenous* can describe anything concrete or abstract: plants, animals, or people *indigenous* to a certain area; ideas or emotions *indigenous* to certain people. Cacti are *indigenous* to arid regions. Lofty ideas are *indigenous* to people of deep religious faith. From Late Latin *indigenus* (native).

indigent (in′ də jent) *adj*. An *indigent* person is needy, impoverished, one who lacks the necessities of life. Our welfare system provides for the *indigent*. The *New York Times* runs a "100 Neediest Cases" feature every Christmas season to help the most *indigent* members of society. From Latin *indigens* (needy), based on *indigere* (to need).

indolent (in′ də lənt) *adj*. An *indolent* person is lazy and slothful and will do anything to avoid exerting himself. The word evokes the image of someone having a nice, easy time—being lazy and loving every minute of it. In a letter to a friend, the Roman author Pliny the Younger (62–113) wrote of "that *indolent* but agreeable condition of doing nothing." *Indolence* (in′ də ləns) is the noun. Plato (428–348 B.C.), in *The Republic*, called wealth "the parent of luxury and *indolence*." *Indolence* comes from the Latin *indolentia* (freedom from pain), based on the Latin negative prefix *in-* plus *dolens*, a form of *dolere* (to feel pain). One wonders whether the person who first thought of the phrase "feelin' no pain" as the equivalent of "mellow" was aware how close he was to the original Latin.

ineffable (in ef' ə bəl) *adj.* This word is capable of two contrary interpretations. It can mean "inexpressible" in a positive sense: A good wife can bring a man years of *ineffable* happiness. It can also mean "unspeakable," in a quite negative sense: Scenes of *ineffable* violence and brutality seem to fill the television screen these days. In *The Charge of the Light Brigade* Tennyson (1809–1892) did his best to glorify what was in fact an instance of *ineffable* bungling. From Latin *ineffabilis* (unutterable).

ineluctable (in ə luk' tə bəl) *adj.* What is *ineluctable* is inescapable, something that cannot be avoided and must happen. Those who believe in predestination are convinced that we must all suffer our *ineluctable* destinies. From a proper consideration and interpretation of all the data, correct conclusions are *ineluctable*. From Latin *ineluctabilis*, which in turn comes from the negative prefix *in-* and the verb *eluctari* (to struggle out of, surmount a difficulty).

ineptitude (in ep' tə tood, in ep' tə tyood—*oo* as in *boot*) *n.* *Ineptitude* can denote unfitness generally, or lack of skill or aptitude for a particular job. The *ineptitude* of Rimsky-Korsakov (1844–1908) for the navy and of Igor Stravinsky (1882–1971) for the law gave the world two great composers. The *ineptitude* of government in handling the problems of the common man is in large part the result of the red tape associated with the ever-increasing bureaucracy. *Ineptitude* can also mean "unsuitability, inappropriateness": The *ineptitude* of a judge's remark can result in the granting of an appeal to a higher court. *Ineptitude* is the noun from the adjective *inept*, from Latin *ineptus* (unsuitable, inappropriate, tasteless). *Inept* and *ineptitude* can also be used where the aura is one of tastelessness: The *ineptitude* of provincials makes them conspicuous in sophisticated urban society. *Ineptitude* is from Latin *ineptitudo*.

ingénue (an zhe noo') *n.* See **ingenuous**.

ingenuous (in jen' yoo əs) *adj.* An *ingenuous* person is free from deceit, artless. *Ingenuous* people shouldn't play poker.

Ingenuous is the opposite of *wily*. Cf. *disingenuous*. The word comes from the Latin adjective *ingenuus* which means, literally, "natural," and came to mean "free-born" and, by extension, "worthy of a free man" (as opposed to a slave), and eventually "honorable, frank." Children are refreshingly—sometimes disconcertingly—*ingenuous*. *Ingénue* (an zhe noo') is the name assigned, in the theater, to the role of an artless, unsophisticated girl. The pronunciation shown is an approximation of its pronunciation in French, where it is the feminine of the adjective *ingénu*, meaning "naive, unsophisticated, *ingenuous*, without artifice."

innate (ih nate', in' ate) *adj*. What is *innate* is inborn. An *innate* quality is one you are born with. Musical prodigies possess *innate* talent which can't be taught. *Innate* can take on the meaning "inherent, built in": If there is an *innate* defect in the system upon which a machine is based, it simply won't work. From the Latin prefix *in-* (meaning "in," not the negative prefix) and *natus* (born), a form of *nasci* (to be born).

innocuous (ih nok' yoo əs) *adj*. Anything *innocuous* is harmless. You can safely take any medicine all of whose ingredients are completely *innocuous*. By extension *innocuous* can mean "harmless" in the sense of "inoffensive": Some people are so sensitive that they can be hurt by the most *innocuous* remarks. *Innocuous* can also take on the meaning "unexciting, vapid": It is terribly boring to have to listen to an *innocuous* account of what must have been an exciting experience. From Latin *innocuus*, based on the negative prefix *in-* plus *nocuus* (harmful). See *desuetude*, for an unusual use of this word.

innuendo (in yoo en' doe) *n*. An *innuendo* is a veiled intimation or insinuation of a derogatory nature, an equivocal or ambiguous allusion, reflecting on someone's character, honesty, ability, etc. Iago, the villain in Shakespeare's *Othello*, who defamed Desdemona and was responsible for her murder and Othello's suicide, was a master of *innuendo*. *Innuendo* is a handy tool with which to destroy a person's reputation without violating the law against libel or defamation of character. It is difficult to prepare a defense against *innuendo*, because of the subtle nuances involved. From Latin *innuendum*, a form of *innuere* (to signal), based on *nuere* (to nod).

inordinate (in or' də nət) *adj. Inordinate* has a number of meanings. It can mean "excessive": Gluttons consume *inordinate* amounts of food. What might have been an interesting novel is spoiled by *inordinate* length. Another meaning is "disorderly": Some people operate their business in a most confusing, *inordinate* manner. A further meaning is "irregular": In some organizations there is no work schedule; everybody works *inordinate* hours. The second and third uses should be avoided; the word would generally be understood to mean "excessive," despite its origin in Latin *inordinatus*, meaning "disorderly, confused."

inscrutable (in skroo' tə bəl—*oo* as in *boot*) *adj.* This word means "unfathomable, mysterious," like the smile on the many images of Buddha or the grin on the face of the Cheshire cat. Matthew Arnold (1822–1888), in *Poor Matthias*, wrote the lines:

Cruel, but composed and bland,
Dumb, Inscrutable and grand,
So Tiberius might have sat,
Had Tiberius been a cat.

We cannot see into the *inscrutable* future, nor can we understand the *inscrutable* laws of human nature. Adventure story writers are prone to refer to "the *inscrutable* East" and newspaper pundits are fond of describing the Russians as "*inscrutable*." *Inscrutable* is the kind of word whose rarely used opposite, in this case *scrutable* (capable of being understood by careful investigation), has not the same figurative flavor, and would not be found in the ordinary desk dictionary. There are other words whose rarely used seeming opposites are not their antonyms, like *impeccable* (faultless—usually applied to manners or dress) and *peccable* (liable to sin); *imponderable* (difficult to estimate) and *ponderable* (weighable). Then there are words like *ineluctable* (inescapable), *impecunious* (penniless), *disgruntled* (discontented), *discombobulated* (upset), and *distracted* and *distraught* (agitated), that have no usable positive form at all. There are, of course, pairs where the negative and positive are not antonyms by any means, but both are perfectly usable words, like *demoralize* (dishearten) and *moralize* (indulge in moral reflections, "preach"). After this mini-treatise, let us not forget that *inscrutable* is from Late Latin *inscrutabilis*, based on Latin negative prefix *in-* plus *scrutari* (to investigate), which gave us *scrutiny* and *scrutinize*.

insouciant (in soo' see ənt) *adj*. One who is *insouciant* is unconcerned and carefree. Happy, *insouciant* people are good company; they don't burden you with worries and problems. *Insouciance* (in soo' see ənts) is the noun. Some people seem to walk through life with enviable *insouciance*, as though they haven't a care in the world. *Insouciance* was taken over bodily from the French, where it is based on a form of the obsolete verb *soucier* (to trouble), related to the noun *souci* (care). *Sans souci* is French for "carefree," and is sometimes seen as the name of a bar or nightclub.

insular (in' sə lər, ins' yə lər) *adj*. Literally, this word means "of or pertaining to islands," as in the *insular possessions* of the United States (e.g., the U.S. Virgin Islands); but its more common figurative use is to describe people who are narrow-minded, like *isolated* island people with resulting narrow, parochial views. (Note that *isolate* [eye' sə late, iss' ə late] comes from Italian *isola*, which in turn comes from Latin *insula* [island] which is the source of *insular*.) It is difficult for a sophisticated person to deal with people of *insular* views and attitudes. *Insular* prejudices create a gap between those holding them and people of liberal views. The noun describing narrow-mindedness is *insularity* (in sə lar' ə tee, ins yə lar' ə tee—*a* as in *hat*).

intangible (in tan' jə bəl). *adj*. See **tangible**.

integument (in teg' yə mənt) *n*. An *integument* is, literally, a natural covering, such as an animal's skin, or the rind or husk of a plant or vegetable; but by extension, it has been broadened to include any covering. One can speak of the *integument* of a book, for instance: In the course of time, ancient books become enclosed in a dried-out brittle *integument* that was originally leather. On a walk in the country one often comes across the cast-off *integuments* of snakes. From Latin *integumentum* (covering).

interdict (in tər dikt') *vb*. To *interdict* is to forbid, especially with the implication of an authoritative prohibition, as by a church or civil authority. In a war, trading with the enemy is strictly *interdicted*. The canons of the Catholic Church *interdict* divorce. The noun in general use is *interdiction* (in tər dik' shən), but there is also the noun *interdict* (in' tər dikt), which is a technical term for certain civil and church prohibitory decrees. From *interdictus*, a form of Latin *interdicere* (to forbid).

interlocutor (in tər lok′ yə tər) *n*. Anyone participating in a conversation is an *interlocutor*, but the term implies that the conversation or dialogue is of an official nature and on a high level, like, for instance, the SALT talks. It is to be hoped that the *interlocutors* at the next Israeli-Egyptian conference make substantial progress. There is a special sense of the word: the center man in a minstrel show who both acts as announcer to the audience and jokes and banters with the two end men. *Interlocutor* comes from Latin *inter* (between) and *locutus*, a form of *loqui* (to speak). The adjective *interlocutory* (in tər lok′ yə tor ee) has the wholly distinct meaning in legal parlance of "intermediate." An *interlocutory* decision given in the course of a lawsuit is not a final disposition of the case. An *interlocutory* decree in a divorce case is temporary, and has to be made final, after a given period, before the marriage is officially dissolved so that the parties can remarry.

interpolate (in tur′ pə late) *vb*. To *interpolate* something into a text is to insert it, especially with the implication that the new material is spurious and has been inserted without authorization and for purposes of deception. It is a simple thing to *interpolate* the little word *not* into a sentence and alter its meaning 180 degrees. The noun *interpolation* (in tur pə lay′ shən) covers both the act of *interpolating* and the inserted word or passage. The unauthorized insertion of material into a text which results in a change in meaning amounts to forgery. *Interpolate* comes from Latin *interpolatus*, a form of Latin *interpolare* (to polish up, and by extension, to falsify).

intractable (in trakt′ ə bəl) *adj*. Anyone or anything that is *intractable* is stubborn, hard to manage, obstinate. The suspicious nature of most primitive people often makes them *intractable* and hard to deal with. *Intractable* children are most unattractive. This adjective can apply as well to material as to people: Understandably, sculptors avoid *intractable* material. From *intractabilis* (unmanageable), based on the Latin negative prefix *in-* plus *tractus*, a form of *trahere* (to drag, pull). *Tractable*, of course, means just the opposite.

intransigent, intransigeant (in tran′ səh jənt) *n*., *adj*. An *intransigent* person is stubborn, unbending, inflexible, unwilling to compromise. When both parties to a dispute are *intransigent*, there is little or nothing their lawyers can do to bring about a settlement. Suspicious people are often *intransigent* and make attempts at persuasion ineffective. This word can be used as a noun denoting a person adamant in his convictions, especially in politics. The adjective is a little like *intractable*, but qualitatively stronger: with hard work you might eventually talk an *intractable* person into a compromise, but never an *intransigent* one. *Intransigent* comes from Latin negative prefix *in-* plus *transigens*, a form of *transigere* (to come to an understanding).

intrepid (in trep′ əd) *adj*. An *intrepid* person is fearless, bold, ready to take recognized risks. That little band of Israeli commandos who descended upon Entebbe were nothing if not *intrepid*. Walt Whitman (1819–1892), in *Song for All Seas, All Ships*, wrote of "all *intrepid* sailors." The British navy named one of their World War II warships *The Intrepid*. William Stevenson, a British secret agent in the same war, called his memoirs *A Man Called Intrepid* (Harcourt Brace, N.Y., 1976). That was his code name. *Intrepid* is derived from the Latin negative prefix *in-* plus *trepidus* (anxious, worried). Cf. *trepidation*.

intuit (in too′ it, in tyoo′ it) *vb*. To *intuit* something is to know it instinctively, i.e., through direct insight without any reasoning, without having to think or be told about it. Sensitive and imaginative people *intuit* the motives of others. Some people, on entering a room and surveying the scene, are able to *intuit* everything that has happened in their absence. People who can do this are called *intuitive* (in too′ ə təv, in tyoo′ ə təv). (It is unlikely that you will run across the uncommon alternative, *intuitable* [in too′ ə tə bəl, in tyoo′ ə tə bəl], but it does exist.) *Intuit* is the result of back formation from *intuition*: The noun came first, and then the verb, just as the verb *to typewrite* was formed from the noun *typewriter*. *Intuition* comes from Late Latin *intuitio*, based on Latin *intuitus*, a form of *intueri* (to contemplate).

inundate (in′ ən date, in un′ date) *vb*. To *inundate* is, literally, to flood or overflow; figuratively, to overwhelm or deluge. Casting directors are usually *inundated* with pleas from aspiring actors. The noun is *inundation* (in un day′ shən). In times of unemployment, help wanted ads result in an *inundation* of applications. From Latin *inundatus*, a form of *inundare* (to flood), based on prefix *in-* (not the negative prefix) plus *unda* (wave).

inure, enure (in yoor') *vb*. To *inure* is to accustom, to habituate. The flood of advertising and public relations has *inured* the public to a false set of values. Life in the tropics *inures* people to the hardships of heat and humidity. The London Blitz *inured* the people of that city to constant danger. This word has a wholly different meaning in law, in the phrase *inure to the benefit of*. A common term in agreements is: "This contract shall be binding upon and *inure* to the benefit of the heirs... of the parties." *Inure*, in this sense, has the effect of *become beneficial* or *advantageous*. From Middle English *enuren*; note the alternative spelling above.

invective (in vek' təv) *n*., *adj*. As a noun, *invective* denotes a violent, abusive attack in words, written or oral, as an adjective, it describes that sort of attack. Prosecutors seem to enjoy hurling *invective* after *invective* at the accused. Communists don't often choose to reason with those of a different political persuasion, they prefer to resort to *invective*. The verb is *inveigh*, which means "to use *invective*, to rail" against someone or something. *Invective* is from Latin *invectio*; the verb is from Latin *invehere* (to attack).

inviolable (in vye' ə lə bəl) *adj*. See **inviolate.**

inviolate (in vye' ə lət) *adj*. Anything *inviolate* is free from attack, desecration, or outrage. Doctors take the professional Hippocratic oath, which contains the words: "...while I continue to keep this oath *inviolate*..." Free men will always fight to keep their homes *inviolate*. The word is also used somewhat less dramatically in the sense of "freedom from alteration": Authors will often resist the suggestions of editors in order to keep their words *inviolate*. From Latin *inviolatus* (unhurt), based on the negative prefix *in*-plus *violatus*, a form of *violare* (to violate). This word is somewhat different from the related adjective *inviolable* (in vye' ə lə bəl), meaning "secure" (from invasion, destruction, corruption, etc.). The church is an *inviolable* sanctuary. Confidences must be kept with *inviolable* secrecy. To be of good character, you must have an *inviolable* conscience. From Latin *inviolabilis*.

irascible (ih ras' ə bəl) *adj*. An *irascible* person is short tempered and easily roused to anger. *Irascible* people, always ready to pick a fight, find it hard to keep friends. Shrews are *irascible*: Petruchio had his hands full with Katharina in *The Taming of the Shrew*. Top sergeants are always depicted in fiction as typically *irascible*. The word comes from Late Latin *irascibilis*, which is based on Latin *irasci* (get angry), which in turn is based on *ira* (anger), from which we get *ire*.

issue (ish' oo) *n.* In addition to its many other common meanings, *issue* means "offspring, descendants." A common legal clause, in wills especially, reads: "If I should die without *issue* . . . " i.e., leaving no children, grandchildren, etc. Shakespeare used *issue* in this sense. In *The Tempest* (act IV, scene 1), Ferdinand hopes "for quiet days, fair *issue*, and long life." Thomas Mowbray, in *Richard II* (act I, scene 2), speaks of his loyalty "to God, my king, and my succeeding *issue*." In *Antony and Cleopatra* (act III, scene 6), Caesar scorns " . . . the unlawful *issue* that their (Antony and Cleopatra's) lust . . . hath made . . . ." *Issue* is derived from Middle French *issir* (to go out), which in turn came from Latin *exire* (to go out). (*Exit* is a form of *exire*.) *Issue*, in the sense of "offspring," *goes out* from the bodies of parents.

iterate (it' ə rate) *vb.* To *iterate* something is to say or do it repeatedly. The commoner form is *reiterate*, which would seem to constitute a tautology, like saying "re-repeat." Once you've made your point, it is unwise to keep *iterating* the argument. (This is sometimes called "flogging a dead horse.") Fourth-of-July orators often bore their audiences by constantly *iterating* the theme of patriotism. All men make mistakes, but wise men do not *iterate* them. It is likely that you will run across *reiterate* much oftener than *iterate*, and that it will mean "say again" rather than "do again." *Iterate* comes from Latin *iteratus*, a form of *iterare* (to repeat), related to *iterum* (again).

jejune (jə joon') adj. This word means "insipid, childish." One can speak of a *jejune* novel, a *jejune* plan of action, a *jejune* idea for a business, implying immaturity, amateurishness and insipidity. The *jejune* remarks we hear on all sides about the economy betray the ignorance and shallowness of the speakers. Literally, *jejune* means "unnourishing," as in a *jejune* diet. The word is derived from Latin *jejunus* (literally, fasting; by extension, hungry, and then on to poor, mean, meager). From this one can trace its current meaning of "insipid." The sense "childish" is a later addition, probably from confusion with "juvenile."

jettison (jet′ ə sən, jet′ ə zən), *n.*, *vb.* *Jettison* is the act of throwing cargo overboard to lighten a vessel, and is also the verb that describes such action. By extension, *to jettison* has come to apply to getting rid of any burden, anything unwanted. In that sense, it is synonymous with *discard*. It is shameful to *jettison* the companions of one's hard times once fortune has begun to smile upon you. We must *jettison* old, outworn ideas and face up to the realities of life as it is. In connection with the original maritime usage, there is the related word *jetsam* (jet′ səm), describing the material thrown overboard; *jetsam* is a variant of *jetson*, a syncopated version of *jettison*. All these words come from Latin *jactura* (throwing away), based on *jacere* (to throw).

jingoism (jing′ go iz əm) *n.* This expressive word describes excessive chauvinism, combined with a bellicose attitude toward foreign countries. A *jingo* or *jingoist* is a person who proclaims far and wide his patriotism, urges preparedness and talks up a tough foreign policy. *Jingoistic* (jing go iss′ tik) is the adjective describing that kind of person and that type of activity. *By Jingo!* was an expression in a British political song urging force against Russia in an 1878 international crisis, and thus gave rise to the epithet *jingo*. President Kennedy warned against "belligerent *jingoism* and narrow isolationism." *Hey Jingo!* was once a magician's "magic" phrase for "Come forth!" but somehow *Jingo* became a euphemism for *God* in the expression *by Jinyo!* and was so used in the 1878 song.

jocular (jok′ yə lər) *adj.* A *jocular* remark is joking, facetious, tongue-in-cheek, jesting, not to be taken seriously. Toastmasters are fond of "roasting" prominent guests by making *jocular* observations about them. *Jocular* implies kidding, rather than unkindness. During spells of bad weather, *jocular* taunts are often made to television weathermen by the rest of the staff. From Latin *jocularis*, based on *jocari* (to joke).

journeyman (jur′ nee mən) *n.* A *journeyman* is a reliable worker, competent but not exceptional. Originally the word applied to a person hired to work for a day, or by the day. In that sense, it came from French *journée* (day, or day's work). It has come to be used where one wants to indicate that the worker in question is capable but far from outstanding. If you can't afford to pay the fancy prices of a top law firm, try to find a *journeyman* lawyer good enough for your purposes. There are lots of error-free baseball players who never really amount to more than *journeymen* members of the team. (In these examples, the word is used in apposition to the nouns with which they are linked.)

juxtapose (juk stə poze') *vb*. When you *juxtapose* two (or more) things, you place them side by side. The implication of this word is to call attention to the combining, whether the objects *juxtaposed* form a bizarre combination or are mutually enhancing. In surrealist painting, the concrete and the abstract, or two objects not found together in real life, are often *juxtaposed* to form interesting combinations. The noun is *juxtaposition* (juk stə pə zih' shən). It sometimes happens that certain pieces of furniture look better in *juxtaposition* than as separate items. Creative writers can produce interesting effects by the *juxtaposition* of words that one would not ordinarily expect to find in combination, the way Homer wrote of the "rosy-fingered dawn" and the "wine-dark sea." T.S. Eliot (1888–1965) wrote of "words . . . *juxtaposed* in new . . . combinations." From Latin *juxta* (close by, near) plus *positus*, a form of *ponere* (to put or place).

karma (kar' ma) *n*. This poetic word, borrowed from Buddhist and Hindu theology, is loosely and commonly used to mean "fate" or "destiny." Technically, the word denotes the sum total of one's deeds in one life which decide his fate in the next incarnation. The American essayist and critic Paul Elmer More (1864–1937) wrote: "As our desires shape themselves, so we act and build up our coming fate, our *karma*."

keen (keen) *vb*. To *keen* is to wail. Used as a noun, a *keen* is an Irish funeral song characterized by wailing, and to *keen*, in Irish folkways, is to utter such a *keen*. A *keener* is a professional mourner, usually a female engaged for wakes. In general usage, quite apart from funerals, *keening* is wailing, and the term is used metaphorically of such things as the *keening* of owls in the night, the *keening* of aerials in the wind, the *keening* of violins in the shadows, the *keening* of bagpipes. *Keen* comes from Irish *caoinim* (to lament).

ken (ken) *n. Ken* is a range of knowledge. This rather poetic word is often found in the expressions *within my ken, outside my ken, beyond my ken.* The concept of relativity is far outside my *ken.* Medieval Italian love poetry was well within the *ken* of Professor Charles Eliot Norton (1837–1908), the great translator of Dante. John Keats (1795–1821) wrote a lovely sonnet entitled *On First Looking Into Chapman's Homer* (George Chapman [1559–1634] translated the works of Homer) with the lines:

> *Then felt I like some watcher of the skies*
> *When a new planet swims into his ken . . .*

Here, *ken* takes on the sense of "range of sight" or "recognition." From Middle English *kennen* (to know); cf. German *kennen* (to know, be acquainted with).

kinetic (ki net' ak) *adj.* This adjective describes anything having to do with motion, caused by motion or characterized by motion. *Kinetic* energy is energy caused by motion. The term is used in the arts as well as in physics: The dance is a *kinetic* art form. Alexander Calder (1898–1976) originated the mobile, a *kinetic* form of sculpture. Derived from Greek *kinein* (to move), which produced *kinetikos* (moving).

kite (kyte) *vb.* A *kite* is a bad check, promissory note, or other piece of negotiable commercial paper that has nothing behind it and is worthless. It is used by a dishonest person to raise money or get temporary credit, and the verb to *kite* is to issue such a check, note, etc. A crook will *kite* one bad check after another, pyramiding his frauds, until the bubble inevitably bursts. From Middle English *kyte.*

kitsch (kitch) *n.* This word, borrowed from the German, describes trashy art, without taste or aesthetic value, usually pretentious, intended to appeal to the popular taste, marked by slick sensationalism or sentimentality or both. A sensitive reader can quickly tell the difference between *kitsch* and good writing. The *nouveaux riches* fill their homes with *kitsch* of every category, from paintings and sculpture to furniture and fixtures. From the German noun *kitsch* meaning "rubbish, trash," from *Kitschen.*

knell (nell) *n., vb. Knell* describes the sound of a bell, rung in a slow beat, usually to mark a death or a funeral. The best known use of this word is in the famous line from *Gray's Elegy (Elegy*

Written in a Country Churchyard, by Thomas Gray [1716–1771]): "The curfew tolls the *knell* of parting day...." (The original use of *curfew*, in medieval times, was the ringing of a bell at dusk, as a signal for extinguishing fires.) The *knell* of buoys deepens the gloom of the fog. *Knell* is also a verb: The funeral bells *knell* and give forth a mournful sound. When an alarm bell is *knelling*, get out! From Middle English *knellen*.

kowtow (kow' tow, kow tow'—*ow* as in *owl*) *vb*. To *kowtow* is to act with servility, show exaggerated respect, behave obsequiously. The verb is usually followed by the preposition *to* or *before*. Once the French Revolution started, the common people no longer *kowtowed* to the aristocracy. It is unwise for a professional to *kowtow* before his clients; it will earn only disrespect. *Kowtowing* is a specialty of head waiters. *Kowtow* is a Chinese word, describing the former custom of kneeling and touching the ground with the forehead as a mark of submission or worship.

kudos (koo' doze) *n*. *Kudos* is praise, honor, glory. The word is always singular—there is no such thing as one "*kudo*." *Kudos* is a performer's reward for a sterling performance. It is the achiever in our society who deserves the *kudos*. *Kudos* sometimes is bestowed upon the one who signs his name to a report, rather than the deserving people who did the hard work. From Greek *kydos*.

lachrymose (lak' rǝ mose) *adj*. The usual meaning of *lachrymose* is "tearful," but it can mean "mournful" as well. Niobe angered the gods; they slew her children and Zeus turned her into stone, in which state she remained *lachrymose*. Much of the poetry of John Milton (1608–1674) is of a *lachrymose* nature, written in a mournful vein. The word comes from Latin *lacrimosus*. The poet Horace (65–8 B.C.) wrote of "fumus lacrimosus" (smoke that causes tears), anticipating Jerome Kern by a good many years. *Lacrima* is Latin for "tear." *Lachryma* or *Lacrima Christi* (Tears of Christ) is the name of a wine produced from grapes grown near Mt. Vesuvius.

laconic (lǝ kon' ǝk) *adj*. A *laconic* person is terse; he uses few words and is the opposite of talkative, garrulous. The *laconic* Vermonter is a stock character of New England folklore. The word comes from *Laconia*, the name of a region of ancient Greece dominated by Sparta, whose inhabitants were noted for their terse and pithy way of speaking. Philip of Macedonia wrote to the Spartan officials: "If I enter Laconia, I will level Sparta to the ground." Their answer: "If." Caesar's famous "Veni, vidi, vici" ("I came, I saw, I conquered") is a famous example of *laconic* speech—not a word wasted.

lacuna (lə kyoo' nə) *n.* A *lacuna* is a gap, a missing part. Some people jump from a questionable premise to a conclusion, leaving a conspicuous *lacuna* in their reasoning. John Cowper Powys (1872–1963), the English author and lecturer wrote: "With a cultured man there is no gap or *lacuna* between his opinions and his life." From Latin *lacuna* (hollow, cavity, and by extension, any gap). One literal meaning of *lacuna* in Latin, "pool," gave us the word *lagoon*. Cf. *hiatus*.

lagniappe (lan yap', lan' yap) *n.* This rather pleasant-sounding word originated in Louisiana. It describes a bonus of one sort or another given to a customer as a token of goodwill, whether extra weight or measure, or a little something different. It is a common custom for grocers to give little children accompanying their parent shoppers a lollypop as a *lagniappe*. A *lagniappe* might be in the form of an extra half-yard of cloth given to the customer as generous measure. Employees of airlines and their immediate relatives travel at a small fraction of the regular fare as a *lagniappe*. More loosely, the term is being used as a synonym for any tip or gratuity. Whatever the form, a *lagniappe* is always welcome. The word comes from American Spanish *la ñapa* (the addition) via Louisiana French. The closest slang equivalent is "gravy."

lambent (lam' bənt) *adj.* This word can be used in a number of ways. It can mean "flickering," playing lightly over a surface: A fire in a fireplace can light the walls of a room with *lambent* tongues of flame. Another meaning is "softly radiant": When Romeo espied Juliet his eyes became *lambent* with adoration. A *lambent* light often fills the skies after a rainstorm. Still another meaning is "brilliantly playful"; Oscar Wilde gives his characters one line after another filled with *lambent* wit. However this word is used, it generates the feeling of light, graceful movement— whether tongues of flame, eyes of love, or brilliant wit. From Latin *lambens*, a form of *lambere* (to lick).

lament (lə ment') *n.* A *lament* is an expression of grief, especially a vivid or passionate one. When Ross informs Macduff of the slaughter of his wife and children in *Macbeth* (act IV, scene 3), Macduff gives way to one loud *lament* after another. As a verb, to *lament* is to feel deep sorrow and regret. William Wordsworth (1770–1850) wrote:

> *Have I not reason to* lament
> *What man has made of man?*

After dear friends have moved away one *laments* their absence. *Lament* gives us the adjective *lamentable* (lam' ən tə bəl) which stresses the regrettable, unfortunate aspect of things and situations in phrases like *a lamentable accident*, *a lamentable occurrence*, *a lamentable court decision*. In that use, *lamentable* expresses the feeling that whatever it describes should never have happened. There is a special use in the expression *the late lamented*, a euphemism for *deceased*. The noun *lamentation* (lam ən tay' shən) describes the act of *lamenting*, expressing grief. *Lamentations* is the title of a book of the Bible ascribed to the prophet Jeremiah. *Lament* (the noun) is from Latin *lamentum*; to *lament* is from Latin *lamentari*; *lamentation* is from Latin *lamentatio*.

languish (lang' wish) *vb.* This word has several shades of meaning: to droop, "take on a melancholy air": Sentimental young ladies in Victorian novels were fond of *languishing* in their boudoirs; "to pine"; A rejected lover *languishes* for the object of his desires; "to suffer neglect": The Count of Monte Cristo *languished* in prison for years. Whether you droop, pine, or suffer neglect, when you *languish* you are miserable. There are several related words. *Languor* (lang' ər) is listlessness. *Languid* (lang' wid) means "listless, lacking in spirit or vitality." *Languishing* describes the air of sentimental melancholy. *Languorous* (lang' ər əs) is synonymous with *languid*, but can also be applied to something that induces *languor*, like a fragrance or a landscape. *Languish* is from Latin *languescere* (become faint); *languor* was taken over intact from Latin, and *languid* is from Latin *languidus*.

lascivious (lə siv' ee əs) *adj.* One who is *lascivious* is lewd and lustful. The *dirty* in *dirty old man* really means "*lascivious*." The word can also be used to describe anything intended to arouse lustful thoughts or sexual desires, like *lascivious* gestures or behavior, or *lascivious* drawings or photographs. From Latin *lascivus*, which in the mother tongue had both a good sense, "playful," and a bad one, "wanton, licentious."

lassitude (las′ ə tood, las′ ə tyood—*oo* as in boot) *n*. Depending on the context, *lassitude* can describe either the unpleasant state of weariness, physical or mental, that results from malnutrition, strain, or oppressive climatic conditions, or a condition of languor, listlessness, and indifference—the desire simply to sit and dream—that seems to prevent certain people from accomplishing anything. There are some diseases, like rheumatic fever, that leave sufferers with a certain degree of *lassitude* though the active phase is over. Long confinement in prison often induces *lassitude* in the inmates. The *lassitude* produced by opium and certain other drugs can cause the wasting of a life. From Latin *lassitudo*, based on *lassus* (weary) and *lassare* (to tire).

latent (lay′ tənt) *adj*. This word describes things that are in existence, but not yet active or apparent, things that are potential but not yet brought to the surface. People often have a great deal of *latent* ability which has yet to be brought out. There are undeveloped countries full of *latent* resources that need exploration and development. People who may behave heterosexually in outward appearance are sometimes spoken of as *latent* homosexuals, meaning that their basic homosexual drive is supressed. From Latin *latens*, a form of *latere* (to be concealed). Cf. *patent*.

laudatory (law′ də tor ee) *adj*. *Laudatory* words and phrases are those that lavish praise. The chairperson of a woman's club being addressed by Adlai Stevenson during his campaign indulged in a lengthy introduction full of *laudatory* remarks. When she finally sat down, Stevenson got up and said, "After that introduction I can hardly wait to hear myself begin!" From Latin *laudator* (one who praises, a Latin term for "character witness"), based upon *laudare* (to praise).

lax (lax) *adj*. People who are *lax* about doing a job are showing a lack of interest in doing it either well or on time. The implication is that they know better, but just don't give a damn. The police, during the latter days of Prohibition, became extremely *lax* about arresting drinkers or purveyors of alcoholic beverages, knowing that everyone (including themselves and the judge on the bench) was equally guilty. Employees who feel overworked and underpaid often become *lax* in their work. *Lax* means "negligent, lacking in strict observance," and is found in the familiar phrase *lax morals*: Once upon a time, ladies who smoked were thought to be *lax* in their morals. (You've come a long way, baby!) From Latin *laxus* (loose, slack), which also gave us *relax*.

lay (lay) *adj*. *Lay* is an adjective applicable to one who is not a member, or connected with, a particular profession, especially law or medicine, but it can apply in its negative sense to any profession, e.g. accounting or architecture. When people pay for advice they are not satisfied with a *lay* opinion, but want to hear from someone with professional credentials. A special use is to describe a person not ordained, i.e., not a member of the clergy, like a *lay* preacher. A common use is found in the term *lay analyst*, describing a person practicing psychoanalysis without benefit of a medical degree. A *layman* (lay' mən) is a person who is not professionally qualified, or not ordained, as the case may be. Such people are known collectively as *the laity* (lay' ə tee). A professional economist or psychologist, for example, might find it difficult to get his point over to the *laity*. From Greek *laikos* (of the people).

lethargic (lə thar' jik) *adj*. A *lethargic* person is sluggish, listless, without pep or energy, has that morning-after feeling. *Lethargic* people get left behind in this competitive world. One *lethargic* person can put a wet blanket on a whole party. The noun is *lethargy* (leth' ər jee). *Lethargic* is from Latin *lethargicus*, taken over from Greek *lethargikos*, based on the Latin and Greek noun *lethe*, from the River Lethe, a mythical river in Hell, referred to in Milton's (1608–1674) *Paradise Lost* as "the river of oblivion." A drink of its waters produced total forgetfulness of the past.

leviathan (lə vye' ə thən) *n*. A *leviathan* is a monster, anything of wondrous size or vast power. *Leviathan* is the biblical name for a sea monster typifying evil (see Psalms 74:14: "Thou breakest the heads of *leviathans* in pieces..."). Hence, the name *leviathan* was used to describe a huge sea monster, especially the whale. Then the term came to mean anything of enormous size and power, like, for instance, the huge ship bearing its name, the U.S.S. *Leviathan*. The American philosopher Irwin Edman (1896–1954) said that America "[looked] like a *leviathan* of mechanical power." The word can be applied to anything huge: It took me forever to read *Anthony Adverse*; it's a *leviathan* of a book. We loved our little red schoolhouse; we don't like modern *leviathan* schools. Cf. *behemoth*.

lexicon (lek' sə kon) *n*. A *lexicon* is a dictionary. The term is taken over intact from the Greek, and is most commonly applied to Greek, Latin, and Hebrew dictionaries. The word is used also to describe the special vocabulary of a particular person, profession, field of knowledge, etc. The legal *lexicon* is full of technical terms and Latin phrases unintelligible to the layman. (See *lay*). Figuratively, it can mean "record": Sadat's visit to Jerusalem was an experience unparalleled in the *lexicon* of international relations. The English novelist and politician Edward Bulwer-Lytton (1803–1873) wrote: "In the bright *lexicon* of youth ...there is no such word as—fail." *Lexicographer* (lek sə kog' rə fər), one who compiles dictionaries (a term applicable to the author of this book) was defined by Samuel Johnson (1709–1784), who wrote the first English dictionary, as "a writer of dictionaries, a harmless drudge." *Lexicography* (lek sə kog' rə fee) is the practice of writing dictionaries.

licentious (lye sen' shəs) *adj*. A *licentious* individual is lewd and immoral, and disregards the proprieties, the rules of human conduct. The word is almost always used to describe sexual excess and immorality, as in a lewd and *licentious* motion picture; a *licentious* way of life; but it is related to *license*, in the sense of undue freedom from the usual restraints of social behavior, and, technically speaking, can be used without sexual connotation. Thus, Thomas Jefferson (1743–1826) wrote of the "lying and *licentious* character of our newspapers." This general use is seen in its derivation from the Latin *licentia*, which means "freedom" (in general, not restricted to sexual matters) but it would be well to restrict its use nowadays to the sexual sense, in which it would be universally understood.

limn (lim) *vb*. To *limn* something is to portray or describe it. This is a literary word, derived from Latin *inluminare* (to light up, and by extension, to make clear), based on *lumen* (light), which gave us Middle English *limene* (to illuminate, especially a manuscript). A ship which is clearly *limned* in the periscope of a submarine is usually an easy victim. *Limning* can be effected by words as well as pictures: An articulate witness who testifies in a way that accurately *limns* the situation is a great help to the court.

linchpin (linch' pin) *n*. Literally, this word applies to a pin through the end of an axle to keep the wheel on. It is used figuratively to characterize anybody or anything deemed vital to hold a situation together. The drafting room is often the *linchpin* of an engineering firm. The testimony of a single witness may be the *linchpin* of a complicated lawsuit. A good chairman is usually the *linchpin* of an effective committee. From Middle English *lynspin*.

limpid (lim' pid) *adj*. *Limpid* means "clear." The word is often associated with pools: One can see to the very bottom of a *limpid* pool. "Your eyes are like *limpid* pools" is a bit of old-fashioned corn from the days of Theda Bara. *Limpid* can be used in a more abstract sense to express linguistic clarity, as a synonym for *lucid*: Abraham Lincoln wrote in a *limpid* style that left no doubt as to his meaning. There is still another use of the word, to mean "serene, untroubled," as in *a limpid childhood, a serene and limpid existence, a limpid conscience*, but this use is not often met with. The word comes from Latin *limpidus*.

lissome, lissom (lis' əm) *adj*. Anyone or anything *lissome* is supple, lithe, agile. It is a rather literary word. Alfred Lord Tennyson (1809–1892) used the phrase "as lissome as a hazel wand." Somehow, the word has a lovely, lingering, wistful sound. One thinks of slender girls who move with grace and suppleness as *lissome*. People fond of cats admire them for their *lissomeness*. *Lissome* is a variant of *lithesome*, a variant of *lithe*, from Latin *lentus*, which had the literary sense of "pliant, supple."

litany (lit' ə nee) *n*. Literally, a *litany* is a form of prayer consisting of a series of supplications to God, each followed by the same response from the worshipers. By extension, it has come to be applied to any monotonously repetitious recital. Every time certain people go on a trip, you have to listen to a *litany* of their adventures. *Litany* is often coupled with the word *complaints*: There are those who bore you to death with their usual *litany of complaints*. The word comes from church Greek *litaneia*.

lithe (lythe—*th* as in *the*). *adj*. See **lissome**.

litigious (lə tij' əs) *adj*. People who are *litigious* are always inclined to litigate (sue), aching for a lawsuit; by extension, argumentative, eager to pick a fight. It is unwise to do business with *litigious* people; they'll take you to court at the drop of a hat. It is best to put your agreement in writing; the slightest ambiguity is a red flag to a *litigious* person. From Latin *litigiosus* (quarrelsome, full of strife), based on *litigium* (quarrel) and *litigare* (to go to law).

logy (loe' ghee) *adj.* When you feel *logy*, you are sluggish and lethargic. Often, when you take a sleeping pill, you feel *logy* all the following day. The seven-course meals eaten by our forefathers made them sleepy and *logy* for the rest of the evening. *Logy* is thought to come from the Dutch word *log* (heavy).

loquacious (loe kway' shəs) *adj.* *Loquacious* people are talkative, garrulous; the opposite of *laconic*. The "truth drug" tends to get the truth out of people by opening them up and making them *loquacious*. *Loquacious* bridge players ruin one's concentration on the game. From Latin *loquacis*, a form of *loquax* (talkative), based on *loqui* (to talk). Cf. the derivation of *colloquy*.

lothario (loe thar' ee owe—*th* as in *thing*) *n.* A *lothario* is a rake, a seducer of women. The word comes from *Lothario*, a seducer in the tragedy *The Fair Penitent*, by Nicholas Rowe (1673–1718), and is often found in the phrase *gay lothario*, from a line in the play: "Is this that haughty, gallant, gay Lothario?" *Gay lotharios* shouldn't be taken too seriously by young ladies; their intentions are not matrimonial.

lugubrious (loo goo' bree əs) *adj.* Anyone or anything *lugubrious* is gloomy, mournful. Some people go about with a *lugubrious* air, no matter what the occasion is. Buster Keaton always affected a *lugubrious* look; it was his trademark. The very word, somehow, sounds mournful. It can apply to things as well as people, like a dismal house, or a foghorn at night. *Lugubriousness* implies unrelieved gloom, and even more of it than the occasion justifies. From Latin *lugubris* (mournful), based on *lugere* (to mourn).

lurid (loor' id) *adj.* This word has several shades of meaning. It is most commonly met with in the sense of "gruesome, shockingly vivid": Some people like to describe an accident without omitting a single *lurid* detail. The word often has the flavor of "sensational," especially in the phrase "lurid account": Tabloid newspapers offer their readers *lurid* accounts of violent crimes and tragedies. Grade B movies delight in presenting *lurid* plots, promoted by *lurid* advertising. Wholly apart from the gruesomeness

implied in the word, *lurid* can be used to describe something
with a fiery flow, garishly red, as in *an incredibly lurid sunset*.
Lurid is not often used in its original meaning, "pallid, wan,"
based on Latin *luridus* (pale yellow; by extension, ghastly). This
sense appears in the work of Virginia Woolf (1892–1941), who
wrote of "leaves [shining] *lurid*... [which] looked as if dipped in
sea water."

macrocosm (mak' rə koz əm) *n.*; **microcosm** (mike' rə koz
əm) *n.* These words mean the opposite of each other; they are
antithetical (see *antithesis*). A *macrocosm* is the great world
around us, the entire universe, and by extension, the *whole* of
something, any great whole, a whole world in itself; while a
microcosm is a *miniature* world, anything seen as a miniature
sample of a whole world, or as resembling something else on a
small scale. Thus, one might regard the state as a *macrocosm* of
the family unit, and the family unit as a *microcosm* of the state.
Van Wyck Brooks (1886–1963) called the boardinghouse "a *microcosm* of a larger world." Describing the island of Penang, off
the Indian Coast, James Morris (*Farewell the Trumpets*, Faber &
Faber, London, 1978) writes: "The great charm of the place...was
its *microcosmic* completeness." (It had a bit of everything that
made up the varied mainland.) The same writer (who became Jan
Morris after a sex change) in *Destinations* (Oxford University
Press, New York, 1981) called Trieste "a *microcosmic* city...whose
anxieties are too often the world's worries in small." A camp has
been called "a city in *microcosm*." The words come from the
Greek: *makros* (large); *mikros* (small); and *kosmos* (order, and
by extension, universe).

maladroit (mal ə droit') *adj.* A *maladroit* person or act is
awkward, bungling, the opposite of *adroit*. The United States
handled the whole Vietnam situation in a *maladroit* way. President Nixon's handling of the tapes was *maladroit* in the extreme.
The running aground of a Soviet nuclear submarine on the
Swedish coast was the result of *maladroitness* on the part of the
captain. From Latin *male* (mah' lay, meaning "badly") plus
adroit.

malaise (ma laze'—first *a* as in *at*) *n.* *Malaise* describes a
general feeling of uneasiness, physical or mental or both. Physical *malaise* usually marks the onset of an illness. There is a

general *malaise* in our society today, uneasy as it is with the prevalence of crime and terrorism. Sometimes you can't quite describe the way you feel; nothing localized or specific; just a general feeling of *malaise*. The word is taken over intact from the French.

malapropism (mal′ ə prop iz əm) *n.* A *malapropism* is a ridiculous misuse of words. Some examples: You could have knocked me over with a fender. Let's play this one an ear at a time. Whew! That's a relief off my mind! Let's burn that bridge when we come to it. The very acne of attainment. *Apropos* (ah prə poe′) means "appropriate(ly)"; the prefix *mal-* (from Latin *male*—prounounced mah′ lay—meaning "badly") changes its meaning to the opposite: "inappropriate(ly)." Richard Brinsley Sheridan (1751–1816) created a character in his comedy *The Rivals* named Mrs. Malaprop, from whom *malapropism* is derived. Among her gems: "A *progeny* [for *prodigy*] of learning"; "the very *pineapple* [for *pinnacle*] of politeness."

malfeasance (mal fee′ zəns) *n. Malfeasance* is wrongdoing, especially misconduct in public office. Richard Nixon's conduct in office is an example of egregious *malfeasance*. Related words are *misfeasance*, the wrongful exercise of lawful authority, and *nonfeasance*, the failure to do what should have been done. (Both are accented on the second syllable.) The words are all common legal terms, and Nixon would appear to have qualified for all three of them. *Malefeasance* comes from French *malfaisance* (evildoing).

malign (mə line′) *vb., adj.* As a verb, to *malign* means "to slander, defame." Senator Joe McCarthy took a special delight in *maligning* innocent men and women. He had senatorial privilege, but if you feel you have been *maligned* by a private individual, your remedy is to sue for defamation of character. As an adjective, *malign* can mean "harmful": Bad company often has a *malign* influence on young people. It can also mean "*malicious*": *Malign* motivation prompted Hitler's desire to burn Paris. From Latin *malignus* (ill-disposed, wicked).

malleable (mal′ ee ə bəl) *adj. Malleable* people are impressionable; applied to material used in manufacture or sculpture, *malleable* means "workable, shapable." Clay is one of the most *malleable* materials for sculpture. The figurative use of the word describes people who can be influenced, those with impressionable or tractable mentalities. It is far easier to deal with the *malleable* character of youth than with the set convictions of adulthood. Demagogues use every effort to hammer away at potentially *malleable* audiences. The word comes from Latin *malleus* (hammer), which also gave us *mallet*.

manqué (mong kay′) *adj*. This word, taken from the French, follows the noun it modifies, and means "unfulfilled, fallen short." A Beethoven *manqué* is a failed composer, one who hasn't made it. A Shakespeare *manqué* is a would-be dramatist who will never attain success. Many a member paying dues regularly to Actors' Equity is an actor *manqué*. *Manqué* is a form of the French verb *manquer* (to miss, fail, lack).

martinet (mar tə net′) *n*. A *martinet* is a strict disciplinarian, one who demands obedience without queston. The term, derived from the seventeenth-century French General Jean Martinet, who invented a new military drill system, is often applied in military circles, but can be descriptive of anyone. Some bosses are *martinets* and run their offices like armed camps. Teachers who act like *martinets* may maintain order but are not always successful in imparting knowledge.

masticate (mas′ tə kate) *vb*. To *masticate* is to chew, to reduce to a pulp. It is advisable to *masticate* slowly and thoroughly, to get the best results from your digestive system. There are several manufacturing processes, as in the making of rubber and cellulose products, where raw materials have to be *masticated*. From Latin *masticatus*, a form of *masticare* (to chew), based on Greek *mastichan* (to gnash the teeth).

matriculate (mə trik′ yə late) *vb*. When you *matriculate* at a college or university, you enroll. After meeting the entrance requirements, one is required to *matriculate* at the institution of learning. From Middle Latin *matriculatus* (person listed), based on *matricula* (list).

maw (maw) *n*. A *maw* is a mouth, jaws, throat, gullet, or the stomach of an animal; figuratively, any great opening resembling an animal's jaws. Robert Browning (1812–1889) used the word literally in the writing of "the *maw*-crammed beast." *Maw* is used symbolically in expressions like the gaping *maw* of hell; the ravenous *maw* of death; the grasping *maw* of television (in its endless need for new material). From Old English *mawe*.

mawkish (maw' kish) *adj*. Anything *mawkish* is cloyingly, insipidly sentimental. The term can apply to persons as well as things. There is no harm in being sweet and sentimental, but people should stop short of being *mawkish*. Some people affect gentility to the point of being *mawkish*. Theda Bara's suitors in those old-time movies now appear side-splittingly *mawkish*. From an obsolete English word *mawk*, meaning "maggot," a curious derivation.

megalomania (meg ə low mane' ee ə) *n*. This word describes delusions of grandeur, exaggerated ideas of one's own importance. A person suffering from this condition is called a *megalomaniac* (meg ə low mane' ee ak), and is obsessed with the need to do things in the grand manner; he is said to be *megalomaniacal* (meg ə low mən eye' ə kəl). The *megalomaniac* Hitler wanted to rule the world. Hollywood became obsessed with *megalomania*; more and more millions had to be poured into films. From the Greek prefix *megalo-*, indicating exaggeration or extravagance, plus Greek *mania* (madness).

mélange (may lonzh') *n*. A *mélange* is a mixture or medley. The implication is that the mixture is a "mixed bag" of diverse and heterogeneous elements. Airplane passenger lists consist of *mélanges* of rich and poor, sophisticated and provincial, old and young. Most home libraries are *mélanges* of every kind of book from Homer to Mickey Spillane. *Mélange* is taken over intact from the French, based on the French verb *mêler* (to mix).

mellifluous (mə lif' loo əs) *adj*. *Mellifluous* sounds are sweet and smooth (literally, flowing with honey). The word is usually found in the phrase *mellifluous voice*, indicating one that is smooth, flowing and sweet. Bing Crosby crooned with a most *mellifluous* voice. Lullabies are usually sung *mellifluously*. On a quiet summer's day the *mellifluous* tones of church bells can be heard from a great distance. The word comes from Late Latin *mellifluus*, based on Latin *mel* (honey) and *fluere* (to flow).

mendacious (men day' shəs) *adj*. Anything or anyone *mendacious* is false, lying, untruthful. Once a person has been proved *mendacious*, it is dangerous ever to trust him in the future. Despite our truth-in-advertising laws, much of what is contained in advertising matter borders on the *mendacious*. The noun is *mendacity* (men das' ə tee). The Archbishop Frederick Temple (1821–1902) said: "There is a certain class of churchman whose mendicity (the practice of begging) is only equalled by their *mendacity*." *Mendacious* is from Latin *mendacis*, a form of *mendax* (lying), based on *mendacium* (lie, falsehood).

mendicant (men' də kənt) *n.* The noun means "beggar"; it can also be used as an adjective to mean "begging." This word is often seen in the expression *mendicant friar*, a monk who depends upon alms for his living. In *The Affluent Society*, John Kenneth Galbraith writes of "The rich man who deludes himself into acting like a *mendicant*," who "will conserve his fortune although he will not be very happy." One is made uncomfortable by people who go around with a *mendicant* air. From Latin *mendicans*, a form of *mendicare* (to beg).

mercurial (mər kyoor' ee əl) *adj.* This word can mean either "lively and sprightly" or "changeable, fickle, erratic," depending on the context. People of *mercurial* cheerfulness can enliven a whole party. Oscar Wilde (1854–1900) was famous for his *mercurial* wit. People of *mercurial* temperament are difficult to deal with. You never know where you stand with unpredictable, *mercurial* individuals. The word comes from the god *Mercury* (*Mercurius*, in Latin, identified with Hermes in Greek mythology), who counted among his attributes not only quick wit, but also sharp dealing and thievishness. Mercury, in Greek mythology, was the messenger of the gods. He is always depicted as having winged feet, a symbol of speed (an admirable, if not always present, quality in a messenger), which gave rise to the use of *mercurial* in the sense of "lively, sprightly." The element *mercury*, also known as *quicksilver*, was aptly named for its fluidity and capacity for rapid separation into small droplets that flow apart in erratic fashion.

meretricious (merr ə trish' əs) *adj.* This word applies to anyone or anything tawdry and insincere, though showily attractive. It is derived from Latin *meretricius*, which in turn comes from *meretrix* (prostitute), so that its literal meaning is "like a prostitute." In its common figurative sense, *meretricious* expresses dishonest, cheap, flashy allure, like that of a harlot, with no real feeling behind it. The new models of some cars are attractive in a *meretricious* way with no sound value behind them. There are altogether too many trashy books of no real substance that are only exercises in *meretricious* titillation from start to finish. *Meretricious relationship* is a phrase commonly used in legal parlance that reflects the literal meaning of the word: Courts are dismissing lawsuits for "palimony" (alimony based on a relationship unblessed by clergy) on the ground that the arrangement between the parties was merely a *meretricious relationship* rather than a marriage.

messianic (meh see an' ik) *adj.* This adjective is applied to a leader (or would-be leader) claiming or expected to be a liberator or deliverer; more loosely, to anyone or any theory claiming or expected to solve whatever the crisis of the moment happens to be. Once in an age there arises a *messianic* leader who can show the people the way to a better life. (Some only claim they can, like Hitler, Peron, Qaddafi, Arafat, and other false prophets.) Genuine leaders have a *messianic* sense of historic mission. Utopian idealists are sustained by a *messianic* expectation of social perfection. *Messiah* (from Hebrew *mashiah*, meaning "annointed") is the name of the deliverer of the Jews promised in the Old Testament. This role is assigned to Jesus in the New Testament (John:25:26). Hence, anyone regarded as or claiming to be a deliverer is called a "messiah," giving rise to the adjective *messianic*.

metamorphosis (met ə mor' fə səs) *n.* A *metamorphosis* is a transformation. It was taken over intact from Greek into Latin, and thence into English. In Greek, the word was formed from *meta-*, a common prefix denoting *change*, plus *morphe* (form). The Roman poet Ovid (45–18 B.C.) wrote a long poem entitled *Metamorphoses* (the plural form) in which people are transformed into animals. In zoology, it is the term describing changes like caterpillar into butterfly, or tadpole into frog. Its common metaphorical use is to denote transformation generally: After one has lived for years in a one-horse town, brief exposure to a big city can bring about a real *metamorphosis* in his manner and appearance. A few new boards here and there and a coat of paint can effect the *metamorphosis* of an old shack into an attractive cottage.

metaphor (met' ə for) *n.* This is a figure of speech in which a word or phrase is used not literally, but in a way that suggests a comparison of the thing described with something else. "A mighty fortress is our God" is one of the world's best-known *metaphors*. Other examples: *The flower of France's manhood was lost in World War I; a skin of ivory; a noble marble brow that stands out* *in a crowd.* In a related figure of speech known as *simile* (sim' ə lee), the comparison is actually made, not merely suggested: a skin white as ivory; a brow white as marble; conduct smooth as silk; eyes like limpid pools. The word *as* or *like* is used in a *simile*, never in a *metaphor*. Other examples of *metaphor*: food for thought; the golden age; the autumn of one's life. From Greek *metaphora*, via Latin.

metaphysics (met ə fiz' iks) *n. Metaphysics* is philosophy, particularly the abstruse variety. It is a technical term in philosophy, denoting the branch dealing with first principles, the nature of existence and knowledge. Its common use, however, often pejorative, is to characterize an argument or theory as too far-fetched and abstruse to prove the point contended for. Stop indulging in *metaphysics*; stick to the facts and probabilities! *Metaphysical* (met ə fiz' ə kəl) is the adjective. People who look away from the facts and rationalize tend to resort to *metaphysical* arguments. Its proper use is seen from its derivation, from the Greek preposition *meta* (after, beyond) plus *physike* (the science of nature); in other words, beyond the real world into the realm of theory and speculation.

mete (meet) *vb.* To *mete* something *out* is to distribute or allot it. It is the judge's function to *mete out* punishment that fairly fits the crime. When food and drink are in short supply, it is the duty of the leader of an expedition to *mete out* rations for the long journey ahead. Related to the German verb *messen* (to measure); from Old and Middle English *metan*.

miasma (my az' mə, mee az' mə) *n. Miasma* is, literally, noxious air or unwholesome exhalations, as from a swamp or any rotting matter. The atmosphere in smoking-cars makes our eyes run and fills our lungs with a *miasma* of stale tobacco smoke. More broadly, the word is used to describe a pervasive atmosphere that tends to harm or corrupt, or an emanation of foreboding and decay. From the minutes of the United Nations sessions there often arises a *miasma* of confusion, desperation, and decay of international morality. From Greek *miasma* via New Latin (stain, pollution).

microcosm (mike' rə koz əm) *n.* See **macrocosm**.

mien (meen) *n. Mien* is bearing, air, especially as an indication of a person's character or mood. Abraham Lincoln was a man of noble *mien*. Arnold Bennett (1867–1931) spoke of "that *mien* of a commercial traveller [British English for *traveling salesman*] who has been everywhere and seen everything." Alexander Pope (1688–1744) wrote:

> *Vice is a monster of so frightful* mien,
> *As to be hated needs but to be seen...*

echoing the words of John Dryden (1631–1700):

> *For truth has such a face and such a* mien
> *As to be loved needs only to be seen.*

Influenced by the French noun *mine* (meen) meaning "expression, appearance"; related to the *-mean-* in *demeanor*.

milieu (mil yeuh'—*eu* like the *e* in *her*) *n*. This word, taken over intact from the French, means "environment, surroundings." First-time prisoners, accustomed to the luxuries of life, are horrified to find themselves in a prison *milieu*. There seems to be a wide market for historical novels set in the *milieu* of earlier centuries. New boys at boarding school often find it difficult to adjust to the new *milieu*.

militate (mil' ə tate) *vb*. To *militate* is to operate or serve as an important influence in favor of or against something. A number of factors *militated* against success in our attempt to rescue the Iranian hostages. The weather can *militate* in favor of or against setting a new track record or a transatlantic crossing. Unfavorable circumstnces can *militate* against the success of any plan. This word comes from Latin *militatus*, a form of Latin *militare* (to serve as a soldier, but by extension, to serve generally). Do not confuse *militate* with *mitigate*.

minutiae (mə noo' shee ee) *n. pl*. The *minutiae* of anything are its smallest details. A careful lawyer will pay close attention even to the *minutiae* of his case. A good worker will apply his skill to the *minutiae* of his craft. From Latin *minutiae* (plural of *minutia*, meaning "smallness").

misanthrope (mis' ən thrope, miz' ən thrope) *n*. A *misanthrope* is a people-hater, a person who dislikes just about everybody. The lack of moral standards and the pervasiveness of corruption in today's world can make a man a *misanthrope*. It seems that *misanthropes* don't even like themselves. *Le Misanthrope* is the title of one of the great comedies of Molière

(1622–1673), produced in 1666. In Shakespeare's *Timon of Athens* (act IV, scene 3), Alcibiades asks Timon, "Is man so hateful to thee...?" and Timon answers, "I am *Misanthropos*, and hate mankind." Lord Macaulay (1800–1859) attributed to Lord Byron (1788–1824) "a system of ethics compounded of *misanthropy* and voluptuousness...to hate your neighbor and to love your neighbor's wife." *Misanthropy* (mis an' thrə pee, miz an' thrə pee) is what characterizes *misanthropes*: hatred and distrust of mankind. The adjective is *misanthropic* (mis ən throp' ik, miz ən throp' ik). *Misanthrope* and its related words come from Greek *misanthropos*, formed from *misos* (hate) plus *anthropós* (man).

misapprehension (mis ap ree hen' shən). *n.* See **apprehend**.

misappropriate (mis ə pro' pree ate). *v.* See **appropriate**.

miscreant (mis' kree ənt) *n., adj.* A *miscreant* is a villain; used as an adjective, the word means "villainous." The word has an interesting derivation from the Middle English word *miscreaunt* (unbelieving), the literal, but uncommon use of the word being to describe a heretic or infidel. Since all who did not "believe" in the Middle Ages were considered base and evil, the word soon acquired the meaning "villain," or as an adjective, "villainous." *Miscreant* might well be added to your store of pejoratives to describe or hurl at people when they behave badly. Shakespeare used *miscreant* often: Early in *Richard II*, Bolingbroke calls Mowbray "a traitor and a miscreant"; early in *King Lear*, the King cries to the Earl of Kent, "O vassal! miscreant!"; in *Henry VI, Part 1* (act V, scene 3), the Duke of York calls Joan of Arc "miscreant," combining in one word the concepts of villainy and heresy; earlier, (act III, scene 4), Basset addresses Vernon as "villain," and Vernon returns the compliment with the epithet "miscreant."

misnomer (mis no' mər) *n.* A *misnomer* is a wrong name of something, or the use of a wrong name. *Vegetable* is a *misnomer* for *tomato*; it is properly classified as a fruit. It is a *misnomer* to call a misty piece of property "Sunny Acres." The Korean involvement was a war; it was a calculated *misnomer* to call it a "police action." From Middle French *mesnomer* (to misname), based on the prefix *mes-* (cf. English prefix *mis-*, indicating error) plus *nomer* (to name), from Latin *nominare* (to name).

misogyny (mǝ soj' ǝ nee) *n. Misogyny* is hatred of women. The adjective is *misogynous* (mǝ soj' ǝ nǝs), sometimes *misogynistic* (mǝ soj ǝ nis' tik), and a woman-hater is a *misogynist* (mǝ soj' ǝ nist). When a man is betrayed again and again by women in unfortunate love affairs, he often becomes a confirmed *misogynist*. To some *misogynists*, the Equal Rights Amendment is a nightmare. Contacts with several Women's Lib extremists have made some men *misogynists*. On close inspection, what looks like *misogyny* turns out to be *gynephobia* (jin ǝ foe' bee ǝ), the abnormal fear of women. "A *misogynistic* prejudice has pervaded the Church's moral thought down through the ages, based on the incident of Eve as the temptress in Genesis...," wrote Francis X. Murphy in "Of Sex and the Catholic Church" (The *Atlantic Monthly*, February 1981). *Misogyny* comes from Greek *misogynia*, formed from *misos* (hatred), plus *gyne* (woman; *gyne* appears in words like *gynecology, gynephobia*).

mitigate (mit' ǝ gate) *vb.* What is *mitigated* is lessened, made less intense or severe. A convicted criminal's contriteness may sometimes cause a judge to *mitigate* the sentence. There are medications that *mitigate* but do not cure the illness. *Mitigating circumstances* is a common phrase describing surrounding facts that explain and partially excuse wrongdoing. In this sense, that phrase has the same effect as the expression *extenuating circumstances*. A pacifist upbringing and news of illness in the family might be taken into consideration as *mitigating circumstances* warranting a less severe punishment for going AWOL. Do not confuse *mitigate* with *militate*. The word comes from Latin *mitigatus*, a form of *mitigare* (to make mild or soft).

mnemonic (nee mon' ik) *n., adj.* A *mnemonic*, or *mnemonic device*, is anything that aids memory. It can consist of something as simple as a string tied around your finger or a knot in your handkerchief. Sometimes it is a rhyme like the familiar one beginning "Thirty days hath September," or a sentence like "Every Good Boy Does Fine," in which the initials are the five ascending notes (E, G, B, D, F) on the lines of the musical treble staff, or an acronym like FACE, the letters being the four ascending notes on the staff spaces. "Spring forward, fall back" is a *mnemonic* that helps people set their clocks properly when daylight saving time starts and ends. From Greek *mnemonikos* (pertaining to memory); *mnemon* is Greek for "mindful," from which we get *amnesia*, the *a* being a negative prefix in Greek.

modicum (mod′ ə kəm) *n*. A *modicum* is a bit, a small quantity. The word is commonly found in negative expressions: That story is a tissue of lies, without even a *modicum* of truth in it. Some people are hopelessly stupid, without even a *modicum* of common sense. From Latin *modicus* (moderate, limited).

molt (mowlt) *vb*. To *molt* (speaking of animals) is to shed the outer covering (skin, feathers, etc.). Take care when you see the skins of *molting* rattlesnakes. Cockateels are pleasant birds to have in your home, though they cover the floor with feathers when they *molt*. It is unwise to fondle a *molting* cat when wearing a blue serge suit. The British spell it *moult*. From Latin *mutare* (to change).

morass (mə ras′) *n*. A *morass* is a marsh or bog; figuratively, anything that bogs you down. In dealing with Big Government, it is easy to become entangled in a *morass* of bureaucracy and red tape. The American journalist Bruce Bliven (1916—) once panned a play as "a *morass* of clumsy exposition and preposterous dialogue." *Morass* is akin to German *Marsch* (marsh).

mordant (mor′ dənt) *adj*. *Mordant* means "sarcastic, biting," and is often used in the phrase *mordant wit*. The comments of George Bernard Shaw (1856–1950) and Oscar Wilde (1854–1900) on English social manners are full of *mordant wit*. The *mordant* analysis by H.L. Mencken (1880–1956) of the American character outraged some and delighted others. The Latin word *mordere* (to bite) produced the French verb *mordre*, a form of which became the adjective *mordant*.

moribund (mor′ ə bund) *adj*. The literal meaning of *moribund* is "approaching death," as in the expression *a moribund patient*. It is more generally used to depict something that is on the verge of collapsing, "going fast," "on the way out." The manufacture of men's hats is a *moribund* industry. Any political party that expends its energy in infighting is in danger of becoming *moribund*. From Latin *moribundus* (dying), based on *mori* (to die).

motif (moe teef′) *n*. The theme of a work of art, whether literary, musical or other, is usually called its *motif*. A recurring *motif* in *Hamlet* is the hero's indecision. The operas of Richard Wagner (1813–1883) are characterized by musical *motifs* that identify the characters. American tourists in the Caribbean are all too prone to wear shirts decorated with tropical *motifs*. This word is taken over from and pronounced as in French.

mottled (mot' əld) *adj*. This word describes anything splotched with spots of different colors and sizes. *Mottled* describes Joseph's Biblical "coat of many colors." The skin of older people is often wrinkled and *mottled*. This word is formed by "back formation" from *motley* (of different colors, varied), which came from Middle English and is akin to *medley*.

mountebank (mount' ə bank) *n*. A *mountebank* is a charlatan and swindler. Originally the term was applied to a pitchman hawking quack medicines (from a platform on the street); by extension, any quack or swindler. In *Hamlet* (act IV, scene 7) Laertes tells King Claudius, "I bought an unction of a *mountebank*." Be cautious about relying on the promises of politicians; so many of them are *mountebanks*. We get this picturesque word from Italian *montinbanco* (literally, a person who climbs up on a bench; in Italian, *montare* is "to climb" and *banco* means "bench").

mulct (mulkt) *vb*. To *mulct* someone is to bleed or milk him of something; to *mulct* something (usually money) is to obtain it by fraud or extortion. Attorneys have been disbarred for *mulcting* estates of money or other assets. People all too often *mulct* insurance companies by padding their losses. There is a rarely seen noun *mulct*, meaning "fine" or "penalty," and the verb can also mean "to punish (someone) by fine or forfeiture." This rare usage is found in the Latin origin of the word: *multa* (a fine), or *multare* (to punish).

mundane (mun dane') *adj*. Anything dull, ordinary or routine is *mundane*. No matter what profession you follow, much of your time is inevitably taken up with *mundane* details. An art critic is not expected to deal with anything so *mundane* as the price of a work of art. You may come across a less common meaning of *mundane*: "worldly" (as opposed to spiritual): Even a priest must learn to deal with people's *mundane* affairs and concerns. From Latin *mundus* (world).

munificent (myoo nif' ə sənt) *adj*. *Munificent* describes anyone or anything extremely generous, bountiful, lavish. The Rockefeller family has been *munificent* in its distribution of wealth to good causes. The *munificent* endowments of Andrew

Carnegie (1835–1919) resulted in the establishment of free libraries throughout the country. From Latin *munificentia* (generosity).

nadir (nay' dər) *n.* The *nadir* of anything is its lowest point. It is a technical term in astronomy, the science from which we also get the word *zenith,* meaning highest point. In his play *The Lower Depths,* Maxim Gorki (1868–1936) achieved the *nadir* of human misery. The Nazi extermination camps represented the *nadir* of human depravity. *Nadir* comes from the Arabic word *nazir,* meaning "opposite" (opposite the zenith, that is).

nascent (nay' sənt) *adj.* Something *nascent* is just beginning to exist. We must encourage the *nascent* democracy of Third World nations. Proper education will bring out children's *nascent* talents. From Latin *nascens,* a form of *nasci* (to be born).

nebulous (neb' yə ləs) *adj. Nebulous* describes anything hazy, indistinct, foggy (in the figurative sense). Some arguments can ramble on and on, *nebulous* from beginning to end. Recalcitrant witnesses seem always to have only the most *nebulous* recollections of the events in question. There is sometimes only a *nebulous* distinction between generosity and ostentation. From Latin *nebulosus* (misty, foggy), based on *nebula* (mist, cloud).

nefarious (nə fare' ee əs) *adj.* A *nefarious* person or deed is wicked, execrable. The Roman Emperor Caligula (A.D. 12–41) is famous for his infamous and *nefarious* deeds. Hitler's *nefarious* conduct represents a nadir in human conduct. From Latin *nefarius* (wicked, abominable), based on prefix *ne-* (not; in this case, against) plus *fas* (divine command).

nemesis (nem' ə səs) *n.* Someone's *nemesis* is his downfall or undoing. It can also denote his unbeatable rival. Sometimes all goes well at college until the oral examination; that can be your *nemesis.* Even if rehearsals proceed smoothly, first-night stage fright can sometimes be an actor's *nemesis.* Jimmy Connors came close to victory at Wimbledon several times, but was always stopped by his *nemesis,* Bjorn Borg. *Nemesis* was the classical goddess of retribution, so called from the Greek verb *nemein,* meaning "to dispense (justice)."

neophyte (nee' ə fyte) *n.* A *neophyte* is a beginner. In church circles, *neophyte* is the name for a new convert, or a novice in a religious order. Its common meaning is "beginner, novice" (in the general sense). Even the president of the United States is a *neophyte* during the early days of office. *Neophytes* shouldn't despair; everybody has to learn the ropes. From Greek *neophytos*, based on prefix *neo-* (new) plus *phyton* (plant).

nether (neth' ər—*th* as in *the*) *adj.* *Nether* means "lower." It is a rather literary word, from Middle English *nethere:* cf. German *nieder* (low). In the *Book of Job* (41:24), God says of the behemoth, "His heart is as firm as stone; yea, as hard as a piece of the *nether* millstone." The lower lip is sometimes called the *nether lip.* The *nether world* is *hell. Nethermost* means "lowest." *The Netherlands,* sometimes referred to as "the Low Countries," are so known because that country lies lower than sea level.

niggardly (nig' ərd lee) *adj.* *Niggardly* people are stingy, loath to part with even the smallest contribution; *niggardly* things are meanly small or scanty. *Niggardly* people try to make themselves scarce or become absorbed in something else when the waiter presents the bill or the collection plate comes around. Underdeveloped countries are provided with only the most *niggardly* public facilities. Do not confuse *niggardly* with *niggling.* From Middle English *nyggard.*

niggling (nig' ling) *adj.* *Niggling* (from *niggle,* to fuss or carp) means "petty." Pedants sometimes make an awful fuss about a *niggling,* hair-splitting semantic difference. *Niggling* can also describe details of work requiring excessive effort: Auditors have to cope with the most *niggling* checking into every detail of voluminous accounts. Etymological research involves *niggling* investigation of the most varied sources. Do not confuse *niggling* with *niggardly. Niggle* is akin to Norwegian *nigla.*

nihilism (ny' ə liz əm) *n.* *Nihilism* is a philosophy that preaches the total rejection of all restraint, all laws, all social and political institutions. A person embracing this creed is a *nihilist* (ny' ə list). Ivan Sergeyevich Turgenev (1818–1883) gave the following definition in *Fathers and Sons:* "A *nihilist* is a man who does not bow to any authorities, who does not take any principle on trust, no matter with what respect that principle is surrounded." Hitler's last days were marked by senseless *nihilism. Nihilistic* (ny ə lis' tik) is the adjective. During the 1960s, many college students acted as though bent on the *nihilistic* destruction of society. Derived from Latin *nihil* (nothing).

nirvana (nir vah' nə) *n.* *Nirvana* is perfect bliss, the state of freedom from all the pain and suffering of the world. Technically, in eastern religions, *nirvana* (a Sanskrit word meaning "a blowing out") is the name of the state attained through the extinction of one's personal passions and delusions; in Buddhism, it marks the end of the cycle of reincarnation. See also *karma.* As used generally, *nirvana* means "perfect peace, heavenly bliss." After seemingly endless exams, vacation comes, releasing the students into *nirvana.* Sometimes a series of unhappy relationships may end with the *nirvana* of a perfect marriage.

nomenclature (no' mən klay chər) *n.* *Nomenclature* is a system of names such as those used in a particular branch of science, philosophy, art, etc. The *nomenclature* of chemistry is filled with unpronounceable names of inordinate length. Heraldry has a *nomenclature* of medieval terms most of which are incomprehensible. From Latin *nomenclatura* (list of names).

non sequitur (non seh' kwə toor) *n.* This Latin phrase meaning "it does not follow," often abbreviated to *non seq.,* is used as a noun describing an unwarranted, unsupported conclusion, a statement made as though logically connected with what has gone before, but which in reality has nothing to do with it. Examples: "Would you like a cup of coffee?" "No thanks, I've come all the way over on my bike." "Her health is very good; she must be awfully rich." *Non sequiturs* are a specialty of politicians answering questions at press conferences.

nostrum (nos' trəm) *n.* A *nostrum* is a quack medicine; by extension, a panacea, a pet scheme recommended for the cure of the ills of the world. *Nostrum* means "our" in Latin, and evokes the image of the pitchman selling "our" drug. You can't trust those *nostrums* with labels that promise a cure for every ill from dandruff to housemaid's knee. Political hacks have a *nostrum* available for any social problem that crops up.

noxious (nok' shəs) *adj.* Anything *noxious* is harmful, physically or morally. Workers in atomic plants run the danger of being exposed to *noxious* radiation. Loose floorboards in a car will expose the occupants to *noxious* fumes coming up from the engine. We must be on guard against the *noxious* teachings of both Communism and Fascism. From Latin *noxius* (injurious).

nuance (nyoo ahns') *n.* A *nuance* is a shade of meaning, a delicate gradation, a subtle difference in expression, feeling, color, etc. It is not enough to know the basic meaning of a word; it is important to recognize the *nuance* imparted by the context. In the course of a long marriage, people become sensitive to every *nuance* of each other's expressions. Taken over intact from the French.

nubile (nyoo' bəl) *adj.* This adjective applies only to girls and young women and means "marriageable, ready for marriage." Girls in tropical countries appear to be *nubile* at an earlier age than those who grow up in cold climates. Lolita, the heroine of the novel of that name by Vladimir Nabokov (1899–1977), may have grown up in a cold climate but certainly was *nubile* at a tender age, and the perfect embodiment of the sexually alluring nymphet. From Latin *nubilis* (marriageable), based on *nubere* (to marry).

nugatory (nyoo' gə tor ee) *adj.* What is *nugatory* is worthless, ineffective, futile. A medicine may have an impressive name and label but turn out to be *nugatory*. At times, our government seems to be taking entirely *nugatory* steps to remedy the economic situation. From Latin *nugatorius* (trifling, vain, frivolous), based on *nugari* (to trifle, be frivolous, talk nonsense).

obdurate (ob' dyoo rət) *adj.* An *obdurate* person is unyielding, inflexible, persistent, especially in the context of resistance to attempts at moral uplifting, as in *an obdurate old rascal* or *sinner*. Victorian novels often featured the prayerful entreaties of a mistreated wife that fell on the deaf ears of the *obdurate*, aloof husband. Lady Macbeth was *obdurate* in her campaign to persuade her husband to seize power. Until his eventual acceptance of the inevitable, Richard Nixon was *obdurate* in his denial of wrongdoing. From Latin *obduratus*, a form of *obdurare* (to hold out), based on *durus* (hard).

obeisance (oh bay' səns) *n. Obeisance* is homage, deep respect; literally, a bow or curtsy showing deference to a superior. To make one's *obeisance* is to make a gesture of deep respect, as in entering a church or advancing to meet a royal personage. In general use it indicates deserved respect or deference: When he returned from the war, General MacArthur enjoyed the *obei-*

sance of the cheering populace. The word can be used with a sardonic nuance: Ambitious composers sometimes play politics by flaunting their *obeisance* to renowned conductors and critics. *Obéissance* is a French word meaning "obedience," and by extension, "submission," based on the verb *obéir* (to obey).

obfuscate (ob fus' kate, ob' fə skate) *vb.* To *obfuscate* something is to make it obscure, to becloud it. James Joyce (1882–1941) *obfuscated* his novel *Finnegans Wake* by inventing words new to the language. Lawyers sometimes *obfuscate* briefs by including all sorts of extraneous points. The noun is *obfuscation* (ob fəs kay' shən). Devious people resort to *obfuscation* in order to evade the issue. From Late Latin *obfuscatus*, a form of *obfuscare* (to darken), based on Latin *fuscus* (dark, and by extension, indistinct).

oblivion (ə bliv' ee ən) *n.* This word can have either an active meaning, describing the state of forgetting, having forgotten, being unaware; or a passive meaning, describing the state of being forgotten. In the active sense: Sleep gives us all a blessed interval of *oblivion*. In the active area, there is the related adjective *oblivious* (unmindful): Children are usually *oblivious* of the sacrifices their parents make for them. After that one drink too many, people become *oblivious* to their surroundings. In the passive sense: In time, the celebrities of the moment will be consigned to *oblivion*. John of Salisbury (d. 1180) called *oblivion* "...that hostile and faithless stepmother to memory." In *Troilus and Cressida* (act IV, scene 5), Shakespeare puts into Agamemnon's mouth these tragic words:

> *What's past and what's to come is strew'd with husks*
> *And formless ruins of* oblivion.

Oblivion is from Latin *oblivio* (forgetfulness), related to the verb *oblivisci* (to forget). *Oblivious* is from *obliviosus* (forgetful).

obloquy (ob' lə kwee) *n. Obloquy* is disgrace and bad repute resulting from public discredit or denunciation. After the death of Mao Tse Tung, the Gang of Four, including Mao's wife, were exposed as subversive and suffered the *obloquy* of those who have betrayed their cause. Benedict Arnold has always borne the *obloquy* of the condemned traitor. *Obloquy* can also be used in the sense of "censure." After his brief moment of triumph, Senator Joe McCarthy was subjected to the *obloquy* of the Senate. Do not confuse *obloquy* with *obsequies* (discussed under *obsequious*). *Obloquy* is derived from Latin *obloqui* (to speak against).

obscurantism (əb skyoor' ən tiz əm, ob skyoo ran' tiz əm) *n.* *Obscurantism* is the deliberate avoidance of clarity. Recalcitrant witnesses who indulge in excessive *obscurantism* may find themselves held in contempt of court. The Administration's "explanations" for the ailing economy are often a study in *obscurantism*. Treatises on economics often amount to nothing more than exercises in *obscurantism*. One who practices *obscurantism* is an *obscurantist* (əb skoor' ən tist). From Latin *obscurans*, a form of *obscurare* (to darken, cover).

obsequies (ob' sə kweez). *n.* See **obsequious**.

obsequious (əb see' kwee əs) *adj.* An *obsequious* person or gesture is excessively deferential and sickeningly servile. An all too common sight in expensive restaurants is the fawning, *obsequious* bowing and scraping of headwaiters greeting big tippers. Rock stars, boxing champions, and professional quarterbacks seem to be surrounded most of the time by retinues of *obsequious* hangers-on. The Roman playwright Terence (190–159 B.C.) in *The Lady of Andros*, wrote: "*Obsequiousness* begets friends; truth begets hatred." From Latin *obsequiosus* (yielding) based on the verb *obsequi* (to comply with). Do not confuse *obsequious* with *obsequies* (ob' sə kweez), meaning "funeral services": The whole world mourned at the *obsequies* of President Kennedy. The word *obsequies* and its meaning came about by accident: *Exsequiae* means "funeral procession" in classical Latin, and through confusion and error, became *obsequiae* in Late Latin; hence, *obsequies*.

obstreperous (əb strep' ə rəs) *adj.* *Obstreperous* people are unruly and boisterous. The term may also be applied to their conduct. Dinner parties can be ruined by the *obstreperous* interruptions of the host's children. During the French Revolution the *obstreperous* crowd outside the palace gates frightened the aristocrats inside. From Latin *obstreperus* (noisy, clamorous), based on the verb *obstrepere* (to make a noise).

obtrude (əb trood'—*oo* as in *noon*) *vb.* To *obtrude* is to force (something, or oneself) on others. One can become unpopular by regularly *obtruding* his opinions on the people around him. There are some people you may like, without wanting to have their ideas *obtruded* on you. The adjective describing such action is *obtrusive* (əb troo' siv), which describes people who *obtrude* themselves (and their opinions) on others, and can be used to mean "disagreeably noticeable": Theatrical agents at Hollywood parties can be terribly *obtrusive* and hard to take for any length of time. From Latin *obtrusus*, a form of *obtrudere* (to thrust upon).

obtrusive (əb troo′ siv—*oo* as in *noon*). *adj*. See **obtrude**.

obtuse (əb tyoos′) *adj*. An *obtuse* person is slow-witted, insensitive, thick-skinned, and thick-headed. You have to be explicit with some people who are too *obtuse* to take a hint. *Obtuse* people don't get the point; anything the least bit subtle is over their heads. From Latin *obtusus* (dull), a form of *obtundere* (thump, beat upon).

obviate (ob′ vee ate) *vb*. To *obviate* something is to make it unnecessary, to make it possible to do without it. The widespread use of calculators *obviates* the tedious solving of arithmetic problems the old-fashioned way. Bridges and tunnels *obviate* the inconvenience of slow ferry trips, though they take some of the fun out of river crossings. *Obviate* is often followed by *the necessity of*, as in a sentence like: The express highway *obviates* the necessity of driving through lots of little towns. This usage would appear to be tautological, since *obviate* has built into it the concept of *rendering unnecessary*. From Latin *obviatus*, a form of *obviare* (to prevent).

occlude (ə klood′—*oo* as in *noon*) *vb*. Anything *occluded* is closed, stopped up. A clot *occluding* a coronary artery can be fatal. The noun is *occlusion* (ə kloo′ zhən). Years of dumping can result in the *occlusion* of a narrow canal. *Occlusion* of the lachrymal duct results in watering of the eyes. The *occlusion* of the mouth of a river forms a delta. From Latin *occlusus*, a form of *occludere* (to close up).

odious (oh′ dee əs) *adj*. *Odious* means "hateful." "Comparisons are *odious*," wrote the English jurist John Fortescue (1395–1476) in *De Laudibus Legum Angliae (In Praise of the Laws of England)*. In a play on Fortescue's famous words, Shakespeare, in *Much Ado About Nothing* (act III, scene 5), has Dogberry say to Verges: "Comparisons are odorous." Shakespeare liked this play on words: In *A Midsummer-Night's Dream* (act III, scene 1), during the rehearsal scene, Bottom recites: "Thisby, the flowers of *odious* savours sweet—" and Quince corrects him: "Odours,

odours." Moral: Do not confuse *odious* with *odors* (or *odorous*)! But Shakespeare knew how to use *odious* correctly: In *Othello* (act V, scene 2) Emilia says to Iago: "You told a lie, an *odious*, damned lie." And in *Henry VI, Part 2* (act IV, scene 4), Lord Say says to the king: "The sight of me is odious in their eyes." From Latin *odiosus* (hateful), based on the verb *odi* (to hate).

offal (aw' fəl) *n.* Literally, *offal* is the term applied to the parts of a butchered animal considered inedible waste. By extension, it has become a term for refuse or garbage in general. Visitors to New York are often appalled at the accumulation of *offal* in the streets. The word can apply, figuratively, to people considered outcasts. Thomas B. Macaulay (1800–1859), the English historian and statesman, decried "the *offal* of the jails and brothels." From Middle English predecessors of *off* and *fall*: things that *fall off*.

Olympian (oh lim' pee ən) *adj.* Anything *Olympian* is majestic, incomparable, lofty. *Olympus* is the name of a mountain in Greece, the supposed home of the greater Greek gods. By extension, *Olympian* became applicable to anyone or anything incomparably superior. One can speak of a countryside of *Olympian* beauty; *Olympian* standards; *Olympian* detachment. Some people live in a world of their own, moving with *Olympian* unconcern through the everyday problems of life that beset the common man.

ombudsman (om' boodz mən—*oo* as in *book*), *n.* This is the term for an official appointed to look into complaints by individuals against public bodies and authorities. It is a Swedish word meaning "commissioner," taken over into English for this specific purpose. It is to be hoped that there is always an *ombudsman* available when one has a valid complaint against discrimination by a public body by reason of race, color, creed, age, sex, or political persuasion.

omniscient (om nish' ənt) *adj.* This is the adjective that describes people who know everything. God is sometimes referred to as The *Omniscient*. The total body of information is so incomprehensibly vast that no human being can be *omniscient* in its literal sense. The term is generally used to describe people who have an amazingly wide fund of information, like successful contestants in television quizzes. *Omniscience* (om nish' əns) is the noun. H. W. Fowler (1858–1933), the great English lexicographer, said in his preface to the *Concise Oxford Dictionary*: "A dictionary-maker, unless he is a monster of *omniscience*, must deal with a great many matters of which he has no first-hand knowledge." From New Latin *omnisciens*, based on Latin *omnis* (all), plus *sciens*, a form of *scire* (to know).

omnivorous (om niv' ə rəs) *adj*. See **carnivorous**.

onerous (awn' ər əs, own' ər əs) *adj*. Anything *onerous* is burdensome. Who would want to be President, and bear the *onerous* cares of state? (Uneasy lies the head....) The head of a household carries the *onerous* responsibility of feeding, clothing, and educating his young. A dictionary-maker has the *onerous* duty of preserving the purity of the language. From Latin *onerosus* (heavy, burdensome), based on *oneris*, a form of *onus* (load), which gave us our own word *onus*.

onomatopoetic (on ə mat ə poe et' ik), **onomatopoeic** (on ə mat ə pee' ik) *adj*. This term describes words that sound like what they mean, like *boom, sizzle, cuckoo, buzz, hiss, bobwhite, hum. Onomatopoeia* (on ə mat ə pee' ə) describes the creation of a word so formed. The use of *onomatopoetic* words in a descriptive passage helps to create atmosphere and dramatize the picture. From the Greek word *onomatopoiia* (making of words), based on *onoma* (name) and *poiein* (to make).

opprobrium (ə proe' bree əm) *n*. This word describes disgrace or infamy suffered as a result of shameful conduct. Oscar Wilde (1854–1900) suffered wretched *opprobrium* as a result of the facts that came out in his libel suit. The *opprobrium* attached to the crimes of the Nazis has cast a lasting shadow over the word *German*. Before his acquittal in 1906, the French Army officer Alfred Dreyfus underwent unwarranted *opprobrium* as a result of his earlier conviction for treason. The adjective *opprobrious* (ə proe' bree əs) means "disgraceful" in a phrase like *opprobrious behavior*, but in expressions like *opprobrious language* and *opprobrious invective* it means "abusive, scornful," i.e., expressive of emphatic reproach, rather than itself being shameful. The context should make the meaning clear. *Opprobrium* was taken over intact from Latin; *opprobrious* is from Late Latin *opprobriosus*.

ordure (or' jər, or' dyoor—*oo* as in *look*) *n*. *Ordure* is dung, excrement; by extension, anything disgusting or degrading. In the Middle Ages, the gutters of towns and villages were befouled by *ordure*. In its extended use, *ordure* can be used as the equivalent of *filth*, as in "feelthy pictures." Some pornographic publications are replete with *ordure* depicting the most depraved and disgusting acts and concepts. *Ordure* comes from Latin *horridus*, which originally meant "rough" and came to mean "uncouth," and later "frightful, horrid."

ostensible (ah sten' sə bəl) *adj*. This adjective applies to things that are pretended, put forward as the reason for something, apparent but not real. Something *ostensible* offers plausibility while concealing the reality of the situation. Lovers have often hurried to an assignation giving as the *ostensible* reason an urgent business meeting. Police authorities sometimes take people into custody for the *ostensible* purpose of protecting them from harm. The adverb *ostensibly* is often used to describe a situation more apparent than real. People are sometimes *ostensibly* frank as to their purposes while concealing the real reason behind their acts. Minor officials are *ostensibly* in charge of an office while the real official remains inaccessible behind a series of doors. From Latin *ostensus*, a form of *ostendere* (to hold out, display).

ostentatious (os ten tay' shəs) *adj*. Anything *ostentatious* is showy and intended to impress. Samuel Johnson (1709–1784), the first English dictionary-maker, encouraged "...an English style, familiar but not coarse, and elegant but not *ostentatious*...." The *ostentatious* display of finery and outrageously expensive jewels by the aristocracy played a part in fomenting the French Revolution. *Ostentation* (os ten tay' shən) is the noun, meaning "showy display." One of the most memorable acts of *ostentation* in history occurred when Cleopatra dissolved a precious pearl in a cup of wine. Thorstein Veblen (1857–1929), the American sociologist and economist, wrote of "conspicuous consumption," a phenomenon akin to *ostentation*. From Latin *ostentatio* (showing off), based on *ostendere* (to show, display).

ostracize (os' trə size) *vb*. When you *ostracize* someone, you exclude him from society or companionship. The act is called *ostracism* (os' trə siz əm). Under the old honor system at West Point, anyone caught cheating had to be *ostracized* by his fellow students. *Ostracism* is often the fate of those convicted of a heinous crime. The word arose from the Greek *ostrakon*, a potsherd (fragment of broken pottery) or tile marked and used as a ballot. The ancient Greeks had a custom of banishing by popular vote any person who achieved power and was thought to be dangerous to the state. The voters favoring banishment wrote the name of the offender on a potsherd. *Ostrakon*, akin to *ostreion* (shell), from which we get *oyster*, developed into *ostra-kizein* (to banish), which gave us *ostracize*.

otiose (oh' shee ose, oh' tee ose) *adj*. This word can mean either "idle, at leisure" or "futile, useless," depending upon the context. *Idle*: A person with a good pension can spend his retirement years in *otiose* comfort. *Futile*: People with poor business sense keep on wasting their money in one *otiose* venture after another. *Useless*: Some plays are encumbered with *otiose* dialogue, and even whole scenes. You may run across the second and third uses, but the first is by far the most common, and closest to the Latin origin of the word: *otiosus* (at leisure), based on *otium* (leisure).

paean (pee' ən) *n*. A *paean* is a song of praise, a shout of exultation, and by extension, any lavish expression of praise or joy. *Paean*, Homer tells us, was the name of a god serving as physician to the other gods, who was later identified as Apollo. The hymn to Apollo began with the words *Io Paean* (Oh, Paean); that phrase was later used in hymns of thanksgiving to any god, and thus *paean* came to signify any song of praise, triumph, or thanksgiving. On the return of our hostages from Iran, Americans joined in a great *paean* to democracy and freedom. As the first astronauts splashed into the sea, millions watching television burst into a *paean* of exultation. In a milder usage: The public united in a veritable *paean* of praise when the great Polish pianist Paderewski (1860–1941) made his first appearance.

palliative (pal' ee ə tiv) *n*. A *palliative* relieves without curing. To *palliate* (pal' ee ate) is to extenuate, lessen, de-emphasize. *Palliative* is often used pejoratively, to indicate that the thing so characterized is not really "doing the job." A *palliative* is like a bandage on a boil: it covers, but doesn't get to the root of the matter. A good example is a pain killer or a placebo. A proffered explanation that does not really explain or excuse a gross error is an unsatisfactory *palliative*. *Pallium* was the name of the large garment worn by men in ancient Greece, and came to mean "coverlet" in Latin. *Palliatus* meant "dressed in a pallium" (as opposed, e.g., to a toga), and by extension, "covered." Hence the word *palliative*, which may *cover* (lessen, relieve) but never cures.

pallid (pal' id) *adj*. One who is *pallid* is pale and wan; by extension, dull, lacking vitality or sparkle. The word can apply to things as well as to people. *Pallor* (pal' ər) is the noun, describing paleness caused by fear or sickness, or even death. People emerging from prison after long confinement look as *pallid* as though they had gone through a long illness. In an extended figurative sense: Sometimes, after a big build-up, an actor disappoints his audience by a *pallid* performance. The excitement of a successful first novel soon dies down, and the next one can seem *pallid* by comparison. From Latin *pallidus*.

palpable (pal' pə bəl) *adj*. Anything *palpable* is easily perceived, obvious. In *Hamlet* (act V, scene 2), after Hamlet claims a hit against Laertes in the dueling scene, and Laertes questions it, Osric cries, "A hit, a very *palpable* hit." The word is usually applied to negative things like lies and absurdities. A nervous manner and incoherent speech are usually the signs of a *palpable* lie. The adverb is *palpably* (pal' pə blee). If you take some statements to their logical conclusions, you can see that they are *palpably* absurd. A phony accent and get-up will soon reveal a person as a *palpable* impostor. The word has an interesting derivation from Late Latin *palpabilis* (capable of being touched), based on Latin *palpare* or *palpari* (to touch); but *palpabilis* came to apply to the sense of sight rather than touch and to mean "capable of being seen," i.e., obvious.

panacea (pan ə see' ə) *n*. A *panacea* is a cure-all. Panacea was the Greek goddess of healing, one of the gods named in the Hippocratic oath taken by prospective doctors. Her name became a common noun in Latin for a fabulous plant, supposed to heal all diseases, and, by extension, any cure-all, and was taken into English as a cure for all ills, a universal remedy, like those old patent medicines that cured everything from dandruff to curvature of the spine. Figuratively, it is used to describe the impossible: a solution to all the problems of the universe. All political platforms purport to be a collection of *panaceas*. Robert Burton (1577–1640) in his *Anatomy of Melancholy* praised tobacco as going "far beyond all the *panaceas*." Those swearing by Panacea today feel quite the opposite.

panache (pə nahsh', pə nash') *n*. *Panache* is verve, flair, style, dash. *Panache* was the name given to a tuft, usually of feathers, attached to a helmet in days of chivalry. From this it came to mean "dash, verve, flamboyance" in manner. After a series of successes in well-publicized cases, some lawyers tend to develop a degree of *panache* that characterizes their later appearances. Actors without sufficient *panache* should know better than to play the lead in romantic musical comedies. To *have panache* is to *have an air about you.* Franklin D. Roosevelt, with his head held high and that famous cigarette-holder tilted upward, had *panache.*

panegyric (pan ə jy' rik, pan ə jihr' ik) *n.* A *panegyric* is a speech or article in praise of someone or something. *Panegyris,* in ancient Greece, meant "public assembly" or "festival" (at which laudatory orations were given) and, via Latin *panegyricus,* gave us *panegyric,* originally a formal oration of praise, and now, by extension, any speech or writing bestowing lavish praise. Our prisoners of war returning from Vietnam were greeted with a round of *panegyrics* that made them blush. The reviews of *My Fair Lady* went beyond raves; they were veritable *panegyrics.*

panoply (pan' ə plee) *n.* A *panoply* is a complete magnificent outfit, a splendid display. Tourists are always impressed by the changing of the guards at Buckingham Palace, as they march by in full *panoply. Panoply* originally meant a "full suit of armor," from Greek *panoplia,* and the term became broadened to include any ceremonial outfit. By extension, it is used figuratively to describe any glittering covering, as in a *panoply* of colorful autumn leaves, or a *panoply* of gleaming, blinding snow.

pantheon (pan' thee on—*th* as in *thing*) *n.* This word describes a preeminent group, those most highly esteemed. Originally, it was the term for a temple dedicated to all the gods—from the Latin, who took it from the Greek *pantheion,* formed from *pan (all)* and *theos (god).* It came to include any public building housing the remains of a nation's illustrious heroes. By extension, the word has come to mean the illustrious group itself. The eminent English novelist Anthony Powell talked of "the place which a contemporary writer will occupy in the *pantheon* of letters," i.e., among the group most esteemed and established. Only a chosen few can hope to achieve a place in the *pantheon* of American painting.

paradox (par' ə dox) *n.* Any self-contradictory statement or contradiction in terms qualifies as a *paradox.* A famous *paradox* is chanted by the witches in the opening scene of *Macbeth:* "Fair is foul and foul is fair." A little later, Macbeth makes his first speech: "So foul and fair a day I have not seen," but all he meant was that the weather was changeable that day. Although a *paradox* disproves itself, sometimes a seeming *paradox* can speak the truth. The English clergyman Thomas Fuller (1608–1661) said, "It is . . . no *paradox* to say that in some cases the strength of a kingdom doth consist in the weakness of it." *Paradoxical* (par ə dox' ə kəl) is the adjective, *paradoxically* (par ə dox' ə kəl lee) the adverb. James Morris, in *Farewell the Trumpets* (Faber & Faber Ltd., London, 1978) characterizes the British people as "*para-doxically* bound together by an ancient class system." A common French *paradox* is to say of an attractive woman, "Elle a du chien." ("She has something of the dog about her.") It has been said that the brain, the most powerful force on earth, *paradoxi-cally* lacks the power to understand itself. From Latin *para-doxum*, based on Greek *paradoxos* (unbelievable).

paragon (par' ə gon) *n.* A *paragon* is a model of excellence, an ideal example of something. Sir Galahad was a *paragon* of virtue, the purest and noblest knight of the Round Table. A *paragon* is perfection personified, whatever the particular virtue may be. Hamlet called man "the *paragon* of animals" (act II, scene 2). In making his decision in the case of the two parties claiming the same baby, King Solomon showed himself to be a *paragon* of wisdom. A *paragon* is the ideal, the acme of perfection, a stan-dard of comparison for all time. Taken over intact from the Greek.

parameter (pə ram' ə tər) *n.* This is not only a highly tech-nical term used in mathematics, statistics, and other sciences, far too complex for definition here, but also a contradiction of the title of this book, for it is important *not* to employ it in general use, the way it is usually misused as the result of confu-sion with the word *perimeter* (pə rim' ə tər). It is frequently *mis*used, in the plural, to mean "limits," in expressions like *within the parameters of the rules of procedure; within the parameters of our constitution; within the parameters of the budget.* A *perimeter* is the outside boundary of a two-dimensional figure, and in that sense, is a *limit,* and even *perimeter* should be confined to its physical meaning and not applied to abstract things. *Parameter* is from New Latin *parametrum; perimeter* is from Latin *perimetros,* taken over from the Greek. To play fair, this entry will not be counted as one of the "1000."

pariah (pə rye' ə, par' ee ə—*a* as in *hat*) *n.* A *pariah* is an outcast, a person rejected by society or his immediate circle.

Despite medical advances in the treatment and containment of the disease, lepers continue to be treated as *pariahs* in most parts of the world. Politicians who disagree with the views of their own party are afraid to speak out, lest they become political *pariahs*. A *pariah* suffers the sting of social ostracism. The word comes from Tamil (one of the many Indian languages) *paraiyan* (drummer). The connection is that *pariah* denotes a member of a low Indian caste of which drumming was a hereditary duty. Englishmen returning from long service in India during the days of the empire brought back many Indian words, which were incorporated into the language and then traveled across the water to America.

parlous (par′ ləs) *adj. Parlous* is a rather self-conscious literary word, which appears to be only a tongue-in-cheek substitute for *perilous*. In fact, it is a Middle English variant of *perlous*, from which we get *perilous*. Latin *periculum* (peril) is at the base of all this. *Parlous* is usually found in phrases like *parlous days, parlous times*. In the prevailing *parlous* state of international relations, we must employ tact and avoid confrontation. These are *parlous* times; all of us have to conserve our strength to face the future.

parochial (pə roe′ kee əl) *adj.* This word is akin to *provincial*, in describing people and outlooks that are narrow, restricted. There are those who are catholic in their tastes, or eclectic; then there are those of *parochial* tastes in music, art, etc. People in small villages, with their *parochial* mentalities, are often unable to grasp the significance of world events. A special use is seen in the term *parochial school*, an institution maintained by a religious organization. This use stems from the literal meaning of *parochial*, "pertaining to a parish"; *parish* is derived from Late Latin *parochia*. Henry James (1843–1926), writing of Henry Thoreau (1817–1862), said "He was unperfect, unfinished, inartistic; he was worse than provincial—he was *parochial*." (After all, a parish *is* narrower than a province.)

paroxysm (par′ ək siz əm—*a* as in *hat*) *n.* A *paroxysm* is a violent outburst. On hearing bad news, Hitler would become convulsed in a *paroxysm* of rage. Macduff reacted to the report of the murder of his family with a *paroxysm* of grief (*Macbeth*, act IV, scene 3). From Greek *paroxysmos* (irritation). In the transition of this word through Middle Latin to English, the meaning would appear to have picked up a degree of intensity.

parsimonious (par sə moe' nee əs) *adj.* *Parsimonious* people are stingy, niggardly. *Parsimony* (par' sə moe nee) is the noun. Some people are so *parsimonious* that they will never invite you to have a meal with them. *Parsimonious* folk tend to look the other way when the collection plate comes around on Sunday morning. Edmund Burke (1729–1797), the Irish statesman, wrote: "Mere *parsimony* is not economy . . .": The word implies excessive frugality, and is clearly pejorative. Sensible people are thrifty; misers are *parsimonious*. From Latin *parsimonia* (thrift), based on *parsus*, a form of *parcere* (to economize).

parvenu (par' və nyoo), *n., adj.* A *parvenu* is an upstart; a person of obscure origin who has recently acquired wealth or position, but not the manners, style, wardrobe, etc., that go with it. The word can also be used as an adjective describing such a person. *Parvenus* look out of place in fashionable restaurants. Persons of breeding feel uncomfortable in the company of a *parvenu*. The word is taken over from the French, where it is a form of the verb *parvenir* (to arrive), from Latin *pervenire*. If *parvenu*, whether as noun or adjective, refers to a woman, it should be spelled *parvenue*, as it would in French.

pastiche (pa steesh') *n.* This word describes an artistic work made up of borrowings from variegated source material, a hodge-podge. There are composers whose work is not original, but rather a *pastiche* of motifs from Handel, Mozart, and Beethoven. Some essays are based on no true research by the writer himself, and end up as *pastiches* of the writings of many scholars. By extension, the word can mean "hodgepodge" generally, a mish-mash, as in *a pastiche of music, poetry, acting, dancing, and mime*; somewhat akin to a *potpourri* (poe poo ree'), which is from the French, meaning "hodgepodge." *Pastiche* is French as well as English; both come from Italian *pasticcio* (literally, pie; figuratively, mess, muddle).

pastoral (pas' tə rəl) *adj.* This word means "rustic, bucolic." It is a lovely word, from Latin *pastoralis*, based on *pastor* (shep-herd; Latin *pastor* gave us our word for *minister of a church*), and evokes the idyllic charm and serenity of a shepherd's life. One speaks of a scene of *pastoral* beauty, a *pastoral* setting, *pastoral* simplicity. Beethoven's Sixth Symphony is called "The *Pastoral*," because programmatically it depicts the countryside. Commuters flee the city each Friday night for the pursuit of *pastoral* pleasures. In narrow ecclesiastical context, it refers to church ministers, as in a *pastoral* letter, a *pastoral* visit to the bereaved family.

patent (pay' tənt) *adj*. What is *patent* is obvious, exposed to view. A lawyer's *patent* lack of preparation may influence a jury heavily against his client's case. Excessive coughing and shuffling of feet indicate an audience's *patent* impatience or disagreement with the speaker's message. From Latin *patens*, a form of *patere* (to lie open).

pathological (path ə loj' ə kəl) *adj*. This word means "caused by disease." The noun from which it comes, *pathology* (pə thol' ə jee), is a general term for the study of diseases, and the name of a course on that subject in medical schools, and is also a term covering abnormality or a diseased condition of any part of the body. The adjective, *pathological*, covers any condition caused by disease, whether of mind or body. A *pathological* condition of the skin requires the services of a dermatologist. A common use is in the expression *pathological liar*, describing a person whose constant tendency or even need to lie arises from a mental disorder. You can't believe a word uttered by a *pathological liar*. Alcoholics are *pathological* drinkers who cannot be talked out of their excesses. From Greek *pathologikos*.

pathos (pay' thos—*th* as in *thing*) *n*. *Pathos* is the quality in human experience or any art form that evokes compassion. The *pathos* in the lot of refugees the world over is almost too much to bear. John Marquand (1893–1960) wrote of the "*pathos* which must always divide a father from his son." The sufferings of Camille are so filled with *pathos* that during a really good performance, there isn't a dry eye in the house. From Greek *pathos* (suffering). Cf. *bathos*.

patrician (pə trish' ən) *n., adj*. A *patrician* is an aristocrat; as an adjective *patrician* means "aristocratic, highborn," and by extension, "characteristic of aristocrats": There are aristocrats with little money who cannot support their *patrician* tastes and aspirations. Cultivated manners, noble bearing, and impeccable attire can stamp a person a *patrician* the moment he enters a room. In ancient Rome, the *patricii* (plural of *patricius*) were the nobility; the word was based on *patres* (fathers; plural of *pater*).

paucity (paw' sə tee) *n*. *Paucity* is a scarcity, poor supply. *Paucity* of raw materials makes Japan vulnerable to blockade.

The people are becoming more and more disillusioned about the wisdom of the government because of the *paucity* of talent visible in high places. From Latin *paucitas* (fewness), based on *paucus* (few; usually in the plural, *pauci*).

peccadillo (pek ə dil' oh) *n.* This is a pleasant word for a petty offense or trivial fault. We're only human; we all have our *peccadilloes*. There are some women who will forgive a husband his sexual *peccadilloes* as long as he cherishes and provides for the family. In Spanish, *pecado* means "sin," from Latin *peccatum* (fault, error, sin), and *-illo* is a diminutive ending, so that a *pecadillo*, in Spanish, is a small sin, or slight fault. (The two *c*'s in the English version hark back to its Latin origin. The same is true of the Italian *peccato* (sin, or as an exclamation—*peccato!*—too bad!)

pecuniary (pə kyoo' nee err ee) *adj.* *Pecuniary* describes anything pertaining to money. People who are motivated solely by *pecuniary* interests miss the simple pleasures of life. Some offenses carry a jail sentence, others a *pecuniary* fine, still others either or both. Abe Lincoln is credited with saying that money in itself isn't important, but that its absence could be mighty inconvenient. He was speaking of *pecuniary* difficulties. From Latin *pecuniarius*, based on *pecunia* (money). Richard Barnfield (1574–1627), in his *Encomium of Lady Pecunia*, wrote:

> *She* [Pecunia] *is the sovereign queen, of all delights:*
> *For her the lawyer pleads; the soldier fights.*

Cf. *impecunious*.

pedagogue (ped' ə gog) *n.* Literally, a *pedagogue* is simply a schoolteacher, but its use implies that the person in question employs pedantic or dogmatic methods. Many of us recall the dreary routines established by our public school *pedagogues*. The adjective is *pedagogical* (ped ə goj' ə kəl). A *pedagogical* approach can discourage learning. *Pedagogy* (ped' ə goj ee) is simply teaching, or the science of teaching. From Latin *pedagogus* (the slave who accompanied the male children of the family to and from school and looked after them at home), which came from Greek *paidagogos* (boy's tutor).

pedant (ped' ənt) A *pedant* is a person who shows off his learning, a nitpicker who insists on strict adherence to formal rules and overemphasizes minor details, an obsessive stickler.

Pedantry (ped' ən tree) is the activity of *pedants*; *pedantic* (pə dan' tik) is the adjective describing *pedants*. A *pedantic* approach sometimes causes people to lose sight of the main point. One can be a scholar without being a *pedant*. A *pedant* is more interested in displaying his learning than in explaining or instructing. From Italian *pedante* (teacher, pedant); the *ped-* comes from Italian *piede* (foot), a reference to the plodding footsteps of a servile follower; and *piede* comes from Latin *pedis*, a form of *pes* (foot).

pedestrian (pə des' tree ən) *adj.* We are familiar with this word as a noun describing a person going on foot. The adjective means "commonplace, dull, unimaginative." The concept of *going on foot* is extended, in the figurative use of the adjective, to "plodding." A *pedestrian* approach to a problem leaves little room for a creative solution. Some books are loaded with *pedestrian* passages that stop the flow of action. From Latin *pedester* (on foot).

pejorative (pə jor' ə tiv) *adj., n.* As an adjective, this word means "disparaging, belittling"; as a noun, it covers any word or expression that disparages, belittles, talks down, puts down, badmouths someone or something. Putting *so-called* or *would-be* in front of a word usually has this effect, as in *Jones, the so-called* (or *would-be*) *actor. Amateurish* is a *pejorative*; so is *indifferent*, in a phrase like *a writer of indifferent poetry*. When one damns with faint praise, one is acting *pejoratively*. Truman Capote said of Jack Kerouac's literary output, "It really isn't writing, is it? It's ... er ... typing." Here, Capote was using *typing* (i.e., mere typing, in contradistinction to *writing*, i.e. *writing ability*) as a *pejorative*. From Latin *pejoratus*, a form of *pejorare* (to make worse), based on *pejor* (worse).

penchant (pen' chənt) *n.* A *penchant* is an inclination, strong liking. There are those who have a *penchant* for exotic foods, while others stick strictly to meat and potatoes. Those brought up in the Quaker faith have no *penchant* for gambling. This word, taken over intact from the French, is based on the French verb *pencher* (to lean).

penultimate (pih nul' tə mət) *adj. Penultimate* means "next to last." The *penult* (pee' nult) of a word is its next to last syllable, like the *-ta-* in *fantasy* or the *-ca-* in *glorification. Penultimate* can be applied to anything in a sequence, e.g., the *penultimate* play in a football game, or the *penultimate* scene in a play; a very handy word. *Penultima* was used in Latin (with *syllaba*—syllable — understood) to mean "penult." Latin *penultimus* was based on *paene*, *pene* (almost) and *ultimus* (last). *Paene*, *pene* is also found in *peninsula*: *paene* (almost) an *insula* (island).

penurious (pə nyoor' ee əs—*oo* as in *look*) *adj.* This word must be used carefully, for it can apply in two entirely different ways, to mean "stingy, parsimonious," or "destitute, poverty-stricken." (Destitute people are sometimes more generous than those well provided with the good things of life.) Silas Marner and Scrooge, both men of wealth, are two of the most *penurious* characters in literature. (Obviously, here *penurious* means "stingy.") We must feed the *penurious* peoples of the Third World. (Here, the meaning is "destitute.") The noun *penury* (pen' yə ree) does *not* reflect the first meaning of *penurious*: *stinginess*. *Penuriousness*, not *penury*, is the word for that. In *Das Kapital*, Karl Marx (1818–1883) described the *penury* of the toiling masses of Britain. *Penurious* is from Middle Latin *penuriosus*, based on Latin *penuria* (lack, want, and hence penury).

peregrination (perr ə grə nay' shən) *n.* Peregrination means "traveling" or "journey." The word is usually found in the plural: Columbus's *peregrinations* in his search for a short route to India led to the discovery of the New World. Shuttle diplomacy has involved *peregrination* of heroic proportions. From Latin *peregrinatio*. There are related words, *peregrinate* (perr' ə grə nate—to travel, impliedly on foot) and *peregrine* (perr' ə grin—foreign), but these are not in common use.

peremptory (pə remp' tə ree, perr' əmp tor ee) *adj.* A *peremptory* order or command is one that is imperious, dictatorial, admitting of no discussion. General Patton was famous for his *peremptory* commands. Some wives used to carry out their husbands' *peremptory* instructions with slavish compliance; Women's Lib has done its best to put an end to that nonsense. From Late Latin *peremptorius* (final, decisive). The poet William Cowper (1731–1800) wrote:

> *He would not, with a* peremptory *tone,*
> *Assert the nose upon his face his own.*

perfidious (pər fid' ee əs) *adj.* A *perfidious* person is faithless, disloyal, treacherous. The most famous use of this word is usually attributed to Napoleon: "Perfidious Albion!" (*Albion* is an ancient name for *Britain*, possibly from the white [*albus*, in Latin] cliffs of Dover.) But it was the French Bishop Bossuet (1627–1704) who wrote, much earlier, "*L'Angleterre, ah! la perfide Angleterre*" ("England, ah! *perfidious* England"). Iago was Othello's *perfidious* subordinate. *Perfidy* (pur' fə dee) is the noun. Judas Iscariot was the incarnation of *perfidy*. *Perfidious* is from Latin *perfidiosus*; *perfidy* from Latin *perfidia*; both are based on Latin *per* (through, in the sense of "beyond the limits of") plus *fides* (faith).

perfunctory (pər fungk' tə ree) *adj.* This word describes anything done routinely, as a duty, without interest or enthusiasm. Club secretaries usually give a *perfunctory* reading of the minutes of the last meeting. Ceremonial awards of distinctions in France are usually embellished with *perfunctory* kisses on both cheeks. The English are famous for exchanging *perfunctory* remarks on the weather. From Late Latin *perfunctorius* (negligent), based on Latin *perfunctus*, a form of *perfungi* (to perform, go through with).

peripatetic (perr ə pə tet' ik) *adj.* People who travel about from place to place are said to be *peripatetic*. The jet set lead a *peripatetic* sort of life. Peddlers' pushcarts are *peripatetic* little shops. *Peripatein* is Greek for "to walk about," and from it was derived the adjective *peripatetikos*, the description given to Aristotle (384–322 B.C.), who taught philosophy while *walking about* in the colonnade in the Lyceum of Athens, called the "peripatos."

peripheral (pə rif' ə rəl) *adj.* This word describes anything touching upon the incidental rather than the essential aspects of a subject. Critics sometimes mislead the public by concentrating on the *peripheral* aspects of a dramatic performance, such as the set and costumes, while ignoring the play's message. In any argument, it is important to keep to the point and not to harp on *peripheral* matters. The noun *periphery* (pə rif' ə ree) means "external boundary," and by extension, the superficial aspects of a subject. From Greek *periphereia* (circumference).

pernicious (pər nish' əs) *adj.* What is *pernicious* is very injurious. Communism and Fascism are both pernicious doctrines. Iago tormented Othello with one *pernicious* lie after another. Hitler's genocidal policy was the most *pernicious* episode in recent history. The meaning is intensified in the expression *pernicious disease* (e.g., *pernicious anemia*), where *pernicious* means "fatal." From Latin *perniciosus* (destructive, ruinous).

peroration (perr ə ray' shən) *n*. A *peroration* is the conclusion of a discourse, consisting of a summing up of the main points and a moving final statement urging acceptance of the argument. In murder cases, both the prosecution and the defense usually wind up with fiery *perorations*. It is well to make one's points succinctly and conclude with an eloquent *peroration*. From Latin *peroratio*.

perquisite (pur' kwə zit) *n*. If you are getting a *perquisite*, you are enjoying a fringe benefit, an allowance or other right incidental and additional to your salary. The free use of a company car is a valuable *perquisite*. Ex-presidents of the United States enjoy a substantial *perquisite* in the form of an allowance covering the expenses of an office staff for life. *Perquisite* is often shortened to *perk*, sometimes *perq*. From Latin *perquisitus*, a form of *perquirere* (to seek for diligently). *Perquisitus* is Latin for "diligently sought" and in Middle Latin acquired the meaning "acquired." (Apparently, seek, and ye shall find.)

persiflage (pur' sə flahzh) *n*. *Persiflage* is banter, a flippant, light-hearted way of dealing with a subject. There are those ne'er-do-wells who spend their days in *persiflage*, with never a moment's serious conversation. Serious subjects require respectful attention and should not be brushed aside with *persiflage*. Witty *persiflage* can be a big help to the hostess at a dinner party. Adopted intact from the French, who based it on their verb *siffler* (to whistle).

persona (pər so' nə) *n*. One's *persona* is his social façade, the "front" he presents to the world at large, as opposed to his real self. The meaning and effect of this word is seen from its meaning in Latin: "mask." There are people nobody really knows; their *persona* changes with every change of ambience. Some can adapt their *persona* to each new situation, but their characters and inner drives remain unchanged.

perspicacious (pər spə kay' shəs) *adj*. A *perspicacious* person is discerning, gifted with keen insight. A lawyer must be *perspicacious* in order to seize upon the relevant issues and brush aside the peripheral ones. *Perspicacious* value judgments are the reward of long experience in the rough and tumble of everyday life among the people. From Latin *perspicacis*, a form of *perspicax* (acute, keen-sighted).

peruse (pə rooz') *vb.* To *peruse* something is to read it through carefully, to go over every word of it. For some reason, many mistakenly believe that *peruse* means somewhat the opposite, to "skim through." *Per-*, as a prefix, implies thoroughness (as in *persist*, *persevere*, etc.). It is a good idea to *peruse* the fine print before signing anything. *Perusal* (pə rooz' əl) is the noun. Good poetry is usually compact, and deserves careful *perusal* rather than a hasty once-over-lightly. From Middle English, where its original meaning was "to use up," showing the effect of the prefix *per-* mentioned above.

pervasive (pər vay' siv) *adj.* *Pervasive* means "spreading about," like an odor you can't get away from or dampness that seeps into every part of your house or your bones. The verb is *pervade* (pər vade'). Mr. Micawber, in *David Copperfield*, spoke of woman as the "*pervading* influence that sanctifies" the family. Dull guests can fill a house with *pervasive* boredom for an entire weekend. From Latin *pervasus*, a form of *pervadere* (to go through).

petulant (peh' chə lənt) *adj.* A *petulant* person is unjustifiably impatient, prone to irritation over trifles, easily annoyed. Some people become *petulant* any time anyone disagrees with them. *Petulance* (peh' chə ləns) is the noun. There are those difficult ones who meet the slightest interruption with *petulance* and annoyance. From Latin *petulantia* (impudence).

philistine (fil' is teen) *n., adj.* A *philistine* is a lowbrow, one who not only lacks culture and is smugly indifferent to it, but tends to attack it. A *philistine* mistrusts any sign of culture in others. The word can be used as a noun or an adjective. *Philistine* was the name of an ancient people of Palestine who warred with the Israelites. (The most famous of them, Goliath, was slain by the youth David—*I Samuel* xviii, 50.) German university students applied the German equivalent of that name, *Philister*, to the townspeople after a "town and gown" fracas in 1693, when the school preacher used as his text "The Philistines be upon thee." (*Judges* xvi, 12). Matthew Arnold (1822–1888) wrote, in *Culture and Anarchy*: "The people who most give their lives and thoughts to becoming rich are just the very people whom we call *Philistines*," and Schopenhauer (1788–1860) defined a *philistine*, in

Personality, or What a Man Is, as "a man who has no mental needs." Babbitt, the hero in the 1922 novel of that name by Sinclair Lewis (1885–1951), is a typical *philistine*; Archie Bunker pushes the outer limits of *philistinism*. *Vulgarian* is a sometimes useful synonym.

phlegmatic (fleg mat' ik) *adj.* If you are *phlegmatic*, you are apathetic, sluggish, slow to be aroused or excited. It is hard to gain the attention of a person who has the *phlegmatic*, indifferent manner of those who have "seen everything" and give up hope for the world. The sad, dull eyes of a wholly *phlegmatic* person can create an atmosphere of gloom throughout the whole house. *Phlegm*, from Greek and Late Latin *phlegma*, is the thick mucus secreted in the respiratory passages, which was believed, in the old days, to cause apathy and sluggishness; hence *phlegmatic*, from Greek *phlegmatikos* (pertaining to phlegm).

piquant (pee' kənt), pee kahnt') *adj.* Pertaining to food, this word conveys the sense of pleasant sharpness in taste: The plainest food can be improved by adding a *piquant* sauce. In a more general sense, *piquant* means "agreeably provocative and stimulating, titillating." Most people like to receive letters full of *piquant* items of gossip. A woman's *piquant* smile and manners can charm a roomful of people. *Piquant* is taken over intact from the French, where it is a form of the verb *piquer* (to prick, sting).

pithy (pith' ee—*th* as in *thing*) *adj.* Anything *pithy* is succinct, meaty, full of substance. *Pith* is the noun, meaning the "heart" or "essential part" of something, as in *the pith of the matter*. A *pithy* remark is one full of force and meaning; it goes to the heart of the matter. Harry Truman avoided digressions and irrelevancies; his remarks were *pithy* from beginning to end. A person pleading a cause should be brief and to the point, should waste no words, and wind up with a vigorous, *pithy* summation. *Pithy* comes from a variety of Middle English, Dutch, etc., words meaning "pit" (of a fruit).

placate (play' kate) *vb.* When you *placate* someone, you appease, pacify, mollify him. Politicians planning tax increases have to put their heads together to find ways of *placating* public opinion. After long and acrimonious negotiations, management has to make realistic concessions to *placate* the union. From Latin *placatus*, a form of *placare* (to soothe).

placebo (plə see′ bo) *n.* This the name given to a substance prescribed by a doctor as though it were medicine, which in fact has no medicinal effect, and is given either for its psychological effect in humoring a patient, or in a controlled experiment to test a real medicine. When there is nothing really wrong with a patient who nevertheless insists that he is a sick man, a doctor will sometimes prescribe a *placebo* in order to satisfy him ("I feel *much* better today, doctor!") *Placebo* is the first person singular, future tense of the Latin verb *placere (to please) and means "I shall please."*

placid (plas′ id) *adj. Placid* people and things are calm, serene, tranquil. *Placid* people are not easily upset. The world loves the *placid* smile of Mona Lisa; she looks as though nothing could ruffle her. How soothing, to sail over *placid* waters on a sunny day! Walt Whitman (1819–1892) wrote:

*I think I could turn and live with animals,
they are so* placid *and self-contained.*

From Latin *placidus* (quiet, gentle, still).

plaintive (plane′ tiv) *adj.* Anything that expresses sorrow, grief, or melancholy, or sounds sorrowful, may be described as *plaintive*. Of all musical instruments, the oboe has the most *plaintive* tone. Children's first letters from a boarding school are often marked by *plaintive* indications of homesickness. From Latin *planctus* (breast-beating, lamentation), which is also a form of Latin *plangere* (to bewail).

plangent (plan′ jənt) *adj. Plangent* describes anything that resounds in a mournful way. The *plangent* tones of a bell buoy in the fog are reassuring though they have a mournful sound. Village church bells summoning mourners create a *plangent* sound that reminds us of the mortality of all men. From Latin *plangens*, a form of *plangere* (literally, to beat, and by extension, to beat the breast, to bewail).

platitude (plat′ ə tyood) *n.* A *platitude* is a trite remark. This term applies especially to observations pronounced solemnly, as though they were profound truths newly discovered and being uttered for the first time. *You can't take it with you*, for example, or *You can lead a horse to water*, etc., or *There's many a slip*, etc., etc. Don Marquis, in *The Sun Dial*, speaks of "stroking a platitude until it purrs like an epigram." From a combination of *plat*, French for "flat," plus *-itude* (as in other words ending in *-itude*, e.g., *attitude*, *magnitude*).

plaudits (plaw' dits) *n. pl.* *Plaudits* are applause and, by extension, any enthusiastic demonstration of approval. When it was introduced, the *Rhapsody in Blue* of George Gershwin (1898–1937) won the unreserved *plaudits* of the critics. A hostess is always delighted when her dinner earns the *plaudits* of her guests. From Latin *plaudite*, a form (imperative plural) of *plaudere* (to clap, applaud).

plethora (pleth' ə rə—*th* as in *thing*) *n.* A *plethora* of anything is an overabundance or an excess of it, and is usually used in a situation when something or other is "too much of a good thing." Sometimes you ask a simple question expecting a simple answer and are overwhelmed by a *plethora* of information that is no help at all. In times of unemployment, help-wanted ads often result in a confusing *plethora* of applications. From Greek *plethore* (fullness). A *plethora* is the opposite of a *dearth*.

poignant (poin' yənt) *adj.* *Poignant* means "moving," in the sense of "very touching." Havelock Ellis (1859–1939), the English psychologist, wrote of "the *poignant* spectacle of a little child without a home." The loyalty of a dog to his master is always a *poignant* sight. Taken over intact from the French.

polemic (pə lem' ik) *n.*, *adj.* A *polemic* is a verbal attack on a doctrine, belief, opinion. *Polemics*, with an *s* but still treated as a singular (like, e.g., *physics* or *economics*), is the art of argument or controversy. *Polemic*, as an adjective, means "argumentative." Fundamentalists are fond of delivering lengthy *polemics* against the theory of evolution. The Russians are past masters of cold-war *polemics*. It sometimes happens that what was intended as an objective lecture develops into a *polemic* attack on the previous speaker's views. From Greek *polemikos* (pertaining to war).

polyglot (pol' ee glot) *n.*, *adj.* A *polyglot* is a person with a command of a number of languages. As an adjective, *polyglot* means "multilingual," and can describe a person (one who knows several languages) or book or other piece of writing (written in a number of languages, like a *polyglot* Bible). People living in small countries, like the Dutch and the Scandinavians, tend to be *polyglot*. From Greek *polyglottos* (many-tongued).

ponderous (pon' dər əs) *adj. Ponderous* can be used in either of two ways: it can apply to anything heavy or unwieldy, or to things like speeches and writings that are labored. The figure of Atlas bearing the world on his shoulders is always shown as bent, because of his *ponderous* burden. Unfortunately, most Ph.D. dissertations are *ponderous* in nature. Due to the nature of the beast, most legislation is couched in discouragingly *ponderous* language. From Latin *ponderosus* (heavy), based on *pondus* (weight).

pontificate (pon tif' ə kate) *vb.* To *pontificate* is to speak pompously, hold forth in a dogmatic way. *Pontifex* is Latin for "high priest," and gave rise to Middle Latin *pontificatus*, a form of *pontificare* (to act as a high priest), so that to *pontificate* is to "speak like a high priest," i.e., speak pompously or dogmatically or both. Columnists often *pontificate* as though they possessed all the wisdom of the ages. What is more exasperating than having to listen to people who *pontificate* on matters they know little or nothing about? *Pontiff* is another word for *pope*.

portend (por tend') *vb.* To *portend* is to foreshadow. The discontented murmurings of an audience *portend* the rejection of a speaker's proposal. There is a confusing miscellany of economic indicators that *portend* better or worse things to come, as the case may be (whereas on the other hand . . .). From Latin *portendere* (to point out, to indicate). A related word is *portent* (por' tent) *n.*, meaning "omen," from Latin *portentum* (sign, token). The lifting of a cloud cover is a *portent* of better weather to come. Winston Churchill (1874–1965) called the V-sign "a *portent* of the fate awaiting the Nazi tyranny." *Portentous* (por ten' təs) *adj.* means "momentous" or "ominously significant," from Latin *portentosus* (monstrous). Lord Byron (1788–1824) wrote:

> *Of all the horrid, hideous notes of woe,*
> *Sadder than owl songs on the midnight blast,*
> *Is that* portentous *phrase, "I told you so."*

Security Council debates often cover *portentous* events, fraught with danger for all mankind.

portmanteau (port man' toe, port man toe') *n.* A *portmanteau* is a traveling bag of a special sort. It is a chiefly British word describing especially the kind of trunk or suitcase that opens into two halves. It comes from the French, where it means "coatrack," and is based on the verb *porter* (to carry) and the noun *manteau* (coat). It has a special use in the term *portmanteau word* (based on the two halves into which this type of traveling bag opens) indicating a word that results from the blending of two other words, like *brunch*. Under the heading *portmanteau*, the author has this to say in his *English English* (Verbatim, Essex, Ct, 1980):

The figurative meaning is that of a made-up word combining the sounds and meanings of two other words, like *squarson*, combination of *squire* and *parson*; ... *smog*, combination of *smoke* and *fog*, etc. One would guess that Lewis Carroll's *slithy toves* had been not only *slimy* but also *lithe*. He invented this usage of *portmanteau* in *Through the Looking Glass*: "You see, it's like a *portmanteau*—there are two meanings packed in one word."

postulate (pos' chə late) *vb.* When you *postulate* something, you assume it to be true. In their reasoning, those against the building of nuclear power stations *postulate* that the inherent danger will inevitably cause enormous loss of life. A *postulation* (pos chə lay' shən) is an assumption. Bertrand Russell (1872–1970) stated: "Life is built on certain *postulations*." Most legal arguments, like theorems in geometry, are constructed on the basis of a series of *postulations*. From Latin *postulatum* (claim, demand), based on *postulare* (to claim).

potpourri (po poo ree') *n.* See **pastiche**.

potter (pot' ər) *vb.* To *potter* is to keep busy aimlessly. Potter is a chiefly British variant of *putter*, and comes from the Middle English word *poten*. It happens all too often that people who seem terribly busy are in reality only *pottering* (*puttering*) about the house or office all day long. *Pottering* in the garden on a sunny day is a pleasant way to spend time whether or not the actual results are rewarding.

pragmatic (prag mat' ik) *adj.* *Pragmatic* activities, especially approaches, deal with situations from a practical point of view. It is more productive to attack a problem in a *pragmatic* way than to spin theories. *Pragmatism* (prag' mə tiz əm) is the mode of thought that puts the emphasis on practical considerations; the matter-of-fact cause-and-effect approach. Instead of arguing in the abstract while trouble is brewing, we should try to reach a result through *pragmatism*. From *pragmatikos*, Greek for "practical. In ancient Rome, *pragmaticus* attained a narrow meaning: "skillful in civil or state affairs," which, of course, implied a practical approach.

prate (prate) *vb.* To *prate* is to babble, to talk too much. Gossips delight in *prating* about one trivial happening after another. The would-be pundit puts on a solemn face and then proceeds to *prate* utter nonsense. Jonathan Swift (1667–1745), the author of *Gulliver's Travels*, described a silly woman in this way:

> *A set of phrases learnt by rote;*
> *A passion for a scarlet coat;*
> *When at a play, to laugh, or cry,*
> *Yet cannot tell the reason why;*
> *Never to hold her tongue a minute;*
> *While all she* prates *has nothing in it.*

From Middle English *praten*. Cf. *prattle*.

prattle (prat′ əl) *n., vb.* To *prattle* is to babble, chatter away. Often, you can't understand a word little children are saying, but they keep on *prattling* endlessly anyway. *Prattle* is sometimes used as a noun, as in the *prattle* of little children, or the foolish *prattle* of the village gossips; or, to indicate a repetitive sound, the *prattle* of the rapids over the stones. From Low German *pratelen*. Cf. *prate*.

precipitate (prə sip′ ə tət) *adj.*; (prə sip′ ə tate) *vb.* As an adjective (note pronunciation), this word has a number of meanings: "headlong": Mountain climbers take the risk of a *precipitate* fall which can be fatal. (Cf. *precipice*.) In another sense, "hasty": At the first sign of real opposition a bully will beat a *precipitate* retreat. Next, "sudden": At the first sight of a motorcycle cop, drivers tend to bring their cars to a *precipitate* slowdown. Finally, "rash": People who enter into a *precipitate* marriage may come to rue it soon after. (Or, to put it in possibly more familiar terms, marry in haste....) The verb *to precipitate* (note last syllable pronounced to rhyme with *late*) means "to hasten, bring about prematurely": Rash words uttered in high places can *precipitate* an international crisis. Do not confuse *precipitate*, however it is used or pronounced, with *precipitous*. From Latin *praecipitatus*, a form of *praecipitare* (to cast down).

precipitous (prə sip′ ə təs) *adj. Precipitous* means "very steep." Tea is grown in India on *precipitous* mountainsides. Old-fashioned houses often have *precipitous* staircases. From Late Latin *praecipitosus*, based on Latin *praecipitis*, a form of *praeceps* (steep). Cf. *precipice*. Do not confuse *precipitous* with the adjective *precipitate*.

precursor (prə kur′ sər, pree′ kur sər) *n*. This word can be used to mean "predecessor, forerunner," or "harbinger" (in the sense of "signal of approach"), depending on the context. The early rocket experiments were the *precursors* of supersonic jet flight. In the second sense: Aches and pains are the *precursors* of flu. The robin is the *precursor* of spring. From Latin *praecursor* (forerunner).

predilection (pred ə lek′ shən) *n*. A *predilection* for something is a liking or preference for it. Some people have a *predilection* for Chinese food; others prefer a simpler cuisine. Most people do not understand the *predilection* of the *avant garde* for atonal music. From Middle Latin *praedilectus* (selection), based on Latin *dilectus* (choosing).

preen (preen) *vb*. This word can be understood in either the sense of "primping, grooming (oneself)" or "priding, congratulating (oneself)." People whose faces are their fortunes often take an irritatingly long time *preening* themselves before their mirrors. In the second sense: Actors *preening* themselves on the receipt of Oscars are a familiar sight on our television screens. In the animal world, *preen* is the word used for "grooming" (dressing fur or feathers with the tongue or beak). Derivation uncertain.

prehensile (pree hen′ səl, pree hen′ sile) *adj*. This word applies to an animal's appendage which is capable of grasping an object. Elephants have *prehensile* trunks; monkeys have *prehensile* tails. Can it be said that Hitler had a *prehensile* attitude toward other nation's real estate? (Perhaps not, if we want to be strict about the proper use of words.) From Latin *prehensus*, a form of *prehendere* (to grasp).

presage (preh′ sij) *n*., *vb*. A *presage* is an omen, anything that foreshadows a coming event. Intermittent riots are sometimes a *presage* of a general uprising of the people. Improved economic conditions are often, but not always, a *presage* of a bull market. As a verb, to *presage* is to foreshadow, portend. Increasing devotion to a lady may *presage* an imminent proposal of marriage. From Latin *praesagium* (presage) and *praesagire* (to presage).

prescience (pree′ shee əns, presh′ ee əns, presh′ əns) *n. Prescience* is foreknowledge. People living close to the land have far more *prescience* of coming weather conditions than urban dwellers. An experienced lawyer has a good deal of *prescience* about the course of a lawsuit. *Prescient* (pronounced all three ways) is the adjective. Seers are *prescient*. The witches in *Macbeth* are *prescient*; they know exactly what is going to happen to Macbeth and the rest of the characters. From Latin *praesciens*, a form of *praescire* (to know beforehand).

presentiment (pree zent′ ə mənt) *n.* A *presentiment* is a feeling that something is about to happen, with the implication that the something is bad or evil; a foreboding. Some people, with nothing to base it on, have cancelled their plane reservations because of a *presentiment* that the flight was ill-fated. There are those who will refrain from investing because of a *presentiment* that nothing will come of the proposed venture. From Latin *praesentire* (to feel beforehand).

prestidigitator (pres tə dij′ ə tay tər) *n. Prestidigitators* are magicians, especially those practicing sleight of hand. *Prestidigitators* can make things appear and disappear at will. The word can be used figuratively, to indicate great or surprising skill: Some lawyers are regular *prestidigitators*; they can concoct a case or a defense out of no hard evidence at all. The art itself is called *prestidigitation* (pres tə dij ə tay′ shən). It helps to spice a children's party with a professional display of *prestidigitation*. When congress and the administration talk about budgets and deficits, they seem to be making huge sums arise or vanish as if by *prestidigitation*. From French *prestidigitateur* (magician), based on Latin *praesto* (ready) and *digitus* (finger).

prevaricate (prə var′ ə kate) *vb.* One shouldn't *prevaricate*: it means "to lie," or at least "to speak evasively." Some people can't tell a straight story; they would rather *prevaricate* than tell the simple truth. The word is just a shade less black and white than *lie*; it covers the making of equivocal or evasive statements for the purpose of misleading. This is seen from its origin in the Latin verb *praevaricari* (to walk crookedly), itself based on *varicari* (to straddle). This gives *prevaricate* the nuance of *hedging*, doing so in such a manner as to mislead. *Prevarication* (prə var ə kay′ shən), is the noun. A sworn witness's *prevarications*, even if not outright falsehoods, can still come dangerously close to perjury.

priapic (pry ap' ik) *adj*. This word, derived from the god Pria (pry ay' pəs) of Greek mythology, describes anyone or anythir over-concerned with male sexuality. Priapus, the son of Dionysus and Aphrodite, was the god of masculine reproductive power, and became the chief deity of lewdness and the personification of the male erection. Some men like to boast about their *priapic* conquests. Sailors are reputedly famous for their *priapic* episodes ashore (a girl in every port).

primogeniture (pry mə jen' ə chər) *n*. This is a system of inheritance under which the eldest son inherited all real property left by his parents, but if there were no sons, the eldest most closely related male inherited everything. How far women's rights have developed: all the way from *primogeniture* to virtual equality under the law! (You've come a long way, baby!) From Late Latin *primogenitura* (first birth).

primordial (pry mor' dee əl) *adj*. *Primordial* means "primeval, first to exist." Life on earth developed from the *primordial* ooze. Is it true that the entire universe originated from a *primordial* mass of gas? From Latin *primordium* (first beginning, origin).

privation (pry vay' shən) *n*. One suffering from *privation* lacks the necessities of life. Only those who themselves experience *privation* can really understand the terrible plight of the starving Cambodians. One really dedicated to the arts or science must be able to stand *privation*. From Latin *privatio* (taking away). Do not confuse *privation* with *deprivation*, which describes the act of withholding something from someone, or taking it away forcibly.

privy (prih' vee) *adj*. To be *privy* to something is to participate in the knowledge of something kept secret from the rest. Only good and trusted friends should be made *privy* to information you want to keep from the world at large. In a long and successful marriage, the couple seem to become *privy* to each other's unexpressed thoughts. The world still wonders whether anyone else was *privy* to Lee Harvey Oswald's plot to assassinate President Kennedy. From Latin *privatus* (private).

probity (pro' bə tee) *n*. *Probity* is honesty, integrity. Abraham Lincoln was a model of the utmost *probity*. Judicial opinions should reflect intellectual *probity*. From Latin *probitas* (uprightness, honesty).

clivity (pro kliv' ə tee) *n*. A *proclivity* toward something is inclination, tendency or proneness to it. Creative work in the sciences benefits from one's *proclivity* to painstaking research (nine-tenths perspiration and one-tenth inspiration). It is difficult to get children interested in an activity to which they have not the slightest *proclivity*. From Latin *proclivitas* (literally, slope; by extension, inclination).

procreate (pro' kree ate) *vb*. To *procreate* is to beget (offspring), to generate. There are those who believe that the only justification for sexual intercourse is to *procreate* the next generation. *Procreation* (pro kree ay' shən) is the noun. The human race shares eating, sleeping, and *procreation* with the rest of the animal word. *Procreant* (pro' kree ənt) is the adjective, describing the ability or tendency to *procreate*, as in the *procreant* breed of rabbits. Walt Whitman (1819–1892) wrote of "the *procreant* urge of the world." From Latin *procreatus*, a form of *procreare* (to beget).

prodigal (prod' ə gəl) *n., adj. Prodigal* (the adjective) has a number of different meanings. First, "recklessly extravagant, wasteful": The financial plight of our cities is the result of years of *prodigal* spending. This is the meaning of *prodigal* in the Biblical story of the *prodigal* son. Next, "lavish": Some people are generous to a fault, always *prodigal* with entertainment and gifts. Finally, "profuse, abundant": In the autumn whole areas are beautified by nature's *prodigal* display of color. From Latin *prodigus* (profuse, extravagant). As to the first meaning, cf. *profligate*. As a noun, it means "one who is *prodigal*."

prodigious (prə dij' əs) *adj*. This word can mean either "enormous" or "amazing, marvelous," depending on the context. Christina Onassis parted with a share of her *prodigious* legacy in favor of her stepmother. Some people spend *prodigious* sums on the maintenance of their yachts. (J. P. Morgan is said to have replied to a question about the cost of operating a yacht: "If you have to ask, you can't afford it.") The rescue at Entebbe was a *prodigious* achievement. Man's first step on the moon was a *prodigious* event. From Latin *prodigiosus* (unnatural; strange; wonderful). The related noun *prodigy* (prod' ə jee) can mean an amazing or wonderful example, as in a *prodigy* of courage, a *prodigy* of knowledge, but its most common use is to describe a person (usually a young person) endowed with an extraordinary gift: Yehudi Menuhin was a musical *prodigy*. Queen Elizabeth I was fluent in Latin and Greek before she was ten; she was a linguistic *prodigy*. *Child prodigy* is a common expression. *Prodigy* comes from Latin *prodigium* (prodigy).

prodigy (prod' ə jee). See **prodigious**.

profane (prə fane') *vb., adj.* As a verb, *profane* means "defile." The barbarians who invaded ancient Rome *profaned* the shrines of the people. One of the twelve "good rules" ascribed to Charles I: "*Profane* no divine ordinances." As an adjective, *profane* can mean either "secular" (as opposed to *sacred*) or "blasphemous, irreverent," depending on the context. In the phrase "sacred and *profane* love," *profane* means "secular." John Bunyan (1628–1688), in *Pilgrim's Progress*, wrote "I will talk of the heavenly, or things earthly; . . . things sacred, or things *profane* . . . ." *Profane* means "blasphemous, irreverent" in usages like this: Upton Sinclair (1878–1968) defied God in the most *profane* and provocative terms. Nixon's tapes are replete with *profane* expletives. The noun *profanity* (prə fan' ə tee) is generally understood to mean "*profane* language." The adjective comes from Latin *profanus*, a combination of *pro* (in front i.e., outside) and *fanum* (temple); outside a temple, hence, not sacred, therefore *profane*, in the sense of "secular." The verb comes from the related Latin verb *profanare* (to profane).

profligate (prof' lə gət) *n., adj.* This word, as an adjective, has two separate meanings: "utterly immoral" and "recklessly extravagant." It can be applied to cases of shameless corruption and vice, without reference to extravagance, or to wild and reckless spending, without reference to vice and immorality, depending on the context. One can speak of a *profligate* person, or simply of a *profligate*, using the word as a noun. In either case, it is a very strong word, not to be used lightly. The Indian maharajahs of olden days had such countless wealth that they could go on being *profligate* without seriously depleting their resources. In *The Picture of Dorian Gray*, Oscar Wilde (1854–1900) depicted a person who became more and more *profligate* under the malign influence of an evil friend. Caligula (A.D. 12–41), the notorious and dissolute Roman emperor, was *profligate* in both senses of the word; there was no limit to either his depravity or his spending. *Profligacy* (prof' lə gə see) is the state of being *profligate* in either sense, "shameless dissipation" or "wild extravagance," but it has still a further meaning: "abundance, lavishness." Thus, one can speak of the *profligacy of nature*, referring to the lavishness of her gifts. Cf. *prodigal*, in its meaning of "profuse, abundant." From Latin *profligatus* (ruined, degraded), a form of *profligare* (literally, to overthrow; by extension to debase). The related Roman noun *profligator* was used in the sense of "spendthrift." The two distinct meanings of *profligate* surely reflect the puritan attitude that reckless spending is in itself immoral.

prognosis (prog no' səs). *n.* See **prognosticate**.

prognosticate (prog nos' tə kate) *vb.* To *prognosticate* is to forecast. From a study of the past action of a stock on the Big Board, investors and analysts think they are able to *prognosticate* its future (depending, of course, on "developments"). *Prognosis* (prog no' səs) is a related word, meaning "forecast, prediction." Its most frequent use is in medicine: the doctor's *prognosis* is his forecast of the probable course of a disease (the *prognosis* is guarded). *Prognosticate* comes from the Middle Latin *prognosticatus*, a form of *prognosticare* (to forecast). *Prognosis* comes from Late Latin *prognosis*. Both are based upon Greek *prognoskein* (to know ahead of time).

proliferate (pro lif' ə rate) *vb.* To *proliferate* is to multiply, spread; literally, to grow (as in budding or cell division) by multiplication of parts; figuratively, to expand. Fears *proliferate* as a result of rumors without facts. Flowers and vegetables should be fertilized and carefully tended; weeds *proliferate* wildly without benefit of any human agency. From Middle Latin *prolifer* (bearing young). The related adjective *prolific* (prə lif' ik) describes anyone or anything producing great quantities, such as a *prolific* apple tree; a *prolific* playwright. Richard Rodgers (1902–1979) and Irving Berlin (b. 1888), are two of America's most *prolific* songwriters. From Middle Latin *prolificus*.

prolific (prə lif' ik). *adj.* See **proliferate**.

prolix (pro liks', pro' liks) *adj. Prolix* people or writings are wordy and tedious, long-winded. *Prolix* speakers, far from exciting their audiences, tend to put them to sleep. There are *prolix* memoirs running hundreds and hundreds of pages which might properly compressed into one-tenth their size. From Latin *prolixus* (widely extended).

prone (prone) *adj*. *Prone* can be used in its literal sense of "lying face downward" (the opposite of *supine*), or in its figurative sense of "inclined, disposed." Practice at a firing range is done from upright, kneeling, and *prone* positions. In the figurative sense: Irascible people are easily upset and *prone* to wrath. Non-achievers are *prone* to envy and rationalization. From Latin *pronus* (inclined forward).

propensity (prǝ pen' sǝ tee) *n*. A *propensity* to something is an inclination or tendency to it. This word is used, for the most part, in connection with the less desirable traits. One would hardly say that Jones had a *propensity* to tell the truth, but it would be natural to say that Smith had a *propensity* to lie. People in tropical countries seem to accomplish less because of a natural *propensity* to indolence. (Wouldn't all people act that way under an endlessly blazing sun?) From Latin *propensio* (inclination), related to *propensus*, a form of *propendere* (literally, to hang down; by extension, to be inclined to).

prophylactic (pro fǝ lak' tik) *n. adj*. As an adjective, *prophylactic* means "preventive," and is descriptive of anything that prevents disease, like a medication. Doctors depend heavily on the *prophylactic* effect of antibiotics to prevent the worsening of a condition. Vaccination is *prophylactic* in the sense of entirely circumventing an affliction. As a noun it applies generally to any preventive, but has a special use as a synonym for *condom*. From Greek *prophylaktikos* (guarding in advance).

propinquity (prǝ pingk' wǝ tee) *n*. *Propinquity* is nearness, whether in space or time. The *propinquity* of an airport to one's home may be convenient at times, but it can also cause a great loss of sleep. A house is often made dark by the *propinquity* of great trees. The *propinquity* of events can make them look like cause and effect when there is no causal relationship between them. From Latin *propinquitas* (proximity), based on *propinquus* (near).

propitiate (prǝ pish' ee ate). *vb*. See **propitious**.

propitious (prǝ pish' ǝs) *adj*. Things that are *propitious* to or for something are favorable to it. Before setting out on a journey, it is a good idea to find out whether the weather report seems *propitious*. In the early days of the Great Society, propounded by

Lyndon Johnson, conditions seemed *propitious* for the relief of the needy. The negative adjective *unpropitious* means, logically enough, "unfavorable," but it is most often used in the sense of "not favorably timed": The announcement of the firm's impending bankruptcy is a most *unpropitious* moment to ask for a raise. The depression of the early thirties made that period *unpropitious* for Republican incumbents seeking reelection. *Propitious* comes from Latin *propitius* (favorable). The related verb *to propitiate* (prə pish' ee ate) means "to make favorable," i.e., "to appease." The ancients made elaborate sacrifices in order to *propitiate* the gods before embarking on important ventures. From Latin *propitiatus*, a form of *propitiare* (to soothe, appease).

proprietary (prə pry' ə terr ee) *adj*. In its general use, this adjective has to do with ownership. A *proprietary interest* denotes ownership of the whole or a part of something. A *proprietary feeling* is a feeling of ownership: A tenant who has lived in a rented house for a great many years develops a *proprietary* attitude toward it. A special use is to describe articles made and sold by a particular company, usually under a patent or a trademark or both, such as *proprietary medicines*. In this sense it is the exact opposite of *generic* as applied to medicines. (See *generic* in this connection.) From Late Latin *proprietarius* (relating to ownership), which came from Latin *proprietas* (meaning property, ownership).

prosaic (pro zay' ik) *adj*. *Prosaic* means "commonplace." This word describes people and things that are dull, uninspired, and uninspiring, humdrum, run of the mill, as opposed to *poetic*, a usage based on the assumption that prose, in general, is less inspired or romantic than poetry. There are, however, many examples to the contrary. The prose of the Gettysburg Address is much less *prosaic* than the poetry of greeting cards. Despite attempts at enthusiasm, corporate annual reports are written in the most *prosaic* of language. The conversation at most country clubs is maddeningly trivial and *prosaic*. From Middle Latin *prosaicus*, based on Latin *prosus* (straightforward).

proselytize (pros' ə lə tize) *vb*. To *proselytize* is to convert (someone) to a new religion, political party, school of thought, etc.; in this sense, to recruit. A person so converted is a *proselyte* (pros' ə lite). Missionaries are in the business of *proselytizing*. Anyone pressing his beliefs upon you is attempting to *proselytize* you. *Proselyte* is from Late Latin *proselytus*, derived from Greek *proselytos* (newcomer). *Proselytize* merely added the verbal *-ize*.

protean (pro' tee ən, pro tee' ən) *adj.* This interesting word, in its literal sense, describes one who is capable of quickly assuming many different forms: figuratively, it means "versatile." Proteus (Pro' tyoos), in ancient Greek legends, was herdsman to the god Neptune. He was an old prophet, able to take on different shapes at will. Hence the adjective *protean*, meaning "ever-changing, variable, versatile." It can be used literally to describe an ameba, which constantly assumes different shapes, but its common use is the figurative one. Laurence Olivier is a *protean* actor—he can play anything from the song-and-dance man in *The Entertainer* to the tragic lead in *Oedipus* or *Othello*. The winner of the decathlon must be a *protean* athlete. The term "Renaissance man" describes a person of *protean* capabilities, skilled in many diverse activities.

protracted (pro trakt' əd) *adj.* To *protract* is to prolong, extend, and a *protracted* meeting or session is one that takes a long time. Most court trials are unduly *protracted* because of jury challenges and later on by endless objections and arguments about admissibility of evidence. The most glaring example possible of a *protracted* speech is a filibuster in Congress or the Senate. *Protracted* implies extensive prolongation. Most sessions at the dentist's seem *protracted* to the patient with his mouth full of paraphernalia. From Latin *protractus*, a form of *protrahere* (to drag on, protract).

proviso (prə vy' zo) *n.* A *proviso* is a reservation, like a clause (usually in a written document, such as a contract or a warranty) that establishes a limiting condition. The word *provision* covers any clause; *proviso* usually sets up a special condition that somehow restricts the operation of another provision. A person can undertake to provide certain services, with the *proviso* that he is still in the employ of the same company. Many contracts contain the *proviso* that there will be no liability for failure to perform in the event of war. From Middle Latin *proviso*, a form of Latin *providere* (to see beforehand, to provide for).

prowess (prow' əs—*ow* as in *owl*) *n.* *Prowess* is exceptional ability or great daring. *Prowess* on the battlefield implies gallantry and daring. The common use is to denote great ability: *Prowess* as a speaker makes one a good debater. The records show that victory on the football field depends largely on the *prowess* of the quarterback. From Old French *prouesse*, which developed into Middle English *prowesse*.

prurient (proor' ee ənt—*oo* as in *look*) *adj. Prurient* people are those who have, or are easily susceptible to, lewd thoughts. Feminine underwear advertisements titillate *prurient* men. *Prurient* people look for a sex angle in every situation. *Prurience* (proor' ee əns) is the noun. *Prurience* is the basis of the voyeur's delight. From Latin *pruriens*, a form of *prurire* (to itch, long for, be lustful).

puckish (puck' ish) *adj.* A *puckish* person is impish, mischievous, whimsical. Puck, whose other names are Hobgoblin and Robin Goodfellow, is the mischievous spirit who is so active in Shakespeare's *A Midsummer Night's Dream.* He got his name from the old common noun *puck,* now almost never used, meaning "mischievous sprite, imp, hobgoblin." *Puckish* people can brighten up any party. A woman's *puckish* little crinkled smile can break a man's heart even if she isn't a raving beauty. *Puckish* comments at a town meeting can shock the staid older folks. *Puck* is from Middle English *pouke,* taken from Old English *puca;* cf. Icelandic *puki* (mischievous demon).

puerile (pyoo' ər ile, pyoo' ər il—*oo* as in *noon*) *adj.* People who are childish, immature and silly qualify for this pejorative adjective. The philosopher George Santayana (1863–1952) said: "Mocking is the first *puerile* form of wit, playing with surfaces without sympathy." Boasting is often only a *puerile* striving for admiration. Teachers can spot an immature mind from the *puerile* style of an essay. From Latin *puerilis* (boyish, childish, silly), based on *puer* (boy).

pugnacious (pug nay' shəs) *adj. Pugnacious* people are belligerent, always ready for a fight, quarrelsome. You can't have a sensible argument with a *pugnacious* person. People with an inferiority complex are often *pugnacious* on the theory that the best defense is an offense. The Doberman pinscher is said to be the most *pugnacious* of dogs. From Latin *pugnacis,* a form of *pugnax* (fond of fighting), based on *pugna* (battle); cf. Latin *pugnus* (fist).

pulchritude (pul' krə tood, pul' krə tyood—*oo* as in *noon*) *n. Pulchritude* is beauty, found often in the phrase *feminine pulchritude.* In a well-performed ballet, the prima ballerina and her corps de ballet present a spectacle of the utmost *pulchritude. Pulchritude* in a woman is God's gift to man. From Latin *pulchritudo* (beauty, excellence), based on *pulcher* (beautiful).

pummel (pum′ əl) *vb.* When you *pummel* someone, you beat him with your fists. The word has an interesting derivation. *Pomum* is Latin for "fruit," and gave rise to Vulgar Latin *pomellum* (ball); that was shortened to *pommel* as the name of the ball terminating the hilt of a sword. When you beat your opponent with the *pommel* of your sword, in the old days, you *pommeled* him. Then when swords became less common and you beat the other fellow with your bare fists, you were still said to be *pommeling* him, and *pommel* gave way to its commoner variant, *pummel*. Regardless of this long derivation, it is highly unpleasant to be *pummeled*. *Pummel* seems somehow to evoke the image of a woman, especially a little woman, going at a big man until he yells, "Uncle!"

punctilious (pungk til′ ee əs) *adj.* A *punctilious* person is one who is extremely strict in observing all the formalities and generally attentive and conscientious. It is comforting to know that your employees are *punctilious* in their attention to the requirements of their jobs. Old-fashioned ladies are particularly pleased when a man is *punctilious* in performing the duties of an escort. *Punctilio* (pungk til′ ee oh) is the noun, and comes from Italian *puntiglio* and Spanish *puntillo*. *Punto* means "point" in both those languages; in Spanish, *-illo* is a diminutive ending, so that *puntillo* means "small point." *Punctilio*, then, is attention to the small points (of conduct). All these words originate in Latin *punctum* (point).

pundit (pun′ dit) *n.* This is the name given to an expert, an authority on a subject, especially one given to holding forth and making authoritative pronouncements. Newspaper *pundits* on competing journals often disagree with one another on everything from the likelihood of war to the best way to make cherry pie. Most of the music *pundits* of the day rejected *Carmen*, the great opera by Georges Bizet (1838–1875), as a negligible piece of musical superficiality. *Pundit* is often used in a semi-jocular, semi-pejorative sense, implying that critics and "experts" are not the source of all wisdom. *Pundit* is taken over from Hindi *pandit* (learned, or learned man).

purgative (pur′ gə tiv) *n., adj.* *Purgative*, as an adjective, means "cleansing," especially of the bowels; as a noun, a "cathartic" or "laxative," or any medicine that has that effect. *Purgative* can be used in a more abstract sense: Confession acts as a *purgative* from sin. *Purgative* is related to the verb *to purge* (cleanse, rid, clear out, eliminate) and comes from Late Latin *purgativus*, based on Latin *purgatus*, a form of *purgare* (to clean, cleanse), based in turn on *purus* (clean, pure).

purloin (pər loin', pur' loin) *vb.* To *purloin* is to steal or filch. The word became familiar from the title of a well-known story by Edgar Allen Poe (1809–1849), *The Purloined Letter. Purloin* implies misappropriation, a breach of trust. Confidential documents *purloined* by those in a position of trust with access to the files are often the source of leaks to the newspapers. Jewelers have been known to *purloin* gems out of jewelry left with them for cleaning, substituting imitation stones for the genuine ones. From Middle English *purloinen*, via Old French from Latin prefix *pro-* plus *longe* (a long way off).

pusillanimous (pyoo sə lan' ə məs) *adj.* A *pusillanimous* person is cowardly, timid, afraid of his own shadow. Walter Mitty, the creation of James Thurber (1894–1961), is the personification of the *pusillanimous* man. Being careful and biding one's time is not necessarily *pusillanimous. Pusillanimous* people are afraid to stand up and be counted, the kind who were willing to name names before the Un-American Activities Committee. From Late Latin *pusillanimis* (mean-spirited), based on Latin *pusillus* (tiny, puny) plus *animus* (spirit).

putative (pyoo' tə tiv) *adj. Putative* is the equivalent of "thought to be, generally regarded as, supposed." In the absence of documentary proof of the relationship, a man can be regarded, under proper circumstances, as a person's *putative* father. Some people coast along on the basis of their *putative* ability. *Putative marriage* involves a special usage: one that is entered into in good faith, though legally invalid, as in the case of a mistaken belief that a former spouse of one of the parties is dead. From Late Latin *putativus*, based on Latin *putatus*, a form of *putare* (to think).

quaff (kwahf, kwaf) *vb.* To *quaff* is to drink heartily, in long drafts (like those virile men in the beer commercials). Some like to pass a whole evening in a cozy pub, *quaffing* all the ale their money can buy. At some dinner parties, toast after toast is an excuse for *quaffing* one drink after another. *Quaff* implies that what is quaffed is intoxicating liquor. Sir Francis Doyle

(1810–1888), in a poem about an English private in the Buffs (a former East Kent regiment), wrote:

> *Last night, among his fellow roughs,*
> *He jested,* quaffed, *and swore.*

Derivation unknown.

quagmire (kwag' mire) *n*. A *quagmire* is, literally, a bog or marsh; figuratively, any situation from which it is difficult to extricate oneself. Rains will turn tilled land into a *quagmire*. In easy stages, we got ourselves stuck in the *quagmire* of the Vietnam War. The SALT talks appear to be a veritable *quagmire* of negotiation. From a combination of *quag-* (dialectal variant of *quake*) and *mire*, which comes from Icelandic *myrr* (marsh).

quail (kwale) *vb*. To *quail* is to flinch or to cower. The strongest courtiers *quailed* before the wrath of Queen Elizabeth I. In Victorian tales about harsh treatment at schools and orphanages, the pupils or inmates always *quail* as the schoolmaster or orphanage owner enters the room. George, later Duke of Clarence, in Shakespeare's Henry VI, Part Three (act II, scene 3), suggests rewards to those who remain faithful to the cause of Richard, Duke of York and says, "This may plant courage in their *quailing* breasts . . . ." From Middle English *quailen*.

qualm (kwahm) *n*. This word can mean either a "pang of conscience" or a "misgiving," depending on the context. In the sense of "pang of conscience" it is often used in the plural, in a negative way: Some people can just sit there and fabricate an entire story, with no *qualms* about the possible effects of the lie. There are those who have no *qualms* about biting the hand that feeds them. *Qualm* can be used in the singular, in an affirmative sentence as well: People do sometimes feel a *qualm* or two when they don't tell the entire truth in their income tax returns. Meaning "misgiving": One sometimes feels a sudden *qualm* about having entered into a marriage or a partnership that seemed so encouraging at first. Derivation unknown.

quandary (kwon' dree) *n*. This is another word for "dilemma," and is an apt way to describe any state of perplexity. On a motor trip, people are often in a *quandary* about whether to take the direct route or the scenic one. When a company is losing money, the owners face the *quandary* about shutting down and putting faithful old workers out of their jobs or continuing in the red. Derivation unknown.

quarry (kwor' ee) *n.* Literally, *quarry* describes a hunted animal, fish, flesh or fowl. Small birds are hawks' *quarry*. In nature, predators are engaged in a never-ending search for *quarry*. The word can be used figuratively to signify anything hunted. Conscientious police keep after their *quarry* with grim determination. Gold ingots on sunken ships are the most prized *quarry* of treasure hunters. The Egyptologist Howard Carter (1873–1939) rejoiced when he at last, in 1922, came upon his long-sought *quarry*: the tomb of Tutankhamen and all its glorious treasures. From Old French *cuiree* (skin, hide), which came from Latin *corium* (hide. (The other kind of *quarry*, where stone is excavated and squared, comes from Vulgar Latin *quadraria*, based on Latin *quadrare* [to square].)

quash (kwahsh) *vb.* In the legal sense, to *quash* is to annul. Convictions are sometimes *quashed* in the appeals court. Indictments can be *quashed* on the presentation of new evidence clearing the accused. In a more general sense, to *quash* is to suppress or quell. During troubled times at the colleges, the university authorities sometimes called in the police to *quash* student riots. Time and again, we read of armies in Third World countries quickly and effectively *quashing* uprisings. From Latin *quassare* (to shatter).

quaver (kway' vər) *vb.* This word has three distinct meanings. First; "to tremble": People on safari, on seeing their first lion, often freeze and *quaver* with terror. In this sense, *quaver* and *quiver* are a matter of choice. Next; "to sing or speak tremulously": At the first sight of a long-lost relative, people's voices usually *quaver* while the tears flow. Finally, in music, "to trill": The *quavering* of a coloratura often brings down the house. From Middle English *quaveren*.

quay (kee) *n.* Wharf. *Quay* was formerly spelled *key* and is still pronounced that way. The spelling was influenced by the French noun *quai* (wharf), the most famous of which is the Quai d'Orsay along the River Seine in Paris, where the French Foreign Office is located. The name *Quai d'Orsay* is the nickname of the French Foreign Office (like *the Hill* for the U.S. Congress). Derived from Old French *cay* (wharf). A *quay* is a strengthened bank or man-made stretch of stone along a waterway for the loading and unloading of ships. Sometimes longshoremen will stand along a *quay* refusing to unload a ship as a protest against the political acts of its country of origin.

quell (kwel) *vb.* This word can mean either "to suppress" or "to allay, to quiet," depending on the context. When you read that "the police quickly *quelled* the incipient riot" or that "the army *quelled* the uprising," you are being told that whatever the disturbance was it was effectively ended. When a doctor *quells* his patient's anxiety by minimizing the importance of an ache or a discoloration, or a daddy *quells* his child's fear of darkness by assuring him that the noises he has heard were being made only by the wind, the person doing the *quelling* is not suppressing anything, but rather allaying or relieving it. From Middle English *quellen*, based on Old English *cwellen* (to kill).

querulous (kwehr' ə ləs) *adj.* *Querulous* people are unpleasant company, because *querulous* means "complaining, grumbling." The Latin poet Horace (65–8 B.C.) described the aging man who praised the good old days and complained about the younger generation (sounds contemporary, doesn't it?) as *difficilis* (from which we got *difficult*) and *querulus* (in the sense of *testy*). In *Pride and Prejudice*, Jane Austen (1775–1817) referred to a character's "usual *querulous* serenity," and H.L. Mencken (1880–1956) wrote that "all successful newspapers are ceaselessly *querulous*...." From Latin *querulus*, which also gave us *quarrel*.

query (kwir' ee) *n., vb.* As a noun, *query* can mean either "question" or "mental reservation." In the first sense: In administrative offices of the government, it is usually rather difficult to get clear answers to your *queries* about the proper procedure. In the other sense: A confused explanation may be acceptable in general, subject to a few *queries* as to aspects to be investigated at a later time. As a verb, *to query* can mean "to inquire about" or "to raise a doubt or question about; to challenge as obscure or doubtful," or "to put questions to, to question directly." In the first sense: When a stranger is lurking about, it is normal and proper to *query* the reason for his presence. Next: It is not at all unusual, at a club or directors' meeting, to *query* items in the treasurer's report. Traveling salesmen don't like to have their expense accounts *queried*. Finally: Public officials must be prepared to be *queried* about their financial dealings. From Latin *quaerere* (to seek, to ask), which gave rise to Latin *inquirere* (to search for, investigate) from which we get *inquire*.

queue (kyoo) *n., vb.* *Queue*, as a noun, denotes a line of people waiting to take their turn. Englishmen quite contentedly form *queues*, at taxi stands, in shops, and the like, rather than scramble to be first in line. (Englishmen like *queues*. It is said that when an Englishman comes upon the tail-end of a *queue* whose purpose is obscure, he joins it automatically, just for the fun of it.) *To queue* is to form a line while waiting turn. Sometimes the expression is *queue up*, but this is substandard. A sign reading FORM LINE HERE in America would more likely read PLEASE QUEUE HERE in Britain. *Queue* is taken over intact from the French, where it means literally "tail," and by extension, *queue* as in English; from Latin *cauda* or *coda* (tail).

quiescent (kwy ess' ənt, kwee ess' ənt) *adj*. When things are *quiescent* they are at rest, inactive. As old age develops, both mind and body grow *quiescent* (or should). When a doctor reassures you that that ache or pain or other symptom "doesn't mean anything," your fears gradually become *quiescent*. From Latin *quiescens*, a form of *quiescere* (to rest).

quintessence (kwin tes' ənce) *n*. Depending on the context, this word can denote either "the essential part" of something or its "embodiment." In the first meaning: The *quintessence* of Darwin's theory is the survival of the fittest. The *quintessence* of man is his ability to think in the abstract. In the sense of "embodiment": Sir Galahad represented the *quintessence* of chivalry and purity. Melody is the *quintessence* of music. The devil is the *quintessence* of evil. Quisling was the *quintessence* of treason. In the Middle Ages, the universe was believed to consist of four elements: air, fire, earth, and water, and the heavenly bodies to consist of ether, the fifth and highest element. *Fifth element* was *quinta essentia* in Middle Latin; hence *quintessence*.

quixotic (kwik sot' ik) *adj*. *Quixotic*, meaning "impractical, visionary," is one of those adjectives (like *herculean*, from Hercules, and *machiavellian*, from Machiavelli) formed from the name of a character in legend, literature, or history; in this case, Don *Quixote*, the super-chivalrous and idealistic but totally impractical hero of the novel of that name by Miguel de Cervantes (1547–1616). (Simon Bolivar (1783–1830) is said to have written: "The three greatest dolts in the world: Jesus Christ, Don *Quixote* and I.") It is *quixotic* to think that the incipient reform movement can, in one fell swoop, purge the city government of waste and corruption. Some incredible projects, like the Entebbe rescue, turn out to be not so *quixotic* after all.

quizzical (kwiz′ ə kəl) *adj.* A *quizzical* look or expression is one that indicates gentle amusement; somewhat puzzled, marked by a bantering air and a degree of mockery; perhaps derisively questioning; usually whimsical. The great actor John Barrymore (1882–1942), with his raised eyebrows and gently mocking way, was famous for his *quizzical* expression and manner. The English are given to *quizzical* understatement and self-mockery. This expressive word is based on *quiz* (to question—derivation unknown) plus adjectival ending *-ical*.

raconteur (rak on tur′) *n.* A *raconteur* is a skilled teller of anecdotes, an interesting storyteller. A skillful *raconteur* is a welcome guest at any gathering. An inexhaustible store of fascinating anecdotes makes one a gifted *raconteur*. If the person in question is a female, the word becomes *raconteuse* (rak on teuz′—*eu* like the *e* in *her*). Taken over intact from the French, where *raconter* means "to narrate."

raffish (raf′ ish) *adj. Raffish* is an unpleasant word, describing people who are low-class, crude, rakish, disreputable. You can tell by an individual's vulgar attire and manner that he is a *raffish* type, crude, with no class at all. *Raffish* fellows, with their devil-may-care attitude and rakish apparel and hairdos, are hardly the sort you'd want to spend an evening with. From *raff*, part of *riff-raff*, which is from Middle English *rif and raf* (things of little value).

rake (rake) *n.* A *rake* is a dissolute person. An example of the awful fate awaiting *rakes* is found in *The Rake's Progress*, a series of paintings and engravings by William Hogarth (1697–1764) and the ballet set by Sir Robert Helpmann (b. 1907) to the opera of that name by Igor Stravinsky (1882–1971). One who lives the life of the perfect *rake*, drinking, gambling, whoring, living off his friends, will come to an untimely end, if the Victorian novelists and playwrights can be believed. (In contemporary literature it ain't necessarily so.) The adjective *rakish* has none of the pejorative quality of the noun *rake*. It is much more innocent, meaning only "dashing" or "jaunty." To give themselves an appearance of smartness, some men wear their hats at a *rakish* angle. Maurice Chevalier (1888–1972) won over his public by his charm and his *rakish* manner. Short for *rakehell*, from Middle English *rakel* (rash, coarse).

rambunctious (ram bungk' shəs) *adj. Rambunctious* means "extremely boisterous, hard to manage" or "noisy and over-active," depending on the context. Obviously, in certain cases it can mean both at the same time. We are all too familiar with the *rambunctious* child who ruins the carefully prepared dinner party or other social event. Parties that start out as pleasant get-togethers can, when stimulated by a few drinks too many, get *rambunctious* and out of hand. From Icelandic intensive prefix *ram-* (very) plus *bumptious* (irritatingly self-assertive).

rancor (rangk' ər) *n. Rancor* is bitter, rankling resentment and ill will. The injuries done to a person in his youth, whether real or fancied, may leave him with a never-ending *rancor. Rancor* has existed between France and Germany for ages. From Middle English *rancour*, which came from Late Latin *rancor* (rancidity, and by extension, grudge) based on Latin *rancere* (to be rancid, to stink).

rankle (rangk' əl) *vb.* To *rankle* is to cause lasting, bitter resentment and annoyance. An insult may *rankle* within you for days and days. *Rankle* can take a direct object: Careless handling of a delicate assignment may *rankle* the boss for weeks. From Middle English *ranclen* (to fester), based on Old French *draoncler*, believed to come from Late Latin *dracunculus* (little serpent), based on Latin *draco* (serpent), from which we get *dragon.* (Apparently little dragons keep wriggling in your bosom when you are *rankled.*)

rapacious (rə pay' shəs) *adj.* A *rapacious* person is greedy, grasping, ready to seize whatever he can. During the Gold Rush of 1849, the *rapacious* prospectors practically trampled each other to stake out their claims. The *rapacious* Hitler wanted the world. Sometimes it seems that *rapacious* conglomerates want to gobble up every company in sight. From Latin *rapacis*, a form of *rapix* (greedy), based on *rapere* (to seize, snatch), which also gave us *rape.* See *rapt.*

rapt (rapt) *adj.* When you are *rapt*, you are absorbed and enraptured. When people are *rapt* in transcendental meditation, nothing disturbs them. A virtuoso's concentration on his performance leaves him with a *rapt* expression. A brilliant lecturer can keep his audience in *rapt* attention. *Rapt* gave us the word *rapture.* From Latin *raptus*, a form of *rapere* (to seize, snatch, tear away), from which we also get *rape.* Cf. *rapacious.*

recalcitrant (rih kal' sə trənt) *adj.* A person who resists authority and is hard to deal with or unmanageable is *recalcitrant*. Sometimes it's necessary to use harsh measures in dealing with *recalcitrant* children. The southern states were *recalcitrant* in insisting on their right to continue slavery. From Latin *recalcitrans*, a form of Latin *recalcitrare* (of a horse—to kick back; figuratively, to deny access). Cf. *refractory*.

recant (rih kant') *vb.* To *recant* something is to disavow it. Joan of Arc refused to *recant* her visions. A witness who *recants* his previous sworn testimony faces the risk of a conviction for perjury. From Latin *recantare* (to recall, recant).

recapitulate (ree kə pich' ə late) *vb.* To *recapitulate* is to summarize. At the end of any long and complicated presentation, especially an oral one, it is advisable to *recapitulate* for the benefit of one's audience. The noun is *recapitulation* (ree kə pich ə lay' shən). A lawyer's *recapitulation* should be brief and put the issues squarely before the judge and jury. From Late Latin *recapitulatus*, a form of *recapitulare* (to summarize), based on Latin *capitulatim* (briefly).

recidivism (rə sid' ə viz əm) *n.* This word means "repeated, habitual backsliding, relapse," especially into criminal, antisocial or other undesirable behavior. Prison statistics show an average *recidivism* rate as high as eighty percent. The unfortunate person so affected is known as a "recidivist," and that word serves as an adjective as well. *Recidivists*, despite the valiant attempts of our social agencies, present society with a seemingly incurable problem. From Latin *recidere* (to fall back).

reclusive (rih kloo' siv—*oo* as in *noon*) *adj.* A *reclusive* person is one who prefers to live alone, avoiding social contact. People who live a *reclusive* life are unaware of what is happening around them. *Reclusive* persons tend to become forgotten and ignored by society. Bereavement causes some people to retire from the social scene and grow melancholy and *reclusive*. *Recluse* (rih kloos') is an uncommon variant of the adjective. As a noun, spelled the same way, but pronounced differently (rek' loos), *recluse* means "a *reclusive* person, a loner." Examples of famous recluses are Howard Hughes (1905–1976) and Greta Garbo (b. 1906). Both words from Late Latin *reclusus* (shut up), based on Latin prefix *re-* and *clusus*, a form of Latin *cludere* (to shut).

recondite (rek' ən dite, rə kon' dite) *adj.* Anything *recondite* is hard to understand, profound, requiring high intelligence to grasp. The concepts underlying the theory of relativity are much too *recondite* for the average man. Applicants for the degree of Ph.D. often write *recondite* treatises, never read except by the examiners. From Latin *reconditus*, a form of Latin *recondere* (to hide).

reconnoiter (ree kə noy' tər, rek ə noy' tər) *vb.* This term started out, and still comes to mind, as a type of military maneuver, to inspect the terrain and get as much information as possible about the strength, position, etc. of enemy forces. It is used quite generally, however, to express the idea of exploring any situation where advance information might be useful. Before setting out on a picnic, it is a good idea to *reconnoiter* the site to see whether it is suitable in every respect. It is always well to do a bit of *reconnoitering* before embarking on any hazardous enterprise. From Middle French *reconoistre*, derived from Latin *recognoscere* (to inspect, investigate).

rectify (rek' tə fy) *vb.* To *rectify* something is to correct it, to put it right. Inaccurate newspaper accounts are all too infrequently *rectified* despite later and more complete information. It is sometimes necessary to *rectify* an overdrawn bank account by making a deposit. Sir John Suckling (1609–1642) wrote: "...when an authentic watch is shown each man winds up and *rectifies* his own...." From Middle Latin *rectificare* (to correct), based on Latin *rectus* (correct).

rectitude (rek' tə tood, rek' tə tyood—*oo* as an *boot*) *n.* *Rectitude* is righteousness, the strict observance of integrity and adherence to a high moral code. We are inspired by leaders like Abraham Lincoln, whose every act was motivated by his *rectitude*. If *rectitude* governed nations, there would be eternal peace on earth. The word has occasionally been used to mean "correctness of judgment." Galileo was absolutely convinced of his *rectitude* in determining that the earth revolved around the sun. (This is not the usual sense of the word.) From Late Latin *rectitudo*, based on Latin *rectus* (straight).

redolent (red' ə lənt) *adj.* *Redolent* means "smelling of," when the adjective is followed by a description of the source of the odor, or "sweet-smelling" when the fragrance is self-evident.

Club cars on railroad trains are *redolent* of stale tobacco smoke and the fumes of alcohol. It is pleasant to walk hand-in-hand through a *redolent* meadow. From Latin *redolens*, a form of *redolere* (to emit an odor, smell of).

redoubtable (rih dowt' ə bəl) *adj.* *Redoubtable* means "formidable," especially with reference to an adversary. Though you have little hope of winning, it must be an exciting challenge to face a *redoubtable* chess champion like Bobby Fischer or a tennis great like Bjorn Borg. When *redoubtable* lawyers face each other, the courtroom is filled with drama. From Middle English *redoutable*, based on Middle French *redouter* (to fear). *Douter* was Old French, and was from Latin *dubitare* (to waver) which gave us *doubt*. Somehow the *b* in *dubitare* found its way into the *-doubt-* in *redoubtable*.

redress (ree' dres, rih dres') *n.*, (rih dres') *vb.* *Redress* is the setting right of something that is wrong. Full back pay is the usual form of *redress* to one who has been wrongfully suspended from his job without pay. As a verb *to redress* is to right a wrong, either by compensating the victim or by eliminating the original cause of the injury. The Ayatollah Khomeini's steps taken to *redress* the abuses of the Shah's regime have been extreme: who will *redress* them? From Middle English *redressen*, taken from Old French *redrecier*, based on *drecier* (to straighten).

refractory (rih frak' tə ree) *adj.* A *refractory* person is difficult or impossible to manage, stubbornly resistant to authority. It is difficult to determine whether harshness or kindness is the better way for a prison warden to deal with *refractory* inmates. *Refractory* children can spoil a family picnic. When a metal is described as *refractory*, it means it has a high melting-point and is hard to fuse or work. From Latin *refractarius* (stubborn), based on *refractus*, a form of *refragari* (to oppose, thwart). Cf. *recalcitrant*, a synonym.

refulgent (rih ful' jənt—*u* as in *but*) *adj.* Anything *refulgent* is radiant, shining, glowing. The Acropolis by moonlight is silvery, *refulgent*, a vision unforgettable. A red, *refulgent* sunset is a thrilling sight, and the sign of good weather on the morrow. This is a word found usually in rather lofty contexts and flights of rhetoric. From Latin *refulgens*, a form of *refulgere*, (to shine brightly).

regale (rih gale') *vb.* To *regale* someone is to entertain him lavishly, or to amuse or delight him, depending on the context. It is the custom of hospitable people to *regale* their guests with good and plentiful food and drink. A good master of ceremonies can *regale* his audience with off-the-cuff anecdotes and jokes for hours on end. From French *régaler* (to regale), based on Old French *regale* (feast).

rejoinder (rih join' dər) *n.* A *rejoinder* is an answer to a reply. "Where do you think you're going?" "What business is that of yours?" "I'm a policeman, and you're trespassing on private property." That last statement is a *rejoinder*. As a legal term, *rejoinder* goes one step further: it is a defendant's answer to a plaintiff's reply, or the fourth pleading: complaint, answer, reply, *rejoinder*, all technical terms. From Middle French *rejoindre*.

remand (rih mand') *vb.* This word has the general meaning of "to order back." It is almost exclusively found in legal usage. It is used most frequently when a prisoner or suspect is sent back into detention: The court refused to grant bail, and *remanded* the prisoner to the custody of the sheriff to await further proceedings. Another legal usage is in connection with appeals: The appeals court *remanded* the case to the lower court, with instructions as to further proceedings. From Late Latin *remandare* (to repeat a command).

remonstrate (ree mon' strate) *vb.* One *remonstrates* when one is pleading in protest against something, presenting arguments in opposition to something. It is usually a waste of energy to *remonstrate* with a confirmed smoker against his dangerous addiction. Teachers often *remonstrate* in vain in their attempts to keep order in the classroom. *Remonstration* (ree mon stray' shən) is the noun, meaning "protest," and is often found in the plural: People's *remonstrations* against the Vietnam War were misktakenly considered unpatriotic. *Remonstrate* is sometimes pronounced *rem' ən strate*, by analogy to *demonstrate*, but that pronunciation is considered substandard, if not incorrect. *Remonstrate* is from Late Latin *remonstratus*, a form of *remonstrare* (to exhibit, demonstrate), based on Latin *monstrare* (to show).

renegade (ren' ə gade) *n.* A *renegade* is one who deserts his own party, group, country, etc., to join another, usually the enemy or a rival. The term also covers those who desert one religious faith for another. In the proper context, *renegade* is synonymous with *turncoat* or *traitor*. Where religion is concerned, it is the equivalent of *apostate*. Leon Trotsky (1879–1940) accused Joseph Stalin (1879–1953) of being a *renegade* form the communist principle of continuous world revolution by the proletariat. (He had to flee and for his pains was murdered in Mexico.) Almost every major cause in history has had its *renegades*, some of them high in the leadership. From Spanish *renegado*, based on Middle Latin *renegatus*, a form of *renegare* (to deny), taken from Latin *negare* (to deny). Cf. *renege*.

renege (rih nig', rih neg', rih neeg') *vb.* In general usage, this word means "to break a promise, to go back on one's word." All too often, a friend *reneges* on paying back a loan and, in the words of Polonius to Laertes (*Hamlet*, act I, scene 3), "...loan oft loses both itself and friend." Nations have been known to *renege* on their promises not to violate a neighbor's borders. In bridge and some other card games, one *reneges* by playing a card from a suit different from the one called for, even though one is holding a card of that suit in his hand. *Renege* is from Middle Latin *renegare* (to deny), taken from Latin *negare* (to deny). Cf. *renegade*.

repartee (rep ər tee', rep ar tee') *n.* *Repartee* is conversation full of fast, witty replies, quick comebacks. The plays of Oscar Wilde (1854–1900) and George Bernard Shaw (1856–1950) are filled with *repartee*. A good example of *repartee* is contained in a conversation between Winston Churchill and Lady Astor. Seated next to Winston at a dinner party, Lady Astor said to him, "If I were married to you, I'd put poison in your coffee." Came the *repartee*: "If I were married to you, I'd drink it." The term can be applied to a single pithy retort as well as to a continuous flow. One of our ex-hostages, asked if he would ever return to Iran, replied: "Only in a B-52." (Let's hope that never happens.) From French *repartie* (retort).

repertoire (rep' ər twar, rep' ər twor) *n.*; **repertory** (rep' ər tor ee) *n.* These two closely related words are sometimes used synonymously, but it is best to keep their meanings distinct. The term *repertoire* applies to the collection or list of works, dramatic, operatic, musical, etc., which a company or performer can perform and which make up the artist's or company's "stock in trade." *Repertoire* need not apply only to artistic endeavors; it is correct, for example, to speak of an acrobat's, magician's, or juggler's *repertoire*. The term can also cover an entire artistic field and apply to the total existing literature in that field, whether dramatic, musical, or other. The D'Oyly Carte Company's entire *repertoire* consists of Gilbert and Sullivan operas. Music consists of a seemingly endless *repertoire* all the way from Gregorian chant to punk rock (if you can call the latter music!). *Repertory* is sometimes used in place of *repertoire*, but its use is better confined to describe theatrical performances of different plays, for relatively short periods, performed in sequence by the same company, known as "repertory theater," performed by a "repertory company." The word is occasionally used to mean "supply" or "store," as in the diverse *repertory* of a country general store. *Repertoire* is taken intact from the French, based on Late Latin *reportorium* (catalogue, inventory); *repertory* is from the same *reportorium*, which was based on Latin *repertus*, a form of *reperire* (to discover, invent), related to Latin *parere* (to bring forth, produce).

replete (rə pleet′) *adj.* Anything *replete* with something is full of it. *Replete* is usually followed by *with*: A great play, wonderfully performed by accomplished actors, can be an evening *replete* with excitement. By itself, *replete* often means "stuffed full of food and drink": "No thanks; I couldn't eat another bite; I'm *replete*." In the proper context, the word simply means "complete": A brief to an appeals court should be *replete* in its citations of authority and persuasive references to past decisions. From Latin *repletus*, a form of *replere* (to fill).

reprehensible (rep rə hen′ sə bəl) *adj. Reprehensible* conduct is blameworthy, deserving of censure. The acceptance of bribes by an official elected by a trusting public is one of the most *reprehensible* acts he can commit. The behavior of some people goes beyond the *reprehensible* into the intolerable. Yellow journalism is *reprehensible* beyond words for the misery it can bring about. From Late Latin *reprehensibilis*, based on Latin *reprehensus*, a form of *reprehendere* (to censure, reprove).

reprobate (rep′ rə bate) *n., adj.* A *reprobate* is an unprincipled person. This word seldom appears as an adjective. A man who leaves his wife and children without a penny, steals from his company, and lives off his friends is a thorough *reprobate*. Charles Dickens (1812–1870), in his novels exposing the terrible conditions under which poor women and children lived in his time, created one fictional *reprobate* after another, like Sykes and Fagin. From Late Latin *reprobatus*, a form of *reprobare* (to reprove).

reprove (ree proove') *vb*. When you *reprove* someone, you are scolding him, not necessarily severely. The verb is used especially when the scolding is done with a view to correcting a fault of behavior and is close in meaning to "rebuke." It is often far more effective for teachers and other disciplinarians to *reprove* rather than to punish young people for lack of effort. Children should be *reproved* for acts of thoughtlessness, especially toward older people. Occasionally this can be accomplished with a *reproving* look. From Late Latin *reprobare* (to reprove).

resolute (rez' ə lyoot, rez' ə loot—*oo* as in *boot*) *adj*. A *resolute* person is one with unshakable determination, firm, determined, steadfast, like the Rock of Gibraltar. Though gentle in manner, Abraham Lincoln, on the question of slavery, was as *resolute* as an Old Testament prophet. The Minutemen of Lexington and Concord were grimly *resolute* in their stand against the British. From Latin *resolutus*, a form of *resolvere* (to resolve).

reticent (ret' ə sənt) *adj*. A *reticent* person is reserved, inclined to keep quiet. There are people who will talk freely about current affairs, but remain *reticent* about their personal lives. *Reticence* (ret' ə səns) is the noun. Calvin Coolidge (1872–1933), thirtieth president of the United States, was a model of *reticence*. He was known as "Silent Cal," and when taxed for his *reticence*, would retort, "You don't have to explain something you haven't said." From Latin *reticens*, a form of *reticere* (to keep silent), based on *tacere* (to be silent).

retrograde (reh' trə grade) *adj*. *Retrograde* means "with a reverse or backward motion," sometimes "in inverse order." Inexperienced skiers climbing a hill often find that their skis begin to slip in a *retrograde* motion so that they're at the bottom before they know it. In reality, the moon's direction is *retrograde* with respect to the earth's rotation, rising an hour later every night. From Latin *retrogradus* (going back), based on *retrogradi* (to go back), formed from *retro* (backward) and *gradi* (to step). The related verb *to retrogress* (reh' trə gres, reh trə gres') means "to go backward," but usually in an abstract sense, as in the expression *to retrogress to infantilism*; in other words, to move back into an earlier and less desirable state. *Retrogress* is from Latin *retrogressus*, a form of *retrogradi*.

retrogress (reh′ trə gres, reh trə gres′). *vb.* See **retrograde**.

retrospective (reh trə spek′ təv) *adj. Retrospective* means "looking back into the past." In a *retrospective* mood, one looks back into his past and reviews his advances and setbacks. In a difficult situation, it is well to take a *retrospective* look at the events that led up to the problem. A *retrospective* exhibition of an artist's work is one that presents examples from every important phase of his development. Such an exhibition is often referred to simply as a *retrospective*, a term in which the word is used as a noun, as in "the Picasso *retrospective*." From Latin *retrospectus*, a form of *retrospicere* (to look back), formed from *retro* (backward) and *specere* (to look).

rhetoric (ret′ ər ik) *n.* In current usage, *rhetoric* is the art of using language effectively. In colleges today, *rhetoric* seems to be a neglected field and is an attribute of only those with a natural gift for words. *Rhetoric* covers both the study of effective prose and the ability to use it. It can also mean the art of oratory. During the Lincoln-Douglas debates on slavery, Stephen Douglas had it all over his tall, ungainly opponent when it came to sheer *rhetoric*, but when it came to plain speech salted with folksy wit, nobody was a match for Abe. From Greek *rhetorike*. *Rhetorical* (rə tor′ ə kəl) is the related adjective, with several meanings: First, "mainly for effect": Some speakers use a great many words and indulge in *rhetorical* flourishes. Next, "bombastic ": A *rhetorical* style, intended to impress an audience, sometimes has the opposite effect. Finally, in the phrase *rhetorical question*, describing a question in form only, really a statement not expecting a reply, like, "What is so rare as a day in June?" or, "Is anything more glorious than to die for one's country?"

ribald (rib′ əld) *adj.* This word applies to persons given to vulgar or indecent humor, or to humor of that sort itself. *Ribaldry* (rib′ əl dree) means "ribald speech or humor." Soldiers traditionally tend to be a *ribald* group. Old-fashioned burlesque comedians were noted for their *ribald* routines. The works of the French satirist François Rabelais (1490–1553) are so full of *ribaldry* that *Rabelaisian* (rab ə lay′ zhən), applied to humor came to mean "coarse." There is a great deal of *ribaldry* in rough peasant humor, and in the peasant scenes painted by the Flemish painter Pieter ("Pieter the Elder") Breughel (1525–1569). From Middle English *ribaud* (lewd person).

rife (rife) *adj*. *Rife* means "present in abundance, in widespread existence." The word expresses abundance, usually not by prior arrangement of those affected. Murder was *rife* in the Old West, when every man wore his own law on his hip. Rumors are always *rife* in Washington. *Rife* is a Middle English word, akin to Old Icelandic *rifr* (abundant).

rigors (rig´ ərz) *n. pl.* *Rigors* has a perfectly good singular, *rigor*, meaning "severity, strictness," but is commonly used in the plural to describe the harshness or severity of weather or climate, or of a particular way of life or activity. A person born and bred in the tropics has a hard time getting acclimated to the *rigors* of a Vermont winter. The *rigors* of mountain climbing are not for the timid. Ballerinas look so soft and gentle on the stage, but to look that way, they have first to endure the *rigors* of ballet training. The adjective *rigorous* can be used in a number of ways. It can mean "harsh, severe": Moslem culture and religion impose extremely *rigorous* laws upon their adherents. Another meaning is "accurate, precise": Mathematical logic must never be loose or relaxed; it must always be *rigorous*. Referring to climate or weather, it means "extremely severe, harsh, inclement." People employed in the construction of the Alaskan pipeline were paid very high salaries to compensate them for their exposure to *rigorous* weather conditions. From Latin *rigor* (literally, stiffness; figuratively, severity; the literal meaning is found in the grim phrase *rigor mortis*, "the stiffness of death").

riposte (rə post´) *n.* A *riposte* is a swift, sharp reply, especially to a challenging or insulting question. "What idiot mailed that letter without a stamp on it?" "You did, Mr. Whipple." See the *riposte* by Churchill to Lady Astor, described under *repartee*. The term is taken from fencing, where a *riposte* is a quick thrust in response to an opponent's lunge. Taken over intact from the French, who got it from Italian *risposta* (response), based on Italian *rispondere* (to answer), from Latin *respondere* (to answer).

risible (riz´ ə bəl) *adj*. Although this word, in a general sense describes anything pertaining to laughter, its usual meaning is "laughable," or more strongly, "ludicrous." When older people try to "do their stuff" in disco dancing, the result is usually *risible*. The little boy with his hand in the cookie jar proclaiming his innocence is a classical example of a *risible* effort. From Late Latin *risibilis* (capable of laughing), based on Latin *risus*, a form of *ridere* (to laugh); *ridere* gave rise to *ridiculus*, which gave us *ridiculous*, an adjective very close in meaning to *risible*. See **deride**, for another example of derivation from Latin *ridere*.

roué (roo ay') *n.* A *roué* is an immoral, dissolute man, a debauchee or rake, especially one who has seduced many women and dropped them for new conquests. In the old-time stage and movie thrillers, innocent young maidens were taken advantage of by *roués* of the city-slicker type. Giovanni Casanova (1725–1798), the Italian adventurer and writer of memoirs, and Don Juan, the legendary Spanish nobleman, both famous for lives devoted to the seduction of women, are two of the best known *roués* in history, whose names have become synonymous with *roué* and *rake*. *Roué* is taken over intact from the French, where it is a form of *rouer* (to break on the wheel—a technique of torture). The profligate Duke or Orléans, Regent of France, invented the use of *roué* in its current sense about 1720. He wanted to collect cronies as dissolute as himself, every one of whom would deserve to be *roué*, i.e., broken on the wheel. The group of ne'er-do-wells he assembled were known as "Orléans's *roués*."

rubicund (roo' bə kund) *adj.* *Rubicund*, meaning "ruddy," is usually found in the description of a complexion, almost always a male's. One thinks of those hearty Pickwickian ale drinkers as men of ample frame and *rubicund* complexions. (Cf. *The Pickwick Papers* of Charles Dickens, 1812–1870.) From Latin *rubicundus*.

rue (roo) *vb.* To *rue* is to regret deeply, to wish something hadn't happened and could be undone. When you are having problem after problem with a troublesome person, you begin to *rue* the day you met him. Looking back, we *rue* our first involvement in the affairs of Vietnam. From Middle English *ruen*; akin to German *reuen* (to regret).

ruminate (roo' mə nate) *vb.* To *ruminate* is to think something over, slowly and thoroughly; to chew over a thought or problem, with concentrated attention, to ponder. It is well to *ruminate* the pros and cons of an intended step fraught with risk (in other words, look before you leap). People often *ruminate* long and hard before throwing away a pile of old letters. The literal meaning of *ruminate* is "to chew the cud," and animals (cows, deer, camels) that do so are called "ruminants" (roo' mə nənts). From Latin *ruminatus*, a form of *ruminare* (to chew the cud); the *rumen* is the first stomach of multi-stomached animals).

sacrosanct (sak' ro sankt) *adj.* Anything *sacrosant* is extremely sacred, inviolable. Literally, this word would be applied to temples, churches, altars, etc., but its most frequent use is figurative, in a nonreligious sense. The maid in the house in which this dictionary is being written is free to clean and tidy up wherever she will—except the author's office, which is *sacrosanct*, with its piles of papers and open reference books strewn all over the place. *Inviolable* is the sense here, as in the case of the studio of a serious musician while he is practicing, or the Oval Office while the President occupies it. From Latin *sacrosanctus* (sacred, inviolable; literally, made sacred by a holy rite).

sagacity (sə gas' ə tee) *n.* *Sagacity* is keen judgment, farseeing wisdom. All who knew Abe Lincoln were impressed above all by his *sagacity*. *Sagacity* in a judge is as important as his knowledge of the law. From Latin *sagacitas* (keenness, acuteness). The adjective is *sagacious* (sə gay' shəs), from Latin *sagacis*, a form of *sagax* (keen, acute).

salacious (sə lay' shəs) *adj.* What is *salacious* is lewd, not merely erotic. This word describes anything obscene, whether conduct or writing, painting, etc. Mae West's performances were merely suggestive; Linda Lovelace's were *salacious*. Conditions are so permissive in most parts of the world today that *salacious* writings and pictures can be openly offered for sale. *Salacious* comes from Latin *salacis*, a form of *salax* (lustful—in its literal use, applied to male animals), a word related to *salire* (to jump). (The connection between jumping male animals and lust should be obvious.)

salient (say' lee ənt, sale' yənt) *adj.* Things that are *salient* are outstanding, conspicuous: they leap to the eye and are therefore important, noticeable. Busy executives don't have time to go into every project in detail; all they want is the *salient* points. One doesn't remember every feature of a face, but only its *salient* traits. The aspect of "leaping to the eye" is clear from the origin of the word, from Latin *saliens*, a form of *salire* (to spring, leap). This also explains why *salient* is used as a noun to describe, in military usage, that part of a fortification or a battle line that projects toward the enemy.

salubrious (sə loo' bree əs) *adj. Salubrious* means "health-giving, healthful, wholesome." Two months in the *salubrious* sunshine of the Caribbean can do wonders to restore a person's health after a long illness. Activity is more *salubrious* than idleness. From Latin *salubris* (healthful). Cf. *salutary*.

salutary (sal' yə terr ee) *adj.* What is *salutary* is healthful, or generally beneficial. A regimen of exercise and diet has a *salutary* effect on the mind as well as the body. In a metaphorical sense: The knowledge that the subways are being patrolled by an increased police force and auxiliary volunteers has had a *salutary* effect on crime statistics. From Latin *salutaris* (healthful). Cf. *salubrious*.

salvo (sal' vo) *n.* A *salvo* is a burst of gunfire, all at once or in rapid succession; a load of bombs dropped simultaneously or one after the other; a broadside, especially in sea battles, from many guns; sometimes, a military salute from a number of guns. When orders are given for a barrage at a given hour, it usually starts with a *salvo* from a large number of guns. Metaphorically, the use of the word has been extended to cover a burst of applause or laughter. A brilliant performance of a coloratura aria is invariably greeted with a *salvo* of applause. The mere appearance of an established comedian is usually hailed by a *salvo* of laughter. From Latin *salve* (hail!), the imperative form of *salvere* (to be well).

sanctify (sangk' tə fy) *vb.* To *sanctify* something is to render it sacred or holy, to consecrate it. In the eyes of the faithful, the presence of a relic of a saint is sufficient to *sanctify* the place where it is contained. Each of the fourteen Stations of the Cross is a place *sanctified* by the fact that Christ stopped there on his way to Calvary. The very ground of the battle of Gettysburg has been *sanctified* by the memory of those who died there. From Church Latin *sanctificare* (to make holy).

sanctimonius (sangk tə mo' nee əs) *adj.* A *sanctimonious* person or air is hypocritically pious, "holier than thou." This word is a pejorative to describe a person who makes a great show of being super-religious and exceedingly righteous. In Shakespeare's *Measure for Measure* (act I, scene 2), Lucio says to one of the Gentlemen: "Thou concludest like the *sanctimonious* pirate, that went to sea with the Ten Commandments, but scraped one out of the table." "'Thou shalt not steal?'" asks the other Gentleman. "Ay," Lucio answers, "that he razed." From Latin *sanctimonia* (holiness).

sang-froid (sahng' frwah') *n*. This word is French for "cold blood." It signifies a cool head, calm and composure in a situation where most people would lose theirs, "If you can keep your head when all about you/Are losing theirs...." from the famous poem "If" by Rudyard Kipling (1865–1936) describes the situation perfectly. In a letter written in 1792 by Thomas Jefferson (1743–1826), the great man said: "Let what will be said or done, preserve your *sang-froid* immovably, and to every obstacle, oppose patience, perseverance, and soothing language."

sanguine (sang' win) *adj*. To be *sanguine* is to be optimistic, confidently hopeful. From Latin *sanguineus* (bloody), it meant, originally, "full of blood," therefore ruddy-complexioned, thus (apparently) showing good humor. It is not a good idea to start out on a venture about which you are not *sanguine*. Mr. Wilkins Micawber, in *David Copperfield*, by Charles Dickens (1812–1870) is the personification of a persistently and hopelessly *sanguine* disposition, to such an extent that *Micawberish* is an adjective describing chronic *sanguineness* in the face of chronic failure.

sapient (say' pee ənt) *adj*. *Sapient* means "wise," and *sapience* means "wisdom." Both are often used ironically: "O *sapient* investment counselor, why, despite thy advice, am I not rich?" Those absent-minded, venerable ivory-tower professors, full of *sapience*, are a dreadful danger driving on the highway. *Sapient* is from Latin *sapientis*, a form of *sapere* (to be wise); *sapience* is from Latin *sapientia* (wisdom).

sardonic (sar don' ik) *adj*. A *sardonic* smile or remark is sneeringly sarcastic, with overtones of scorn or bitter mockery: a *sardonic* expression is derisive. "Aha, my proud beauty!" was always said by the villain in old-time melodrama with a *sardonic* twist of the mouth. Lawyers who expose a false witness on cross-examination tend to wear a *sardonic* grin, expressive of disdain. From Greek *sardinios* (Sardinian), via Latin *sardinius*, influenced by French *sardonique*. The Greek adjective referred to a Sardinian plant which, when eaten, was alleged to cause spasms of laughter that were eventually fatal.

sartorial (sar tor' ee əl) *adj*. This is the adjective used to describe anything pertaining to clothing, dress, style (particularly in men's attire). Ambassadors are required to maintain high standards of *sartorial* elegance. Johnny Carson always makes his initial appearance in full *sartorial* splendor. Top corporate executives are, as a rule, extremely attentive to *sartorial* details. From Latin *sartor* (tailor).

saturnine (sat' ər nine) *adj*. A *saturnine* person is gloomy, taciturn, and sluggish. Misanthropes habitually wear a surly, *saturnine* expression. William Congreve (1670–1729), the English dramatist, asked: "Is there in the world a climate more uncertain than our own?" and blamed on it the fact that the British were "...apt to discontent...*saturnine*, dark and melancholic." *Saturnine* was originally an astrological term, applied to those born under the sign of Saturn, and therefore, according to old superstition, taciturn, gloomy, and forbidding.

savoir-faire (sav ər wahr fare') *n*. Tact, polish, wide knowledge of the ways of the world, and of how to behave in any company and in any situation—these are the attributes of a person with *savoir-faire*. *Savoir-faire* is an exceedingly important asset of a man of the world. A career of even the most brilliant person can be wrecked by a lack of *savoir-faire*. *Savoir faire* is a French phrase meaning "to know how to do," or more freely, "to know how to act."

savor (say' vər) *n*., *vb*. As a noun, *savor* means "taste" or "smell," nearly always in a favorable sense: The *savor* of French cooking, as it wafts its way through the kitchen door, excites the appetite. The *savor* of meat cooked outdoors on charcoal is a special experience to both nostrils and palate. Metaphorically, *savor* can mean any particular quality, especially the power to arouse interest or cause enjoyment: Often, after a bereavement, life loses its *savor*. The *savor* of the first bright, shining day of spring gives life a fresh meaning. As a verb, *savor* can mean "to enjoy the taste or smell of (something)," or "to taste or smell like (something)": We all *savor* the fragrance of hot coffee in the cold morning air. A burning yule log *savors* of comfort and coziness. *Savor*, as a verb, can be used in a metaphorical way, in connection with abstract things that have no taste or odor: A reply can be responsive and still *savor* of impertinence. The adjective *savory* (say' və ree) is always complimentary: How pleased the hostess is when the guest exclaims: "A *savory* dish indeed!" From Middle English *savour*, taken from Latin *sapor* (taste).

saw (saw) *n.* A *saw* is a well known saying or proverb, a wise adage. We all know the old *saw*: once bitten, twice shy. Some people can muster an old *saw* to suit any occasion, and others can dig up another that gives the opposite advice: Nothing ventured, nothing gained—but look before you leap. A Middle English word, akin to German *Sage* (legend, fable) and Icelandic *saga*; akin to *say*.

scabrous (skab′rəs) *adj.* This word has a variety of meanings, and it is not always easy to see the relationship between them. First, "having a rough surface": Some plants are *scabrous*, and unpleasant to the touch. Next: "knotty, difficult, tricky": *Scabrous* situations need tactful and delicate handling. Next: "risqué, obscene": The most *scabrous* magazines are openly displayed on the newsstands these days. Finally, "of depraved manners, behaving indecently": Gambling casinos usually attract a *scabrous* crowd to the resorts where they are located. From Latin *scaber* (scabby, rough), related to *scubere* (to scratch); but *scab* has Scandinavian origins, and what has "having a rough surface" to do with being "obscene" or "behaving in a depraved manner?"

schism (siz′ əm) *n.* A *schism* (note pronunciation) is a split or division into opposing factions caused by disagreement on matters of doctrine or policy. One of the great *schisms* in history was the division of the Christian faith into Catholicism and Protestantism. *Schism* relates mostly to religious bodies but can be used generally: The extreme views of the left wing caused a *schism* in the British Labour party, which resulted in the formation of the Social Democratic party. The word can also mean either of the factions or parties created as a result of such a split, but it is not commonly used that way. From Greek *schizein* (to cut, to cleave). The odd pronunciation is the result of the Middle English form *scisme* or *sisme*.

scion (sy′ ən) *n.* A *scion* is a descendant, usually a son of a noble or "important" family; rarely applied to a female. In botany, the word is used to describe a cutting from a plant, suitable for use in growing a new one. *Cion* is an uncommon alternative spelling. A *scion* of the Rothschild clan would be expected to go into banking as a matter of course. *Scions* like Edsel Ford and Henry II don't have to worry much about getting a start in the automobile business. From Old French *cion*.

score (skore) *n.*, *vb.* This word has multiple meanings, both as noun and verb. As noun: The *score* is the tally in a game; from an earlier sense, a mark or notch cut in wood, etc., for keeping *score*; a *score* of anything is twenty of them (the Gettysburg address begins: Four score and seven years ago ..."; cf. the Biblical three score and ten); a *score* in music is a written or printed musical composition; *score* can describe a significant success that gains some great material reward: Bernard Baruch (1870–1965) made a tremendous *score* in his earliest ventures into Wall Street. The word is often used figuratively in the expression *to settle old scores*, and colloquially in describing an experienced person: That guy really knows the *score*. As a verb: to *score* is to make a point in a game, like crossing home plate in baseball; to win a point in an argument, i.e., to *score off* someone; to make a shallow cut in a material like cardboard or leather so that it can be torn or folded easily; to raise welts (on someone's skin) by whipping; to make superficial cuts, as on meat (the way "cube steaks" are made); in an altogether different use, to criticize cruelly—the word is much used this way in newspaper headlines: PRESIDENT SCORES CONGRESS FOR DELAY; in another use: to write out the individual instrumental parts of a musical composition, as in *scoring* a piece for a reduced orchestra. A recent slang use is "to succeed in seducing a new (usually female) companion": "Well, did you score last night?" "I'll say!" It is obvious that in interpreting or using this word, one must *know the score*. From Icelandic *skor* (notch—see the first noun-use given above).

scourge (skurj) *n.*, *vb.* A *scourge*, literally, is a whip used for severe punishment, but its common use is to describe a person or thing considered to be a great affliction or source of heavy punishment or damage. Not for nothing was Attila the Hun (406–453) known as "the *Scourge* of God": His boast was, "Where I have passed, not a blade of grass will grow again." (He was the particularly vicious King of the Huns who invaded Europe.) Cholera and the Black Plague were the *scourges* of Europe in the Middle Ages. The verb follows the literal noun meaning, "to flog with a whip"; figuratively, it means "to afflict, punish, or criticize severely": Headmasters, in the old days, would *scourge* pupils not only with the cane, but by depriving them of all privileges for very long periods. For generations, dust storms have *scourged* the prairie states. The American economist and writer Stuart Chase, (b. 1888) said that television would "*scourge* the phonies out of politics." (Was he right?) From Late Latin *excoriare* (to flay).

scurrilous (skur' ə lus) *adj.* A *scurrilous* attack (the usual phrase) is one that is nastily, grossly insulting and abusive. Politicians, particularly, when under attack, almost automatically characterize the accusation as *scurrilous*, implying that the attack is unwarranted. The word can also mean "coarsely humorous": A number of television caricatures of President Carter were nothing more than *scurrilous* jests. From Latin *scurrilis* (mocking, jesting).

scuttle (skut' əl) *n., vb.* Apart from its meaning as a noun to describe a container for coal kept in a room, and its verb meaning "to scurry," as in *he scuttled out of the room*, a *scuttle* is a small hatch in the deck, side, or bottom of a boat; and the verb means to "open the seacocks of a vessel in order to sink it." That is its literal meaning, but it is now more often used figuratively meaning "to destroy," deliberately and completely, in a fairly short time: The report of the acceptance of a bribe or scandalous relations with a secretary, can effectively *scuttle* a politician's career. After looking into the facts, a lawyer will sometimes *scuttle* the client's hopes for quick success in litigation. From Middle English *skotel*.

seamy (seem' ee) *adj.* Literally, *seamy* means "showing the seams," like the inside of a garment; therefore, rough and not meant to be seen; now heard only in the figurative sense of "disagreeable" or "sordid." People who are born into wealth and luxury know little about the *seamy* side of life. The poor have to live in *seamy* neighborhoods, like those near the gashouse or the docks. *Seam* is from Middle English *seme*, and akin to German *Saum* (hem); *seamy* merely added the adjectival-*y*.

secular (sek' yə lər) *adj. Secular* can mean either "worldly" (as opposed to *spiritual*, *sacred*, or *religious*) or "lay" (in the sense of *nonclerical*). In the first sense: Some people devote themselves entirely to *secular* affairs, without ever a thought to the spiritual. Those wholly immersed in mundane, *secular* matters lose a great deal of what life has to offer. In the second sense: *Secular* schools offer a much wider curriculum than denominational institutions. From Latin *saecularis* (relating to a particular age, as opposed to *eternal*), based on *saeculum* (literally, one generation; in a wider sense, the longest a person can live—a hundred years, i.e., a century). *Secular* is synonymous with *temporal*.

seminal (sem' ə nəl) *adj.* Literally and technically, *seminal* means "containing, or pertaining to, semen": The *seminal* fluid is contained in the testes of the male. In botany, it means "pertaining to seed." In general use, *seminal* has a figurative sense of "original," with the clear implication that whatever is so described is likely to give rise to future growth and development —nearly always in a favorable way. Pablo Picasso (1881–1973) was one of the truly *seminal* artists of the twentieth century; for three decades there was scarcely an artist that did not owe something to his example. The formulation of the theory of relativity was a *seminal* event in science. From Latin *seminalis*, based on *semen* (seed).

sententious (sen ten' shəs) *adj.* A *sententious* person is too fond of putting on a show of wisdom, especially in the form of sage maxims and truisms, and usually in a smug and righteous manner. After hearing that the early bird gets the worm, a penny saved is a penny earned, and all about a stitch in time, one gets somewhat bored with the other fellow's *sententious* moralizing. From Latin *sententiosus*, based on *sententia* (way of thinking, opinion).

sentient (sen' shənt) *adj.* A *sentient* being is one capable of perceiving and feeling by means of the senses. When Shylock, in *The Merchant of Venice* (act III, scene 1), asks rhetorically, "Hath not a Jew eyes? Hath not a Jew hands, organs, dimensions, senses . . . ?" he was passionately declaring himself to be as *sentient* as the next person. In science fiction, all sorts of planets are inhabited by *sentient* beings equipped with all sorts of sensory organs. From Latin *sentiens*, a form of *sentire* (to feel).

septic (sep' tik) *adj.* Anything that causes or has to do with infection by microorganisms may be described as *septic*. The formation of pus is a sure indication that a wound is *septic*. This word is often found in the term *septic tank*, into which sewage is conveyed and which makes use of bacteria to decompose it. From Latin *septicus*, which came from Greek *septikos*, based on *septos* (rotted). Do not confuse *septic* with *sceptic* (a variant spelling of skeptic) (skep' tik), a person with a doubting, questioning attitude toward things in general.

sequel (see' kwel) *n.* A *sequel* is a follow-up of either an event, an action, or a work of literature, film, etc. Columbus's later voyages of exploration were *sequels* to his discovery of America.

The later James Bond novels constitute a series of *sequels*. When, after the *sequel Son of Frankenstein*, they kept going on to more distant members of the family, most people's interest in that horrendous clan began to flag. *Sequel* can be used as well in the sense of "consequence, result": Poverty in old age can be the *sequel* to reckless extravagance in youth. From Latin *sequela* (that which follows), based on *sequi* (to follow).

sequester (sə kwest' ər) *vb.* To *sequester* is to remove and keep separate; most commonly a matter of legal usage. Funds or other assets held by a trustee should be *sequestered*, never commingled with the trustee's own funds or property. The property of a debtor can, under certain circumstances, be legally *sequestered* from his possession until the claim is settled. Lawyers must *sequester* client's funds in special accounts. Juries are often *sequestered* overnight in a hotel or other housing. More generally, maiden aunts sometimes live out their lives *sequestered* in the family home. And teenagers frequently remain *sequestered* in their rooms for hours at a time listening to rock 'n'-roll records. From Late Latin *sequestrare* (to set aside, for safekeeping), based on *sequester* (depositary, one appointed to hold property pending a dispute).

serendipity (serr ən dip' ə tee) *n. Serendipity* is the making of a pleasant discovery by accident, the good luck of finding something agreeable that you weren't looking for, especially when you were looking for something else. This word was coined by the English writer Horace Walpole (1717–1797), based on a Persian fairy tale entitled *The Three Princes of Serendip*, who kept having such adventures. A stupendous example of *serendipity* was Columbus's discovery of the West Indies while searching for a route to the East Indies. The discovery of a rich uranium deposit under a lead mine that had petered out was a stroke of *serendipity* that made the owners rich. The adjective is *serendipitous* (serr ən dip' ə təs), as in a *serendipitous* discovery. *Serendip*, also spelled *Serendib*, was the old name for Ceylon, now Sri Lanka.

serpentine (sur' pən teen, sur' pən tyne) *adj.* Anything *serpentine* is curved and sinuous, shaped like a snake. Some rivers run in a relatively straight line; most wend their *serpentine* way through the countryside or town. Of their *serpentine* roads, the English say: "The rolling English drunkard made the rolling English roads." (All those who object to this as slander blame it on the lowing herd mapping out its own cowpath.) From Latin *serpentinus* (snakelike).

servile (surv' əl, sur' vile) *adj.* A *servile* person is slavish, submissive, cringing. Headwaiters are either arrogant or *servile*, depending on their assessment of the forthcoming tip. Celebrities attract a throng of *servile* hangers-on. An aspiring writer should be able to perceive what is great in the literature of the past without resorting to *servile* imitation. From Latin *servilis* (slavish), based on *servus* (slave).

shibboleth (shib' ə ləth) *n.* A *shibboleth*, originally a peculiarity of speech or a custom or usage distinctive of a particular group, is a catchword or slogan characteristic of a party or sect. It has come to mean any such slogan empty of real meaning, an outworn bit of dogma. Older party members often continue to cling to their *shibboleths*, though discredited. The word, ancient Hebrew for *ear of wheat* or *stream*, appears in a Biblical story (Judges, xii, 4–6) as the test word used by the Gileadites on the fleeing Ephraimites when they were challenged at the River Jordan. The Ephraimites couldn't pronounce the -sh- sound; when asked to say "shibboleth," the best they could do was *sibboleth*. They thus revealed themselves as the enemy and were slain. *Shibboleths* reveal your origins, good or bad, but the word has a generally pejorative meaning.

sibilant (sib' ə lənt) *adj.* A *sibilant* sound is a hissing sound: the word is nearly always used to describe a sound uttered in human speech, like the letter *s*. When people have a gap between their two front teeth, their conversation may be notable for its wealth of *sibilants*. The English comedian Terry Thomas's trademark is such a gap and its *sibilant* consequences. A hissing snake makes a *sibilant* sound. In the field of phonetics, *sibilant* is the word for certain consonants or consonant combinations that produce a *sibilant* sound: *s, z, sh, zh, ch* (as in church), *j*. There are lots of *sibilants* (as well as a lot of alliteration) in the following lines from the *The Mikado* (W.S. Gilbert, 1836–1919):

> *To sit in solemn silence in a dull, dark dock...*
> *Awaiting the sensation of a short, sharp shock*
> *From a cheap and chippy chopper on a big black block.*

From Latin *sibilans*, a form of *sibilare* (to hiss, whistle).

simile (sim′ ə lee) *n.* A figure of speech that compares two things using the word *like* or *as*. See *metaphor* and the examples there given. Additional examples: as pretty as a picture; as like as two peas in a pod; hair like spun gold (or black as a raven's wing). From Latin *simile* (resemblance, comparison), a form of *similis* (like, similar).

simulate (sim′ yə late). *vb.* See **dissimulate**.

sinecure (sin′ ə kyoor) *n.* This is the word for a job or appointment requiring little or no actual work, though paying a salary or other compensation (especially if it pays well). Honorary chairmen of the board, with good salaries and no duties, enjoy *sinecures* envied by hard-working executives. The Vice Presidents of the United States may fade into such obscurity that the good citizens forget their names, but the job is no *sinecure*— they often have a lot to do. From two Latin words, *sine cura* (without care).

sinuous (sin′ yoo əs) *adj.* Sinuous means "very curved, winding, undulating." In the dark or in a fog it is very difficult to follow a *sinuous* path or drive along a *sinuous* road. The celebrated female figure divine is always, slim, lissome, and *sinuous*. The word comes from Latin *sinuosus* (full of windings), based on *sinuare* (to curve) and *sinus* (curve); the first syllable has nothing whatever to do with *sin*.

skeptic, sceptic (skep′ tik) *n.* Originally, this word was the name of a member of an ancient Greek philosophical school that denied that man could ever know anything with certainty: now, it applies to anyone who makes a practice of doubting and insists on examining all beliefs, including widely accepted ones. A special application of the word occurs in the matter of religious beliefs. Colloquially, *skeptics* are "from Missouri." *Skeptics* travel under the banner "seeing is believing." The adjective is *skeptical*. It is terribly irritating, when you are truthfully giving the reason for missing a date, to be met with a *skeptical* look. From Latin *scepticus*, taken from Greek *skeptikos* (thoughtful, of an inquiring mind).

skittish (skit′ ish) *adj.* Skittish means "frisky, extremely lively," with the implication of nervous readiness to be triggered into action. The word is associated with horses, and in that connection implies that the animal is easily startled. Most thorough-breds are quite *skittish*, apt to shy at any bit of paper blown across the road. The safety man in the moment before kickoff usually exhibits a *skittish* mood. Derivation uncertain.

slake (slake) *vb.* To *slake* is to quench, and the most common use of the word is in the expression *to slake one's thirst*. It brings up the image of a cool running stream or, more prosaically, the office water fountain. Thirst, however, is not the only thing that can be *slaked*; its more general meaning is "to allay" by doing something that satisfies the situation: A soft answer can *slake* someone's wrath. Sweet surrender can *slake* desire. Success may *slake* aggressive ambition. *Slake* has a special use with respect to lime: It describes the treatment of lime with water, causing disintegration, resulting in *slaked* lime, a powder used in making plaster and cement. It is called "*slaked*" because the water treatment makes the lime inactive. Of uncertain Old English derivation.

slew (sloo) *n., vb.* As a noun, a *slew* of anything is a lot of it, an abundance, "oceans." In this use, *slew* is an informal word. One makes slow progress leaving a sports stadium surrounded by a *slew* of people. Those big family reunions are usually treated to a *slew* of food. As a verb, *slew* is a variant of the more common form *slue*, and in that sense it means "to swing around," usually on one's own axis, with the implication that the swinging is done in haste, probably in response to an urgent need. The endless series of television movies with a police motif expend a *slew* of footage in which one car after another *slues* around during a frantic chase. The noun *slew* is from Irish *sluagh* (army, multitude); the verb *slue*, or *slew*, is of unknown derivation.

slue (sloo) *vb.* See **slew**.

smug (smug) *adj.* A *smug* person is self-satisfied, especially to a degree or in a manner that irritates others. People whose predictions come true are all too apt to be *smug* about it, as they pronounce those inevitable words, "I told you so." What is more irritating than the *smug* expression on the face of a person uttering old saws, or reminding you how much better things were in his youth? Thought to be derived from Dutch *smuk* (neat), akin to German *smuck* (tidy, trim). These sources seem more likely in view of the occasional, though very uncommon, use of *smug* to mean "trim, spruce, sleek."

sobriquet (so' brə kay, so' brə ket, so brə kay', so brə ket') *n.* A *sobriquet* (however pronounced) is an assumed name or a nickname. The early Russian Communist leaders assumed *sobriquets*: Josif Vissarionovich Dzhugashvili (1879–1953) became "Stalin"; Lev Davidovich Bronstein (1879–1940) chose "Trotsky." In the case of authors, the term for an assumed name is *pen name* or *nom de plume* or *pseudonym* rather than *sobriquet*, but *sobriquets* are frequent: "George Eliot" for Mary Ann Evans (1819–1880); "George Sand" for Amandine Aurore Lucie Dupin Dudevant (1804–1876). Those are all names chosen by the individuals concerned. *Sobriquet* applies as well to, and is more commonly understood, as a nickname that sticks to a celebrity, with or without his contrivance. The characters glorified by Damon Runyon (1884–1946) were made all the more picturesque by their *sobriquets*: Harry the Horse, Nicely Nicely, Big Jule, and the rest. Cassius Clay changed his name to Muhammad Ali (a real change of name, rather than a *sobriquet*) but enjoys the *sobriquet* "The Greatest" as a result of his boasting. Jack Dempsey became "The Manassa Mauler"; Luis Firpo "The Wild Bull of the Pampas"; Joe Louis "The Brown Bomber." These were all *sobriquets*, even if the boxers weren't or aren't acquainted with the word. Taken over from the French, which got it from Old French *soubriquet*, the way the word is sometimes spelled in English.

sodden (sod' ən) *adj.* *Sodden* describes the condition of utter saturation, the ultimate degree of wetness, usually with unpleasant implications. Bread that has been soaked in water becomes so *sodden* as to fall apart at a touch. When you're out in the rain in sneakers, they eventually get *sodden*. A special use of the word is found in the expression *sodden drunk*, which is about as drunk as you can get. It is a very old word, an obsolete Middle English form of the verb *to seethe*, which (to the surprise of many) means "to soak," but is normally used to convey a state of extreme agitation, foaming at the mouth with anger.

solecism (sol' ə siz əm) *n.* This is a useful term for any erroneous or ignorant use of words, whether the error relates to grammar, usage, or pronunciation. By extension, *solecism* can include any breach of good manners. Some examples of the narrower meaning: "I *seen* an accident today." "Either of them *are* good enough." "He is a man *whom* I think will succeed." *Mischievious* is an all too common *solecism* in pronunciation. As to a breach of etiquette: It would be a *solecism* to wear a flashy necktie at a funeral—but the word is almost always used in the narrower sense, relating to grammar, etc. It has an interesting derivation, from Latin *soloecismus* (grammatical error), taken from Greek *soloikismos*, based on *Soloi*, a city in Cilicia (an ancient country in southeast Asia Minor) whose Athenian colonists spoke bad Greek. Do not confuse *solecism* with *solipsism*.

soliloquy (sə lil′ ə kwee) *n*. A *soliloquy* is a speech, usually in a play, expressing a person's thoughts aloud and addressed to no one in particular. The most famous *soliloquy* is Hamlet's, beginning, "To be, or not to be; that is the question." During a particularly long filibuster, a senator who thought he was making a speech might look around him and discover he was making a *soliloquy*. From Late Latin *soliloquium*, based on Latin solus (alone) and *loqui* (to speak).

solipsism (sol′ əp siz əm) *n*. Technically, *solipsism* is a term in philosophy covering the theory that only the self exists or can be demonstrated to exist, because all we can know of the world is what we can get through our own five senses. This technical usage would hardly be met with in everyday speech, where, by extension, *solipsism* has come to mean "self-centeredness," with its adjective *solipsistic* (sol əp sis′ tik) to describe the attitude that you are the only one in the whole wide world that counts. Excessively self-indulgent people can be said to be *solipsistic*, with no consideration for anyone else. People who are (or were) in exalted positions, like the late Papa Doc in Haiti and Idi Amin (late of Uganda), are extreme examples of *solipsism*. [People who practice] *solipsism* are known as *solipsists* (sol′ əp sists), and do not spend any time casting their bread upon the waters or sending out get-well cards. Do not confuse *solipsism* with *solecism*. From two Latin words: *solus* (alone) plus *ipse* (himself).

sop (sop) *n*. Literally, a *sop* is something like a piece of bread soaked in a palatable liquid like sugar-water or broth, given to a baby, for instance, to pacify it: figuratively, and now more often, the term covers anything given, such as a trivial bribe or concession, to keep someone or something appeased or quiet for the time being. The boss might distribute minor bonuses as *sops* in an attempt to keep the staff from demanding higher wages. Most people tend to praise an actor friend who has given a poor performance as a *sop* to his vanity, or at least his self-respect. A person sometimes has to do a great deal of rationalizing as a *sop* to his conscience. From Old English *sopp*.

sophism (sof′ iz əm—*o* as in *pot*) *n.* A *sophism* is a specious statement or argument made to deceive someone; one that sounds plausible but is actually a clever distortion of the facts. In ancient Greece the *Sophists* were a class of instructors in various branches of learning who eventually began to lean more to finding ingenious methods of reasoning and quibbling than to sound, sincere logic. A *sophist* (sof′ ist) is a person who reasons cleverly but speciously, and *sophistry* (sof′ ə stree) describes the method of reasoning used by *sophists*—tricky, plausible, but essentially fallacious. People arguing an unsound position will often resort to *sophism* and false premises. *Sophism* is from Latin *sophisma*, taken intact from the Greek; *sophist* is from Latin *sophista*, based on Greek *sophistes* (sage, wise); *sophistry* came from the Middle English form *sophistrie*, based on the earlier Latin and Greek. *Sophisticate* (originally "to adulterate") is from the same source.

sophomore (sof′ ə mor, sof′ mor—*o* as in *pot*) *n.* Most of us know that a *sophomore* is a second-year student in high school or college. The adjective *sophomoric* (sof ə mor′ ik, sof mor′ ik) however, is used to describe the intellectual pretensions and overconfidence of the typical *sophomore* who thinks he knows a lot more than he actually does. It was Alexander Pope (1688–1744) who said: "A little learning is a dangerous thing." Some people mean well, but their *sophomoric* solutions of the world's problems and freely offered panaceas can be irritating. Speakers are sometimes interrupted by callow youths shouting *sophomoric* questions. The word has an amusing derivation: It is a combination of two Greek words, *sophos* (wise) and *moros* (foolish—we get the word *moron* from *moros*). In other words, a *sophomore* is a wise fool. Do not confuse *sophomoric* with *soporific* (even though *sophomoric* pronouncements do induce yawns).

soporific (sop ə rif′ ik) *n., adj.* The adjective means "sleep-producing," and the noun means "sleep-producing drug". There are speakers whose speeches are so *soporific* that you can hear people snoring all over the place. In *Romeo and Juliet* (act IV, scene 1) Friar Laurence gives the heroine a *soporific* or sleeping-draught ("Take thou this vial," he says, "being then in bed/ And this distilled liquor drink thou off;/ When presently through all thy veins shall run/ A cold and drowsy humour....")—and then the trouble starts. From Latin *sopor* (sleep) and suffix *-ficus* (-making), i.e., sleep-making.

soupçon (soop son') *n.* This is the French word for "suspicion." In English it means the very merest dash, trace, or hint of something, usually said of a flavor in cooking. Never overdo the use of spices—just a *soupçon* makes all the difference. It has been used in connection with matters other than cooking, in phrases like *a soupçon of sarcasm, a soupçon of deviousness*. This is a highly literary use, but a good one—to be encouraged.

spate (spate) *n.* A *spate* is a sudden outpouring, of overwhelming proportions. It can be applied literally to a huge and unexpected rush of liquid, like a flash flood, but in general use it can describe an outpouring of almost anything, like an argument that develops into a *spate* of wrathful words and abuse. At mealtimes, successful fast-food establishments are overwhelmed with a *spate* of orders. As a result of the 1848 potato famine in Ireland, our country experienced a *spate* of Irish immigration. The long-suffering American television audience is being subjected to a *spate* of violence and mayhem. (How about a nice quiet series about an accountant—or even a dictionary maker?) From Middle English *spate*.

spleen (spleen) *n.* The *spleen* is an important organ of the body, acting on the blood, and once believed to be the seat of melancholy and ill humor. In common speech, *spleen* has come to describe spiteful bad temper, and when a person turns in anger upon another, he is said "to vent his *spleen*" upon him. A person "full of *spleen*" is one who is chronically irritable. "Thou're such a touchy, testy...fellow; so much...*spleen* about thee. There is no living with thee...," wrote the English essayist Joseph Addison (1672–1719). From Latin *splen* (spleen), taken intact from the Greek. *Lien* was a Latin variant.

sporadic (spo rad' ik) *adj.* This word describes anything occurring here and there, now and then; occasional, scattered. *Sporadically* (spo rad' ə klee) is the adverb. From time to time the world appears to be entirely rid of a disease, only to have it reappear *sporadically*. Success requires sustained efforts; *sporadic* bursts of energy are often a waste of time. From Greek *sporadikos*.

spurious (spyoor' ee əs) *adj.* What is *spurious* is counterfeit, not authentic, not the genuine article, phony. People used to bite coins to tell the genuine ones from the *spurious* ones. *Spurious* reasoning is the tool of sophists. Art dealers and even museums have been plagued by *spurious* works of art. *The Protocols of the Elders of Zion* was an entirely *spurious* work published in Russia in 1905, based on an earlier forgery, purporting to serve as blueprint for "secret Jewish plans for achieving world power." Their *spuriousness* was exposed in 1921; nonetheless, they provided a tool for Hitler. From Latin *spurius* (false).

squalid (skwol' əd) *adj.* Miserably dirty and unpleasant, usually from neglect or poverty, wretched, sordid. In shocking proximity to the splendid homes of the rich, we often find slums so *squalid* as to jolt our consciences. Charles Dickens (1819–1870), in novel after novel, exposed the *squalid* living conditions of the poor. The noun is *squalor* (skwol' ər). From Latin *squalidus* (dirty) and *squalor* (dirtiness) respectively.

stentorian (sten tor' ee ən) *adj.* A *stentorian* voice is extremely loud and penetrating; it is always said of a male voice. *Stentor* was a Greek herald during the time of the Trojan War. Homer (eighth century B.C.) says in *The Iliad* (V, 783) that Stentor's voice was equivalent to that of fifty men combined. Daniel Webster (1782–1852), the great American statesman and orator, is said to have had a voice of such *stentorian* proportions that it carried to the farthest corner of any chamber, no matter how large. Top sergeants are known for their *stentorian* voices.

stolid (stol' id) *adj.* A *stolid* person is unemotional, impassive, unexcitable, unresponsive, not easily roused. The typical Maine farmer is said to be laconic and *stolid. Stolid* people appear to take things as a matter of course. *Stolid* resistance to an Oriental merchant in the bazaar is the best way to get the price down; walking away helps a lot, too. From Latin *stolidus* (stupid, dull, obtuse.)

strident (stride' ənt) *adj.* Anyone or anything *strident* is loud and harsh, grating, creaking. *Strident* sounds are harsh and shrill, insistent and discordant. Summer nights are sometimes filled with the *strident* sound of croaking frogs. Oil is the remedy for *strident* hinges. The sounds of a symphony orchestra tuning up may be *strident*, yet they give the audience a feeling of anticipatory pleasure. From Latin *stridens*, a form of *stridere* (to make a harsh noise).

stultify (stul' tə fy) *vb.* To *stultify* someone's mind is to make it dull, ineffectual, torpid, especially by long and boring work or a boring environment. The *stultifying* inactivity of a small rural community can deaden even the mind and spirit of a potentially creative person. Monotonous menial labor is *stultifying*. From Late Latin *stultificare* (make stupid), based on Latin *stultus* (stupid).

sublimate (sub′ lə mate) *vb*. To *sublimate* is to transform impulses, feelings, etc., leading to forbidden behavior, usually sexual, into socially acceptable activity; the process being generally unconscious, and for the purpose of avoiding censure, punishment, or guilty feelings. Without realizing it, we often *sublimate* our erotic feelings by plunging into feverish activity, whether creative or menial. It is said that many great works of art are the result of the artist's *sublimating* his sexual impulses toward his models or other erotic needs. The noun is *sublimation* (sub lə may′ shən). It is said that the music of Tchaikovsky (1840–1893) was in large part the result of the *sublimation* of his physical needs. There is a wholly distinct use of *to sublimate* in chemistry: to vaporize right from the solid state, without first liquefying. From Latin *sublimatus*, a form of *sublimare* (to elevate).

sub rosa (sub ro′ zə) *adj., adv*. These are two Latin words which mean, literally, "under the rose." In Roman times, hanging a rose over the table, at a secret meeting, was a symbol that the participants were sworn to secrecy. Legend has it that Cupid gave a rose to Harpocrates, the god of silence, to keep him from revealing the indiscretions of Venus; hence the rose as a symbol of secrecy, and the meaning of *sub rosa* as "secret(ly), confidental(ly)." The expression is applied particularly to actions that must be hidden from the public eye. When conspirators meet, the proceedings are always strictly *sub rosa*, with never a whisper to reach the world outside. Clandestine lovers, like Romeo and Juliet, must meet *sub rosa*.

succor (suk′ ər) *n., vb*. Succor is help, aid, usually with the implication that one is coming to rescue somebody from a fairly dangerous or wretched predicament. The giving of such aid or relief is expressed by the use of the word as a verb. Whether it be the cavalry, the marines or the posse, there is usually an episode in western films when they get there just in time to give *succor* to the beleaguered good guy. Brilliant planning and incredible daring made it possible for the Israeli commandos to *succor* the distressed hostages at Entebbe. From Latin *succerrere* (to come to the aid of).

succubus (suk' yə bəs) *n*. See **succumb**.

succulent (suk' yə lənt) *adj*. Literally, *succulent* means "juicy," usually as applied to food and often with the sense of "appetizing." *Succulent* plums and peaches are hard to resist. A *succulent* Sunday roast might be the climax of a week's dining. In botany, a *succulent* plant is one that, like cactus and other desert plants, is provided with thick, porous tissues that can store up water. Figuratively, the word is sometimes applied to a young woman full of sparkle, freshness, and vitality and meant as a compliment, despite possible feminist objections to this use as an unacceptable sexist term. From Late Latin *succulentus*, based on Latin *succus* (juice).

succumb (sə kum') *vb*. To *succumb* is to yield, give way. One can *succumb* to a disease, a mood, persuasion, an adversary, etc. A person can *succumb* to despair, to the strains of the rat race, to the flu, to almost anything. A company can *succumb* to the effects of an economic depression, just as a person can *succumb* to the effects of a mental depression. A nation can *succumb* to a foe with superior military strength. Standing alone, *succumb* can mean "to die": After years of life in the tropics, plagued by one exhausting malady after another, he finally *succumbed*. From Latin *succumbere* (to yield, fall down). The related Latin verb *succubare* (to lie under) gave us the curious word *succubus* (suk' yə bəs), the name given in the Middle Ages to a demon who was believed to have assumed female form to have sexual intercourse with sleeping men. In later days, the word *succubus* was applied to any demon or fiend. There are those who come to dread sleep itself, for fear of the nightly visit of their *succubus* (here used in the figurative sense of "nightmare"). The Late Latin form *succuba* meant "prostitute," a meaning explained by the origin of the word in Latin *succubare* (to lie under). See also the discussion of *incubus*, the converse of *succubus*, under *incumbent*.

sully (sul' ee—*u* as in *but*) *vb*. To *sully* is to stain, blemish. Even though groundless, and later publicly retracted, a *scurrilous* newspaper story can *sully* a reputation forever. No scandal ever *sullied* the image or name of Abraham Lincoln. From

Middle French *souiller* (to soil), which also gave us *soil*. The adjective *unsullied*, though negative in form, is positive in meaning, and is the equivalent of "spotless, immaculate" (themselves negative in form); usually found in the phrase *unsullied reputation, unsullied name*.

supercilious (soo pər sil′ ee əs) *adj*. A *supercilious* person is haughty and contemptuous of supposed inferiors, disdainful, arrogantly superior. The English butler is usually portrayed as a very solemn man with a *supercilious* expression. Marie Antoinette (1755–1793) is generally depicted as the most *supercilious* of royal figures, famous for the haughty (if apocryphal) phrase, "Let them eat cake." Camels, with their heads at a jaunty angle while they slowly chew their cud, always seem to be exhibiting a disdainful, *supercilious* air. From Latin *superciliosus*, based on *supercilium* (literally, eyebrow; figuratively, arrogance).

supine (soo pine′, soo′ pine) *adj*. *Supine* can be used in its literal sense of "lying on one's back, face up" (the opposite of *prone*), or in its figurative sense of "passive," to describe a person who does not react in the face of provocation, threat of danger, etc. Used in this latter sense it is a pejorative, implying that to behave *supinely* is wrong, and sometimes even cowardly. If the leaders of France and England had not remained so *supine* during the Spanish Civil War and the early stages of Hitler's aggression, World War II might never have occurred. From Latin *supinus* (lying on one's back; inert).

supplicate (sup′ lə kate) *vb*. To *supplicate* is to beg, beseech, petition humbly and prayerfully. We are all familiar with the image of George Washington *supplicating* God for better weather and victory. For centuries the afflicted have gathered at Lourdes to *supplicate* the Virgin for relief. It is not uncommon for a lawyer to *supplicate* a judge for compassion toward a first offender. From Latin *supplicatus*, a form of *supplicare* (to kneel, beseech).

surfeit (sur′ fit) *n., vb*. A *surfeit* of anything is an excess of it, especially of food or drink. This word is sometimes applied to the sensation of disgust and distress caused by such excess. In *A Midsummer Night's Dream* (act II, scene 2), Lysander says:

a surfeit *of the sweetest things*
The deepest loathing to the stomach brings.

Novels with a *surfeit* of sub-plots are hard to follow. *To surfeit* is to supply (someone) with an excess of something. The public eventually became *surfeited* with revelations during the Watergate scandals. From Middle French *surfait*, a form of *surfaire* (to overdo).

surmise (sər mize') *n., vb.* To *surmise* is to suppose, without certain knowledge, to infer on scanty evidence. Intuitive people often learn that what they had formerly *surmised* turns out to be the truth. It is always risky to *surmise* another's thoughts. A *surmise* is a belief based on slight evidence, a conclusion with no firm basis. Be careful of expressing random *surmises*; others may repeat them as fact. Shakespeare's *King Henry IV, Part 2* begins with an "Induction" (introduction) in which a character called "Rumour" says:

> *Rumour is a pipe*
> *Blown by surmises, jealousies, conjectures . . .*

And in act III, scene 4 of *Cymbeline*, Shakespeare has Imogen say to Pisanio, "I speak not out of weak *surmises*, but from proof. . . ." *Surmise* comes, via late Middle English *surmisen*, from Latin *supermissus*, a form of *supermittere* (to throw upon).

surreptitious (sur əp tish' əs) *adj.* *Surreptitious* means "stealthy, clandestine." Because of the feud between their families, Romeo and Juliet could meet only *surreptitiously*. Children often like to indulge in *surreptitious* reading in bed, long after the lights are supposed to have been turned out. Lovers delight in exchanging *surreptitious* glances. Referring to pirated publications, the word means "unauthorized": *Surreptitious* copies of musical tapes and records are flooding the market. From Latin *surrepticius* (stolen —cf. the familiar phrase *stolen glances*).

sybarite (sib' ə rite) *n.* A *sybarite* is a person who lives mainly for pleasure and luxury, a sensualist or voluptuary—often with the implication that he can afford not to work for a living. The term comes from the ancient Greek city of Sybaris, in the south of Italy, noted for the luxurious ways of its inhabitants. The adjective is *sybaritic* (sib ə rit' ik). The Roman philosopher and dramatist Seneca (4 B.C.–A.D. 65) tells of a Sybarite (inhabitant of Sybaris) who complained of restlessness at night, because he found a rose-leaf doubled under him, and it "hurt him!" The travel companies are always inviting us to come to this or that island paradise and live the life of a *sybarite*. The *sybaritic* element of our society is currently known as the "jet set."

sycophant (sik′ ə fənt) *n.* A *sycophant* is a flatterer, a most unpleasant type, a self-seeking, servile, sniveling hanger-on, a toady. Sudden fame attracts *sycophants*. Boxing champions and rock stars seem to be constantly surrounded by a swarm of *sycophants* whenever they appear in public. Courtiers of old were a special breed of *sycophant*. William Allen White (1868–1944), the journalist known as the "Sage of Emporia" (Kansas), wrote of a lame duck president: "...the *sycophants* were gone, for the outgoing president had nothing to give." Don't take the praises of a *sycophant* seriously. From Latin *sycophanta,* based on Greek *sykophantes* (informer). The legend is that *sykophantes* originally meant "one who showed figs" (*skyon* is *fig*, and *phantes* came from *phanein* (to show); they informed against illegal fig-exporters; hence they were tattletales, hence flatterers). Scholars are skeptical about this derivation.

sylph (silf) *n.* A *sylph* is a slim, graceful girl. Originally the term was applied to an imaginary soulless creature who inhabited the air. The word is most frequently met with in the adjective *sylphlike*: A *slyphlike* figure is ideally suited to show off the latest fashions in bikinis. From New Latin *sylphus*.

symbiosis (sim bee oh′ sis) *n. Symbiosis* is the term for the living together of two different organisms which creates a mutually advantageous situation. The adjective that describes such an arrangement is *symbiotic* (sim bee ot′ ik). Without the beneficial bacteria that dwell in intestinal tracts, animals couldn't digest their food; in this *symbiotic* relationship, the bacteria take what they need from the food, and let animals digest the rest. Taken over intact from the Greek; a word composed of the prefix *sym-* (variant of *syn*—together) and *bios* (life).

syntax (sin′ tax) *n.* This term covers both sentence structure and the study of the formation of sentences; the branch of grammar that deals with the arrangement of words in a sentence. When you begin to study a new language, it is far easier to memorize lists of words than to master the *syntax*—the formation of sentences. Matthew Arnold (1822–1888), in his essay *On Translating Homer* (the eighth-century-B.C. Greek epic poet), wrote: "...he is eminently plain and direct...both in his *syntax* and in his words...." From Greek *syntaxis*, based on *syntassein* (to put in order, arrange).

synthesis (sin' thə sis—*th* as in *thing*) *n*. Synthesis is the combining of elements to create a whole. It can apply to the combining of chemical elements to create a compound, and has a special application to the production of a substance that may or may not occur in nature. It is by no means limited to chemistry: Opera is a *synthesis* of music and theater. It was the *synthesis* of the ideas and talents of a great many scientists in the "Manhattan Project" that produced the atom bomb. *Synthetic* (sin thet' ik—*th* as in *thing*) is the adjective, used more in common speech than the noun from which it is formed. Literally, it describes anything produced by *synthesis*, such as *synthetic* rubber; but informally, it has come to mean "artificial, imitation," in a phrase like *house built in synthetic Elizabethan style*. *Synthetic* is also used as a noun, describing substances like nylon or rayon. The verb *to synthesize* (sin' thə size) describes the act of combining elements to form a new whole, called *synthesization* (sin thə sə zay' shən). *Synthesis* was taken over intact from the Greek via Latin; *synthetic* from New Latin *syntheticus*, based on Greek *synthetikos*.

tacit (tas' it) *adj*. What is *tacit* is understood without being expressed in so many words; understood, implied (by the circumstances, or by silence). If I am permitted to walk across your lawn every day while you look on, I can assume that I have your *tacit* approval. Even during the bitterest part of World War I, there was a *tacit* agreement that neither side would fire on Christmas Eve. From Latin *tacitus*, a form of *tacere* (to be silent). Cf. *taciturn*.

taciturn (tas' ə turn) *adj*. A *taciturn* person is uncommunicative, inclined to keep silent; the opposite of *voluble* or *garrulous* or *loquacious*, not disposed to participate in conversation. *Taciturnity* (tas ə turn' ə tee) is the noun. The typical Maine farmer is said to be the personification of *taciturnity*. Calvin Coolidge (1872–1933) was a man so *taciturn* that when his death was announced, Dorothy Parker (1893–1967), the American writer famous for her sardonic wit, asked: "How can they tell?" Aldous Huxley (1894–1963) used the expression "from self-revealing sociability to *taciturn* misanthropy." When Polonius, in giving advice to his son Laertes (*Hamlet*, act I, scene 3), included the admonition to "Give every man thine ear, but few thy voice," he was praising the virtues of *taciturnity*; and Sir William Osler (1849–1919), the Canadian physician and philosopher, admonished people to "cultivate the gift of *taciturnity*"; but *taciturn* people are often considered cold and unfeeling. From Latin *taciturnus*, based on *tacitus*, a form of *tacere* (to be silent). Cf. *tacit*.

tactile (tak′ təl, tak′ tile) *adj*. *Tactile* describes anything pertaining to or using the sense of touch, or anything perceptible to touch, i.e., tangible. Some animals, especially sea creatures, have only a *tactile* relationship to their environment. When a person is blind from birth, his *tactile* sense becomes greatly enhanced. The Braille system was created as a means of *tactile* communication of written words and symbols for the sightless. From Latin *tactilis*, based on *tactus*, a form of *tangere* (to touch), also the source of *tangible* and *tangent*.

tangential (tan jen′ chəl) *adj*. Anthing *tangential* is a deviation or digression from the main point or subject; it wanders or strays off from the real or basic issue. the word can also mean "incidental," to describe something that touches only lightly on another subject; it is based upon *tangent*, which means "touching" generally, and as a noun has various meanings in geometry, like a straight line that just touches a circle at only one point. A good deal of time is wasted in television interviews by the subject's drifting off into one *tangential* point after another, particularly if he is trying to evade the issue. From Latin *tangens*, a form of *tangere* (to touch).

tangible (tan′ jə bəl) *adj*. Literally, *tangible* describes anything that can be felt, perceived by touch; but it has been extended, in its normal use, to mean "actual, substantial," (rather than imaginary), "definite" (as opposed to vague). In law, especially in the phrase *tangible assets*, the adjective describes those things that have an actual physical being, like real estate, furniture, and jewelry, as opposed to "intangibles" like bank accounts and securities, which exist only on paper. Even the diehards abandoned President Nixon upon the presentation of the *tangible* evidence—the "smoking gun" of the taped conversations. The knowledge of foreign languages is a *tangible* advantage to international travelers and diplomats. The creation of a work of art is a *tangible* achievement. From Latin *tangibilis*, based on *tangere* (to touch). *Intangible*, literally speaking, is the opposite of *tangible*, describing things that cannot be perceived by touch, but has been extended to mean "vague" or "elusive," like an *intangible* feeling of imminent disaster or an *intangible* sense of uneasiness.

tautology (taw tol′ ə jee) *n. Tautology* is the unnecessary use of words that merely repeat a thought and perform no other function, words that add nothing by way of additional information or clarification. Examples: *an inexperienced beginner; a hot scorcher of a day; a widow woman.* When the sports announcer tells you the score is tied at five to five, he is guilty of *tautology*: all he had to say was "tied at five." The adjective is *tautological* (tawt ə loj′ ə kəl). It is *tautological* to speak of "a patriot who loves his country" or "a novice who has just started." The speeches of politicans are filled with *tautological* flourishes that often diminish rather than enlarge the force of their oratory. From Late Latin *tautologia*, taken over from the Greek, based on *tauto* (the same) plus *logos* (word).

tawdry (taw′ dree) *adj.* Anything *tawdry* is cheap, showy, and gaudy, without real value or taste, while trying to appear elegant: often implying a pathetic attempt to seem better off than one is, without the necessary money or taste to bring it off. A faded beauty who has fallen on hard times decked out in her *tawdry* best is a pathetic sight. *Tawdry* is a corruption of *St. Audrey*, at whose annual fair in Ely, England, cheap flashy lace, called *St. Audrey's lace*, was offered for sale. The word was eventually applied to anything cheap, showy, in bad taste. In Shakespeare's *The Winter's Tale* (act IV, scene 4) the shepherdess Mopsa says to Clown, "Come, you promised me a *tawdry*-lace, a pair of sweet gloves." (*Tawdry*, as an adjective, came into use after Shakespeare's time.)

tedious (tee′ dee əs, tee′ jəs) *adj. Tedious* means "boring." Some people can make the most trivial incidents interesting; others can make their account of the most unusual adventure *tedious*. A long train ride through a dull landscape, when you have nothing to read and no one to talk to, can be one of the most *tedious* experiences of your life. In Shakespeare's *King John* (act III, scene 4) the dauphin Lewis says to King Philip:

Life is as tedious *as a twice-told tale*
Vexing the dull ear of a drowsy man.

Anatole France (1844–1924) said: "All the historical books which contain no lies are extremely *tedious.*" *Tedium* (tee' dee əm) is the noun. H. W. Fowler, in *A Dictionary of Modern English Usage* (Oxford University Press, Oxford, 1926), under the heading *Quotations,* writes: "pretentious quotations are the surest road to *tedium.*" From Latin *taedium* (boredom) and Late Latin *taediosus* (boring).

temerity (tə merr' ə tee) *n. Temerity* is rashness, reckless lack of fear, unthinking boldness, foolhardiness, especially when motivated by an underestimation or disregard of consequences. It is not often that one meets a private with the *temerity* to argue with a top sergeant. Only a foolish schoolboy would have the *temerity* to recite without having done his homework. Six hundred men died in *The Charge of the Light Brigade* (Tennyson, 1809–1892) as a result of their commander's *temerity.* From Latin *temeritas.*

temporal (tem' pə rəl) *adj.* Like its synonym *secular, temporal* can mean either "worldly" (as opposed to spiritual), or "nonclerical." Before St. Francis experienced revelation and gave himself to the church, his life was devoted to *temporal* pleasures. Churches sometimes resort to *temporal* activities like fairs and bingo games to support their financial needs. Anxiety can be relieved by formal ecclesiastical confession and sometimes by the *temporal* revelations one makes to the psychoanalyst. From Latin *temporalis* (temporary—as opposed to eternal).

tendentious (ten den' shəs) *adj.* Anyone or anything *tendentious* is biased, tending to favor a particular cause or point of view. Newspaper reporters can be quite *tendentious* under the guise of objective journalism. It is important to distinguish between accurate communication and *tendentious* expression. In any investigation it is important to stick to the proven facts and avoid *tendentious* assertions. From Middle Latin *tendentia* (tendency), based on Latin *tendere* (to tend, be inclined).

tenet (ten' ət) *n.* A *tenet* is a belief, an opinion, doctrine, position on a given matter, held as true. If you accept the divinity of Mahomet, you must be prepared to accept every *tenet* of Islam. It is a basic *tenet* of the physical sciences that one must observe and deduce. From Latin *tenet* (he holds), a form of *tenere* (to hold).

tenuous (ten' yoo əs) *adj*. Literally, *tenuous* means "very thin" in either form or consistency, but by extension it has come to mean "of little substance," "thin" in the sense of "not convincing, of little validity." One solid convincing truth is of more substance than a hundred *tenuous* arguments. It is unwise to expect people to accept *tenuous* evidence on faith. Pedants are inclined to make *tenuous* distinctions so they can show off their learning. In the sense of "weak": Toward the end, hunger strikers have only a *tenuous* hold on life. From Latin *tenuis* (thin, slight).

terse (turs) *adj*. *Terse* means "concise, brief, short and sweet," as applied to speech or writing. If you are working for a harried executive it is advisable to make your memoranda as *terse* as possible. A famous example of *terse* communication was the message radioed by an American carrier pilot in World War II: "Sighted sub, sank same"—also, incidentally, a nice example of alliteration. An even *terser* message was dispatched to London in 1843 by Sir Charles Napier (1782–1853), a British general fighting in India. His opponent was the elusive Sind. *Peccavi* is Latin for "I have sinned," and was used as an acknowledgment of guilt or sin in circles with a classical education. When Napier captured Sind, to announce his victory he cabled one word: "Peccavi." From Latin *tersus* (clean, neat), adjective taken from a form of *tergere* (to wipe, cover, clean).

testy (tes' tee) *adj*. A *testy* person is impatient, irritable, easily annoyed and quick to show it, equipped with a short fuse. Long bumper-to-bumper delays make motorists *testy*. Those simple easy directions (translated from the Japanese) for assembling toys and gadgets can make the most easygoing person *testy*. From Middle English *testif* (headstrong).

timorous (tim' ə rəs) *adj*. *Timorous* is a somewhat stronger word for *timid*, implying a higher degree of fear and uncertainty, and a consciousness of weakness in the face of danger. A *timorous* man cannot be trusted in a position of command. The New York subways at midnight are certainly no place for the *timorous*. From Middle Latin *timorosus*, based on Latin *timor* (fear).

titular (tit' yə lər, tich' ə lər) *adj*. *Titular* means "having the title but without real authority." The *titular* head of an organization is without authority; his alleged subordinates are really running the show. Queen Elizabeth is the *titular* head of state, but the prime minister makes the decisions. From Latin *titulus* (title of honor).

toady (toe' dee) *n., vb.* A *toady* is an obsequious flatterer who fawns on someone and caters to his every whim in order to get into or stay in favor. Almost everybody appreciates an admirer, but sensitive people are put off by *toadies*. When someone becomes a celebrity, *toadies* spring up around him like mushrooms after a shower. The verb, *to toady*, describes the acts of a *toady*, who engages in excessive deference toward another purely from self-interest. An unknown composer may *toady* to a great conductor in the hope of getting his composition played. Old acquaintance may *toady* to one who has won the sweepstakes or has inherited money, in the hope that crumbs may fall from the tabletop. Some people prefer proud, independent cats to demonstrative *toadying* dogs. *Toady* is formed from *toad* in its figurative sense of "object of aversion," by simply adding the adjectival *-y*.

torpid (tor' pəd) *adj.* A *torpid* person or animal or mind is slow, sluggish, lacking in vigor, apathetic, dull. In the early-morning hours, many insects seem too *torpid* to move; as the sun warms their nests, they become active again. All too often, the vigorous youth of yesterday becomes the overweight, *torpid* gentleman of today. An organ of the body, too, can become *torpid* and cease to function properly. Life in the tropics often makes the natives too *torpid* to work efficiently. From Latin *torpidus* (numb).

tortuous (tor' choo əs) *adj.* This word describes anything, like a road or path, that is full of twists and turns; figuratively, it means "devious, not straightforward." The *tortuous* country lanes in England were originally cowpaths made by the meandering herds. The path to success is steep and *tortuous*. Sophists engage in *tortuous* reasoning. Recalcitrant witnesses give *tortuous* testimony. From Latin *tortuosus* (full of turns and windings). Do not confuse *tortuous* with *torturous* (causing or marked by torture).

traduce (trə doos', trə dyoos') *vb.* To *traduce* is to slander, malign, vilify, accuse falsely of some base acton. By his relentless innuendo, Iago *traduced* the character of Desdemona. Richard Nixon *traduced* the very name of the Democratic party by accusing it of "twenty years of treason." In Shakespeare's *Henry*

VIII (act I, scene 2), Cardinal Wolsey complains to King Henry and Queen Katharine of being "*traduced* by ignorant tongues, which neither know my faculties nor person...." From Latin *traducere* (to expose).

transcend (tran send') *vb.* To *transcend* is to exceed, surpass, rise above, go beyond. This word is nearly always used in a favorable sense. Your kindness *transcends* the bounds of hospitality. Some poetry *transcends* mere individual experience; it deals with the experience of all mankind. *Transcendent* (trans send' ənt) and *transcendental* (tran sen dent' əl) are the adjectives. *Transcendent* means "surpassing, exceeding the limits of ordinary human experience": To the average man who loves his comfort, the courage of explorers in remote and dangerous places seems *transcendent*. *Transcendental* has a number of technical applications in philosophy, but can be used as synonymous with *transcendent*. The currently popular system of "*Transcendental* Meditation" professes to *transcend* the normal workings of the mind, to go above and beyond it. From Latin *transcendere* (to climb over); the adjective is from the form *transcendens*.

travesty (trav' ə stee) *n.* A *travesty* is, literally, a comic imitation of a serious work of art, generally a literary or dramatic work, poking fun at it; in this sense, *travesty* has about the same meaning as *burlesque*. By extension, it is used to denote any grotesque or degraded imitation. The *travesty* can be intentional, as in the case of a "fun" production of an ancient classic, complete with contemporary political allusions, telephone props, and other anachronisms; or unintentional, as in a case where the judge is so biased that the trial is a *travesty* of justice. There are elections so conducted, with the buying of votes and intimidation of voters, as to amount only to a *travesty* of democracy. In this latter category, there belongs as well any work of art so poorly done that it may be characterized as only a *travesty* of the original, which it sought, sincerely but inadequately, to imitate. From French *travesti* (disguised), based on Latin *trans* (across, to the other side of) plus *vestire* (to dress), from which we also get *transvestite* and *transvestism*, a special kind of *travesty*.

tremulous (trem' yə ləs) *adj.* One who is *tremulous* is trembling with nervousness or timidity. The word often describes someone who is nervously hesitant about saying or doing something, or fearful of some imminent event. Actors wait to read the first night reviews and turn *tremulously* to the theatrical section of the newspapers. Most of us have been in the *tremulous* state in which we walk into the boss's office to ask for a raise. A knock on the door in the dead of night produces a *tremulous* reaction. From Latin *tremulus*.

trenchant (tren' chənt) *adj*. Originally, *trenchant* meant "cutting, sharp," but it is now used only in its figurative sense of "forceful, incisive, effective," sometimes even "caustic." The plays of Oscar Wilde (1854-1900) and George Bernard Shaw (1856-1950) are full of *trenchant* wit. The crisis facing President Franklin D. Roosevelt at his inauguration called for a *trenchant* policy of financial and social reform. The success and fame of the great lawyer Clarence Darrow (1857-1938) were based on his ability to present *trenchant* arguments in a powerful way. From Old French *trenchant*, a form of *trenchier* (to cut).

trepidation (trep ə day' shən) *n*. *Trepidation* is anxious uncertainty, fear and anxiety, nervous agitation. People who invest on thin margin look at each day's market reports with some degree of *trepidation*. *Trepidation* marks the faces of those poor refugees seeking immigration visas to safe havens. From Latin *trepidatio*, based on *trepidus* (anxious). Cf. *intrepid*.

truculent (truk' yə lənt) *adj*. A truculent person is aggressively hostile, belligerent, ready to fight or take offense on very small provocation, defiant. Originally, it meant "brutal, fierce, ferocious," but this use is seldom heard now. Idi Amin was characteristic of the boasting, *truculent* tinhorn dictator. *Truculent* is just the adjective for the little boy who says his big brother can lick anybody. Don't try to reason with anyone who stands there with clenched fists and a *truculent* expression. The noun is *truculence* (truk' yə ləns). From Latin *truculentus* (rough, ferocious).

truism (troo' iz əm) *n*. A *truism* is a statement so obviously true as to seem hardly necessary to put into words; something one would think everyone would have to agree with, without argument. Most *truisms* are hackneyed. Examples: Nothing lasts forever; we're all human; Rome wasn't built in a day. All truisms are clichés, or platitudes; the reverse isn't necessarily so: it isn't inarguably true that you can't make a horse drink (just get him thirsty enough) or that there's many a slip (just be careful holding the cup). *True* is from Middle English trewe; akin to

German *treu*; *truism* merely omits the *e* and adds the noun ending *-ism*.

truncate (trung' kate) *vb*. To *truncate* is to shorten by cutting off an end or cutting out a part. It is usually heard in the form of the adjective *truncated*, meaning "shortened," but almost always in the figurative sense of "incomplete." It is necessary for newspaper make-up men to *truncate* some news items to fit into available space. Some think that *though* is a *truncated* form of *although*; it isn't so: *although* is a contraction of the early form *all though*, originally an emphatic or intensive form of *though*. To a well-versed Shakespearean, *truncated* versions can be irritating, especially as he waits expectantly for a favorite line that has been cut. From Latin *truncatus*, a form of *truncare* (to shorten by cutting off, to mutilate).

turgid (tur' jid) *adj*. *Turgid* can be used in its literal sense of "swollen, distended," or in the figurative sense of "pompous, ostentatious, overembellished," particularly as applied to language. Gum or tooth infection can make one's whole cheek *turgid*. A good many editorials can be made less *turgid* by cutting out half the words. The prose (and poetry) in the love letters of adolescents is often overblown and *turgid*. From Latin *turgidus*.

tyro (tie' roe) *n*. A *tyro* is a beginner, a novice, especially in some skill or trade. Watching an expert at work is a useful way for a *tyro* to spend his time. If a *tyro* is serious about learning his craft, you must be gentle in correcting his mistakes. Sometimes spelled *tiro*, which is the Latin noun from which we get *tyro* (recruit; by extension, novice).

ubiquitous (yoo bik' wə təs) *adj*. A *ubiquitous* person or thing is one that is everywhere at the same time (or seems to be). The *ubiquitous* sea surrounded the ancient mariner but he almost died of thirst ("Water, water, everywhere/Nor any drop to drink" —Samuel Taylor Coleridge, 1772–1834, in *The Rime of the Ancient Mariner*). On a warm summer evening, we must often flee indoors because of the *ubiquitous* gnats. Our big cities are becoming frightening because of the *ubiquitous* crime. From Latin *ubique* (everywhere).

umbrage (um' brij) *n.* *Umbrage* is a feeling of offense, resentment, extreme displeasure and annoyance, usually found in the expression *to take umbrage*, meaning "to take offense," although one can *give umbrage* or *feel umbrage*, but *take* is the usual verb. Sensitive older ladies often take *umbrage* at the unintentional rudeness of little children. One has to take great care in issuing invitations to a wedding; for each person you invite, there might be two to take *umbrage* by being left out. The comedian Jackie Gleason gives this advice: "Never take *umbrage* unless you can lick the guy." From Latin *umbratus*, a form of *umbrare* (to shade), which also gave us *umbrella*.

unconscionable (un kon' shən ə bəl) *adj.* This adjective describes actions, attitudes, etc., that are unscrupulous, not restrained by one's conscience; excessive, extreme, improper to the point of outrage; always in a bad sense. In their attempts to cover up the criminal acts of the Watergate burglars, President Nixon and his immediate staff were guilty of *unconscionable* behavior. A shocking amount of government money is spent on *unconscionable* cost overruns. The adverb is *unconscionably* (un kon' shən ə blee). Even the most devout parishioners begin to squirm when the sermon is *unconscionably* long. From the combination of the negative prefix *un-*, plus *conscion* (formed by "back formation" from *conscience*) plus adjectival ending *-able*: *conscience* is from Latin *conscientia* (awareness, conscience). As is so often the case with negative adjectives, the positive form, *conscionable*, is rarely used.

unctuous (ungk' choo əs) *adj.* An *unctuous* manner is oily, over-earnest and excessively considerate, overly pious. Literally, *unctuous* is used to describe anything actually oily or greasy, but in common usage the word implies an affectation of sincerity for an ulterior purpose, usually to ingratiate oneself in order to gain some unstated goal. The *unctuous* manner of subordinates often earns disrespect rather than promotion. Even in their bereavement, many people are disquieted, rather than soothed, by the unctuous posture of most funeral directors. Do not confuse the noun *unctuousness* with *unction* (anointing with oil; figuratively, affected earnestness; *extreme unction* is the Catholic rite of anointing the dying). From Middle Latin *unctuosus*, based on Latin *unctun* (ointment), from *unctus*, a form of *ungere* (to anoint, besmear). According to the author's *English English* (Verbatim, Essex, CT, 1980), the British use the slang word *smarmy* to mean "oily" in the sense of "*unctuous*": *Smarmy* is undoubtedly related to *smear*, which is what one does with both oil and flattery.

unfathomable (un fath' əm ə bəl—*th* as in *the*) *adj.* Anything *unfathomable* is incomprehensible; something whose meaning you cannot penetrate. The word is based on the verb *to fathom*, meaning "to measure the depth of," and by extension, "to understand." (In its literal application, *fathoming* is measuring in units of *fathoms*, one *fathom* being equal to six feet, and this usage is exclusively nautical.) Philosophers of different schools often find each other's reasoning to be *unfathomable*. Even ardent admirers of Robert Burns (1759–1796) find a good deal of his poetry *unfathomable*, and even those who most loudly proclaim the virtues of James Joyce (1882–1941) agree that *Finnegans Wake* without a key is largely *unfathomable*. *Fathom* came from Old English *faethme*, the measure equal to the length of outstretched arms. *Unfathomable* is one of those negative adjectives whose positive form is rarely heard.

unflagging (un flag' ing) *adj.* *Unflagging* means "untiring, persistently determined, not about to quit." The verb *to flag* means "to become weary, slow down from fatigue," and can be applied either to physical energy or interest. The form *flagging* is met with in phrases like *flagging spirits, flagging efforts*. Mountaineers are notable for their dogged and *unflagging* exertions in the face of the most adverse weather conditions. The invention of the electric light bulb was the result of the *unflagging* efforts of Thomas Edison (1847–1931). See *unconscionable* for comment on negative adjectives. The derivation of the verb *to flag* is said by some to be from the blending of *flap* and *fag*. Maybe.

unmitigated (un mit' ə gāte əd) *adj.* What is *unmitigated* is absolute, not modified or diminished in any degree; used almost always in a pejorative sense. Judas Iscariot is the universal example of the *unmitigated* traitor. The Johnstown flood (1889), the Chicago fire (1871) and the San Francisco earthquake (1906) were *unmitigated* natural disasters. Karl Friedrich Hieronymus, Baron von Munchhäusen (1720–1797), known familiarly in the English-speaking world as "Baron Munchausen," was one of the most *unmitigated* liars in history—a teller of tales as tall as a mountain. Simon Legree, the brutal slave dealer in *Uncle Tom's Cabin* (Harriet Beecher Stowe, 1811–1896), is the prototype of the merciless, *unmitigated* scoundrel. See **mitigate** for derivation.

unpropitious (un prə pish' əs) *adj*. See **propitious**.

unseemly (un seem' lee) *adj*. *Unseemly* means "improper," particularly in behavior or manners; especially describing actions socially inappropriate in a specific situation. Dirty jokes are *unseemly* in the presence of a clergyman. It is *unseemly* to make unfavorable ethnic comparisons in the presence of a member of the minority involved. Midnight is an *unseemly* hour for a casual visit. The positive adjective *seemly* is less frequently used than *unseemly*, which comes from prefix *un-* plus *seemly*, based on Middle English *semeli*.

unsullied (un sul' eed) *adj*. See **sully**.

untenable (un ten' ə bəl) *adj*. What is *untenable* is impossible to defend or maintain; usually applied to theories, arguments, and positions taken. If you keep piling supposition on supposition you will soon find yourself in an *untenable* position. There is a school of thought that Darwin was wrong; the argument of its adherents, based on emotional fundamentalism, flies so directly in the face of scientific evidence as to be *untenable*. In the face of the new tank assault, the infantry platoon's position rapidly became *untenable*. The positive adjective *tenable* is less often used; it was taken over intact from the French, which was based on Latin *tenere* (to hold). *Untenable* is a combination of prefix *un-* plus *tenable*.

untrammeled (un tram' əld) *adj*. *Untrammeled* means "not restricted or hampered," often in the phrase *free and untrammeled*. *Trammel* is a noun whose figurative meaning is "hindrance, impediment," and the verb *to trammel* means "to hamper, restrain." Neither the noun nor the positive verb is at all common; see *unconscionable* for comment on negative adjectives. The natives of those idyllic South Sea islands have a free and easy life-style *untrammeled* by the demands and conventions of life in the developed countries. Our dreams are *untrammeled* by the confines of reality. This word has an interesting derivation: a *trammel net* is a three-layered fishnet; *trammel* comes from Middle French *tramail* (three-mesh net), based on Late Latin *tremaculun*, which came from a combination of Latin *tres* (three) plus *macula* (mesh of a net). *Untrammeled* is a combination of prefix *un-* plus *trammeled*, a form of the verb *to trammel*.

uxorious (uk sor′ ee əs, ug zor′ ee əs) *adj*. An *uxorious* husband is one who obsessively dotes on his wife, and is slavishly submissive to her. Macbeth and Mark Antony are portrayed in some accounts as the victims of their *uxoriousness*. Though it is unusual for an *uxorious* husband to rebel, worms have been known to turn. From Latin *uxorius*, based on *uxor* (wife).

vacillate (vas′ ə late) *vb*. To *vacillate* is to waver, hesitate, be indecisive, swing back and forth between feelings or opinions, be unable to make up one's mind. Originally it meant "to sway to and fro." People who *vacillate* make poor executives and even poorer generals. The noun is *vacillation* (vas ə lay′ shən). The *vacillation* of a head of state on matters of disarmament sends ambiguous signals to the other nations of the world. From Latin *vacillatus*, a form of *vacillare* (to totter, sway to and fro).

vacuous (vak′ yoo əs) *adj*. Anyone or anything *vacuous* is inane, empty-headed, without substance. A book or a conversation or a look or a person can be characterized as *vacuous*. There is no point in arguing with a *vacuous* mind. Audiences listening to incomprehensible contemporary music often just sit there with *vacuous* stares. The contents of many of the tracts handed out on the streets by well-meaning disciples are *vacuous* to the point of bewilderment. When applied to a face, a look, a stare, a person's eyes, *vacuous* means "expressionless." From Latin *vacuus* (empty), which gave us *vacuum*.

vagary (va ger′ ee, və gay′ ree, vay′ gə ree) *n*. This word, meaning "unpredictable, erratic turn of events," is almost always used in the plural. People unwilling to chance the *vagaries* of spring weather should not make elaborate picnic plans in April. Broadway angels must take their chances with the *vagaries* of the theater. From Latin *vagari* (to wander, ramble). From the same source we get *vagrant* and *vague*.

vapid (vap′ id) *adj*. What is *vapid* is insipid, flat, dull. What is more painful than a long plane ride sitting beside a garrulous, *vapid* passenger who won't let you read? It is irritating to recount an adventure that seems exciting to you, only to be met by a fixed, patient, *vapid* smile. Shaggy dog stories have intentionally *vapid* tag lines. The noun is *vapidity* (vəpid′ ə tee). From Latin *vapidus* (spiritless, flat).

variegated (var′ ee ə gate əd) *adj.* This term is narrowly applied to anything marked by a variety of patchwork colors and, more generally, to things that are varied in other ways. Some common synonyms in the narrower sense are *dappled*, *motley*, *parti-colored*. *Variegated* autumn leaves make a dazzling show in the setting sun. In the more general sense: The supporters of the French revolution were a wildly *variegated* lot, drawn from all classes of society. Here, the closest synonym would be *diversified*. From Late Latin *variegatus*, a form of *variegare* (to make [something] look varied).

vehement (vee′ ə mənt) *adj.* *Vehement* means "impassioned, intensely emotional, violent, extremely forceful." The abolitionists toured the countryside making one *vehement* speech after another attacking slavery. "No! No! *A thousand times no!*" was the form of the heroine's *vehement* rejection of the villain's lecherous advances in old-time melodrama. The noun is *vehemence* (vee′ ə məns). Churchill's many speeches defying the Nazis were delivered with his special brand of *vehemence* that so greatly stirred his people. Like so many persons who eventually admit their guilt, Vice President Spiro Agnew at first *vehemently* denied all charges. From Latin *vehemens*.

venal (veen′ əl) *adj.* A *venal* person is capable of being bought, susceptible to bribery. *Venal* public officials were the curse of the corrupt administration of Boss Tweed (1823–1878). Beware of *venal* journalists who slant their stories. From Latin *venalis* (for sale; by extension, venal). Do not confuse *venal* with *venial*.

veneer (və neer′) *n.* Literally, *veneer* is the term for a thin layer of finer wood laid over cheaper material in furniture, walls, etc. Figuratively, the word is used to describe a superficial show or pretense of a good quality to cover up something disreputable or undesirable. Some of the world's most notorious criminals put on a *veneer* of piety and respectability. Even in advanced cultures, there is only a thin *veneer* of refinement covering up people's primitive instincts. From German *Furnier* (veneer).

venerate (ven′ ə rate) *vb.* To *venerate* is to respect deeply, to honor as sacred or noble, to revere. This word is mostly used when describing the feelings inspired by someone or something honored and usually fairly old. It is a custom of Oriental people to *venerate* their ancestors. We *venerate* the monuments of ancient lands. Abraham Lincoln exhorted his listeners to *venerate* both the battleground and the brave men who fell at Gettysburg. From Latin *veneratus*, a form of *venerari* (to revere, worship). The adjective *venerable* (ven' ə rə bəl) is applied to someone or something worthy of being *venerated*, commanding respect because of great age or great accomplishments, like a *venerable* member of the Senate, a *venerable* church or a *venerable* redwood tree; from Latin *venerabilis*.

venial (veen' yəl) *adj*. What is *venial* is pardonable, forgivable, not serious. This word is heard mainly in the phrase *venial sin* (as opposed to *mortal sin*—both as defined in the teachings of the Roman Catholic Church). A white lie motivated by kindness is merely a *venial* sin. Doing forty on a wide, straight road with a thirty-five m.p.h. limit, in light traffic when the weather is fine, should be considered a *venial* offense. Erasers are attached to the end of pencils for the correction of *venial* errors. From Middle Latin *venialis*, based on Latin *venia* (indulgence, forgiveness). Do not confuse *venial* with *venal*.

veracious (və ray' shəs) *adj*. When applied to a statement, *veracious* means "true"; applied to a person, "truthful." Disguised as fiction, novels are sometimes *veracious* accounts of actual incidents. When a person is described as *veracious*, it means that he habitually speaks the truth. A *veracious* reporter who fears no special interests commands the respect of the public. The noun, *veracity* (və ras' ə tee), meaning "truthfulness, accuracy," is used more often than the adjective. It is up to the jury to determine the *veracity* of a witness. Emile Zola (1840–1902), in *J'accuse*, successfully challenged the *veracity* of the "incriminating" documents in the Dreyfus case. From Latin *veracis*, a form of *verax* (truthful), and Middle Latin *veracitas*, respectively. Do not confuse *veracious* with *voracious*.

verisimilitude (verr ə sim il' ə tood, verr ə sim il' ə tyood) *n*. This word expresses the quality of appearing to be true or real or plausible, especially applicable to the representations of reality in fiction or painting. In historical novels, conversations that could not possibly have been recorded are believable only if they possess *verisimilitude*. Despite impressionistic technique, the still lifes and landscapes of Paul Cézanne (1839–1906) succeed in establishing *verisimilitude*. From Latin *verisimilitudo* (probability).

veritable (verr′ ə tə bəl) *adj.* Something *veritable* is not simply true, it is absolutely and positively so, no way to be denied. An argument that started out with mild insults might turn into a *veritable* battle royal, with fisticuffs and smashed furniture. A wife who seemed all sweet compliance can, in the fullness of time, become a *veritable* tyrant in the home. The word is taken over without change from Middle French *véritable*, going back to Latin *veritas* (truth), still heard in the proverb "*In vino veritas*" (literally, "In wine there is truth"; in other words, liquor loosens tongues).

vertigo (vur′ tə go) *n.* *Vertigo* is dizziness, giddiness, the feeling that one, or the world about him, is whirling about. When some people look down from a height they suffer from *vertigo*. *Vertigo* can be used figuratively to mean "bewilderment, extreme confusion": A country boy's first exposure to the big city can produce such a feeling of *vertigo* that he wants to rush back to the farm. Taken over intact from the Latin, where its literal meaning is "whirling around" and its figurative meaning is "giddiness."

vicissitude (və sis′ ə tood, və sis′ ə tyood) *n.* This word is almost always heard in the plural, *vicissitudes*, meaning the "ups and downs" of life, the unpredictable changes of fortune. Hoboes somehow manage to remain cheerful in spite of the *vicissitudes* of life on the road. Real friendships endure despite the *vicissitudes* of many years. From Latin *vicissitudo*.

vignette (vin yet′) *n.* This word was originally applied to those old photographs or portraits shaded off gradually at the edges, or to decorative designs representing branches and leaves (*vignette* is French for "little vine"); now commonly applied to a brief literary sketch, by itself or as part of a larger piece. Literary *vignettes* are chiefly descriptive and are usually characterized by delicacy, charm, and wit. The novels of Agatha Christie (1891–1976) are full of vignettes of English country life that embellish the scene without holding up the action. The word is sometimes loosely applied to a brief scene in real life that amounts to a typical "slice of life": for instance, mother berating child, boss ogling secretary, furtive petty criminal eluding policeman.

vilify (vil′ ə fy) *vb.* To *vilify* is to speak ill of, to defame, with the implication that the charge is unfair. Dr. Samuel Johnson (1709–1784), author of the first standard English dictionary, remarked that "the vulgar mind ridicules and *vilifies* what it cannot comprehend." The noun is *vilification* (vil ə fə kay' shən). the Ayatollah Khomeini's *vilification* of our President and people whipped up the frenzy of the Iranian "students." From Late Latin *vilificare* (to vilify), based on Latin *vilis* (cheap, of little value) plus *-ficare*, compound form of *facere* (to make, do).

virago (vir ay' go) *n*. A *virago* is an extremely quarrelsome, loud-mouthed, scolding shrew. Xanthippe (zan tip' ee), who lived in the late fifth century and was the wife of the Athenian philosopher Socrates (469–399 B.C.), was such a *virago* and so well known as such that her name became a synonym for a scolding, ill-tempered wife. One of the most famous *viragoes* in literature is Katharina, the heroine of Shakespeare's *The Taming of the Shrew*. An interesting derivation, from Latin *virago* (a man-like woman, female warrior) based on *vir* (man), from which we get *virile* and *virility*.

virtuoso (vur choo oh' so) *n., adj*. A *virtuoso* is a person of outstanding skill; a term usually applied in the field of music, but not necessarily so. At the age of four, Mozart (1756–1791) was already enough of a *virtuoso* to astound his elders. Laurence Olivier (b. 1907) can play almost any role; he is a true *virtuoso*. As an adjective: Every concert conducted by Arturo Toscanini (1867–1957) was a *virtuoso* performance. Benjamin Franklin (1706–1790) set an example of *virtuoso* diplomacy. To be technically correct, a female qualifying for the adjective should be known as a *virtuosa*, but this usage should be discouraged as pedantic, like the shouting of "Brava!" at the opera or ballet. The practice, if not pedantic, is at least precious. The noun expressing a *virtuoso*'s capability is *virtuosity* (vur choo os' ə tee—*o* as in *pot*). The *virtuosity* of Leonardo da Vinci (1452–1519)—to say nothing of his versatility: painter, sculptor, engineer, architect, musician, mathematician—has set a standard for all time. Taken over intact from the Italian, based on Middle Latin *virtuosus*, drawn from Latin *virtus* (excellence), from which we get *virtue* and related words.

virulent (vir' yə lənt—*i* as it *bit*) *adj*. *Virulent* means "poisonous, extremely noxious"; medically, "highly infective"; figuratively, "violently hostile, bitter, spiteful." The venom of a cobra is *virulent* to the point of being deadly. An epidemic of bubonic plague (the "Black Death"), which spread over Europe in the fourteenth century, was so *virulent* that it killed an estimated quarter of the population. Senator Joseph McCarthy

(1909–1957) was far-famed and ill-famed as the master of *virulent* accusation of innocent people. *Virulence* (veer' yə ləns) is the noun: The *virulence* of Hitler's ranting orations marked him as a madman. From Latin *virulentus* and *virulentia*, respectively, based on *virus* (poison).

visage (viz' əj) *n*. This term is applied to the face of a human being, usually with reference to its features, expression, or size. The expressions on the *visages* of the figures of Botticelli (1444–1510) seem truly to be the product of divine inspiration. The stern *visage* of the judge on the bench may well belie his human sympathy. In Shakespeare's *Measure for Measure* (act V, scene 1) Lucio cries to the Duke, disguised as a friar: "Show your knave's *visage*, with a pox to you." Taken over intact from the French, who pronounce it vee zahzh'.

visceral (vis' ər əl) *adj*. In its literal sense, *visceral* (from the noun *viscera*, denoting the internal organs of the body, especially the intestines) would be used in medical references, but it is far more commonly used figuratively, relating to intuitive, inward feelings, instinctive response, "gut reaction." People with long experience in a field are often guided more by *visceral* reactions than by intellectual reasoning. People who can't look you in the eye impart a *visceral* feeling of distrust. *Visceral* is from Middle Latin *visceralis*, based on Latin *viscera* (internal organs).

vitriolic (vih tree ah' lik) *adj*. *Vitriolic* (based on *oil of vitriol*, which is sulphuric acid) is used commonly to mean "scathing, savagely hostile, venomously biting," usually used to describe that kind of verbal attack or attacker. It was the *vitriolic* denunciation by Edward R. Murrow (1908–1965) of Senator Joseph McCarthy (1909–1957) that eventually brought about the latter's downfall. Hitler's *vitriolic* fulminations against his enemies produced a thunderous chorus of "*Sieg heil!*" The *vitriolic* speeches of the Communist delegations to the United Nations are unseemly outbursts at an organization devoted to world peace. *Vitriolic* is the adjectival form based Middle Latin *vitriolum*.

vituperative (vye tyoo' pə rə tiv) *adj*. Anything *vituperative*, particularly speech or language, is harsh or abusive. *Vituperative* language is the language of vicious and violent denunciaton. It is embarrassing to overhear the mutually *vituperative* shrieks of fishwives. The Communists are given to hurling *vituperative* abuse at those who differ with them in matters of political opinion. The verb is to *vituperate* (vye tyoo′ pə rate), and the noun is *vituperation* (vye tyoo pə ray′ shən); neither is quite so common as the adjective. Toward the end of a long and wearing presidential campaign, the hitherto somewhat restrained candidates finally let go and heap *vituperation* upon each other. From Latin *vituperatus*, a form of *vituperare* (to blame, scold, censure).

vociferous (vo sif′ ər əs) *adj.* *Vociferous* shouting is clamorous, unrestrained, insistent in expressing one's views. "Extra! Extra! Read all about it!" was the *vociferous* cry of the old-time corner newsboy. Union leaders can become quite *vociferous* in stating their demands. An adoring audience becomes more and more *vociferous* in its cries of "Encore! Encore!" as the cast repeats its bows. From Latin *vociferari* (to cry aloud). The verb to *vociferate* (vo sif′ ər ate) is less common than the adjective.

voluble (vol′ yə bəl) *adj.* A *voluble* person is very talkative, prone to use a great volume of words, usually a rapid talker (and not much of a listener). *Voluble* is the opposite of *taciturn*. Iago, in Shakespeare's *Othello* (act II, scene 1), lying to Roderigo about Desdemona's passion for Cassio, calls Cassio "a knave very *voluble*," or what in today's slang might be called a "fast talker." A *voluble* person can be the life of a party, or an annoying nuisance, depending on the circumstances. From Latin *volubilis* (rapid, fluent in speech).

voracious (vo ray′ shəs) *adj.* This word has a special narrow meaning relating to food and eating: "ravenous, craving and consuming great amounts of food." Most teen-agers have *voracious* appetites. Gluttons are *voracious*. In its general sense, it means "insatiable, eager to get and consume (almost anything)." Many youngsters are *voracious* readers of comic books. William Randolph Hearst (1863–1951), the newspaper publisher, was a *voracious* collector of all kinds of works of art. From Latin *voracis*, a form of *vorax* (gluttonous). Do not confuse *voracious* with *veracious*.

votary (vo′ tə ree) *n.* A *votary* is a person devoted to a particular religion, cause, ideal, subject, pursuit, etc. More narrowly, it applies to those vowed to the service of God, like a priest, nun, or monk. In its general sense, it can denote any ardent adherent. Every sport has its *votaries*. The extreme enthusiasm of the *votaries* of rock-'n'-roll is usually quite puzzling to the older generations. Gambling casinos are crammed with the *votaries* of chance. From Latin *votum* (vow) which also gives us *vote* and *devoted*, which *votaries* most definitely are.

votive (vo' tiv) *adj.* *Votive* describes anything given in fulfillment of a pledge or vow; now most often found in the phrases *votive offering* and *votive Mass*, but applicable to other things: At times, a *votive* monument is erected to the memory of a benefactor. Churches often glow with the light of a multitude of *votive* candles. The faded beauty in *The Lady Who Offers Her Looking-Glass to Venus* (Matthew Prior, 1664–1721), a devotee of that goddess, says:

> *Lady, take my* votive *glass,*
> *Since I am not what I was,*
> *What from this day I shall be,*
> *Venus, let me never see.*

A *votive Mass* is one said outside the priest's customary schedule, for some special purpose or occasion. From Latin *votivus*, based on *votum* (vow).

waft (waft) *vb.* To *waft* is to travel or carry lightly through the air. It is pleasant when the aroma of freshly cut grass *wafts* across the field. Music is especially pleasant when it is *wafted* by gentle breezes over water. The smell of freshly brewed coffee *wafting* through the house is one of the pleasures of life. Derivation uncertain; may be from Middle English *waughten* (to convoy).

wag (wag) *n.* A *wag* is a roguish wit, a person given to droll humor. Court jesters were professional *wags*. Shakespeare's clowns are *wags*, whose roguish wit relieves the starkest tragedy. "We wink at *wags* when they offend," wrote John Dryden (1631–1700). *Waggish* is the adjective, *waggery* (wag' ə ree) the noun for the conduct of a *wag*. The writings of the English clergyman and novelist Laurence Sterne (1713–1768), particularly *Tristram Shandy*, are full of *waggish* humor. The tale is told of S.J. Perelman (1904–1979), the American humorist, who, when beset by a horde of ladies of the evening on leaving a restaurant in Taipei, remarked to his apologetic native companion, "Think nothing of it; it's just a case of the tail dogging the *wag*." Derivation uncertain.

wanton (wahn' tən) *n.*, *adj.* As an adjective, *wanton* has a variety of uses. It can describe an act committed deliberately, without justification and maliciously: It is shocking to see the results of *wanton* vandalism committed on our city streets. The guards at the Nazi concentration camps committed one act of *wanton* cruelty after another. *Wanton* can mean "uncalled-for, willful": People often throw away opportunities in a *wanton* way. Another meaning is "careless, reckless": Avoid *wanton* remarks that may offend the sensibilities of others. A special and frequent meaning relates to sexual morals and behavior: "loose, lewd, lascivious; sexually without restraint." Casanova (1725–1798) and the legendary Don Juan are the prototypes of the *wanton* male. An old-fashioned use is made of *wanton* as a noun, denoting one who acts *wantonly*, almost always describing a female, a "loose woman," reflecting the sexist prejudices now happily much less prevalent than in the days when this usage was coined. From Middle English *wantowen* (ill-reared).

waspish (wahs' pish) *adj.* A *waspish* person is ill-tempered, sharp-tongued, ready to snap at others. It is a term that can be applied to writing or speech as well as individuals. Many people are inclined to be a bit *waspish* in the morning, before they've had their first cup of coffee. Intemperate foremen and typical drill sergeants can dismay you with their *waspish* comments. Obviously based on the antics of the wasp of the Vespidae and Sphecidae families of insects; *wasp* itself is from Middle English *waspe*, which came from Latin *vespa* (wasp). (Come to think of it, don't those Vespas roaring by without mufflers sound as annoying as wasps?)

welter (wel' tər) *n.*, *vb.* A *welter* is a condition of turmoil, wild confusion, a jumble, a muddle. A speaker calling for audience reactions is sometimes greeted by a *welter* of dissenting opinions. People tend to run about in a *welter* on the occurrence of an emergency. The verb *to welter* means "to wallow," like pigs in a muddy sty, but can be used figuratively with considerable impact: Some people are born losers; they seem to *welter* in setbacks and bewilderment. Far from being ashamed, rakes and roués actually *welter* in their sinful way of life. From Low German *weltern* (to roll).

winnow (win' oh) *vb.* To *winnow* something is to separate the desirable part from the worthless. Wheat or other grain is *winnowed* by tossing it into the air or otherwise exposing it to a draft in order to blow away the lighter chaff, dirt and other impurities. *Winnow* can be used effectively in a figurative sense: When a job is offered, it is important to *winnow* the applicants' letters in order to find the most promising person for the position. It is up to the judge and jury to *winnow* false testimony from the truth. From Middle English *win(d)we(n)*, akin to Latin *ventilare* (to fan, wave in the air).

winsome (win' səm) *adj*. A *winsome* person is engagingly attractive, charming, usually with the implication of lightheartedness; more likely to be said of a woman than a man. In Victorian novels, *winsome* young ladies are always softening the hearts of old curmudgeons. The term can also be applied to appearances: A *winsome* smile goes a long way toward breaking the ice. *Winsome* is synonymous with *winning* used in that sense. From Middle English *winsom*; *wyn* means "joy" in Old English.

wizened (wiz' ənd) *adj*. A *wizened* person or face is shriveled, full of wrinkles, withered: usually applied to the old and unhealthy, very occasionally to fruits, etc. Witches in fairy tales are usually depicted as *wizened* old women, gnomes as *wizened* old men. *Wizened* features are a sign of age and decrepitude. From Middle English *wisen* (to wither).

wont (wont—*o* as in don or don't) *n*., *adj*. As a noun, *wont* means "custom, practice." It is some people's *wont* to sleep all day and work all night. In this sense, *wont* usually appears in the form *It is (someone's) wont* (to do so-and-so). It has an adjectival use as well. The example given above could be rephrased: Some people are *wont* to sleep all day (etc.). Young lovers are *wont* to stay out after dark on summer evenings. *Wont*, as a noun, is often used negatively: On festive occasions, most people eat more than is their *wont*. From Middle English *woned*; cf. German *gewöhnt* (accustomed).

wry (rye) *adj*. The original, literal meaning of this word is "twisted, distorted," and it is still used that way in the expression *wry neck*; one can also speak of a *wry* nose or mouth. Its more common use is to describe an expression of disdainful irony: Young people's awkward and ineffectual attempts to explain embarrassing situations are usually met with *wry* faces on the part of their more sophisticated elders. It is customary for experienced Washington pundits to make *wry* observations about politicians. *Wry* humor is dry and twisted humor. Too many television shows have the all-wise wife making *wry* jokes about her husband's bumbling efforts about the house. From Greek *rhoikos* (crooked), which went through various changes in Old and Middle English: *wryen*, *wrigian* (to swerve), etc. *Writhe* is from the same source.

xenophobia (zeen ə foe' bee ə) *n*. *Xenophobia* expresses morbid fear and distrust of strangers or foreigners, or of anything new, strange or foreign. The adjective is *xenophobic* (zeen ə foe' bik). A *xenophobe* (zeen' ə fobe) is a person who hates or fears foreigners or strangers, or new ways or strange or foreign customs. *Xenophobia* is the hallmark of backwoods people. The whole character of Archie Bunker is based on his *xenophobia*: Archie is the *xenophobe* par excellence. The insular Englishman of yore was *xenophobic* in his distaste for foreign dress, foreign food (especially garlic) and foreign sounds. From two Greek words, *xenos* (stranger, *n.*, foreign, *adj.*), and *phobos* (fearing).

yen (yen) *n*. A *yen* is a powerful desire or craving, a longing or yearning. Overweight people find it hard to overcome their *yen* for fattening foods. Office workers are often distracted by a *yen* for a staffer of the opposite sex. *Yen* is an informal word and is thought to be derived from the Cantonese word *yan* (craving), associated with opium.

zealot (zel' ət) *n*. A *zealot* is a fanatic, especially a fanatical follower of a radical cause or leader. *Zeal* (zeel) is the fervor that motivates a *zealot*, and *zealous* (zel' əs) means "ardent, diligent," but neither *zeal* nor *zealous* has the force of *zealot*, which implies devotion beyond bounds, even at the risk of one's safety. In the sixties, many young people were *zealots* for a cause they had only dimly defined for themselves. Today's extremists all over the world are the worst kind of *zealot*—the ones you can't reason with without risking your life. From Greek *zelotes*.

zenith (zee' nith). *n*. See **nadir**.

Authoritative Guides to Better Self-Expression: